# Palgrave Studies in Life Writing

Series Editors
Clare Brant
Department of English
King's College London
London, United Kingdom

Max Saunders
Department of English
King's College London
London, United Kingdom

This series features books that address key concepts and subjects, with an emphasis on new and emergent approaches. It offers specialist but accessible studies of contemporary and historical topics, with a focus on connecting life writing to themes with cross-disciplinary appeal. The series aims to be the place to go to for current and fresh research for scholars and students looking for clear and original discussion of specific subjects and forms; it is also a home for experimental approaches that take creative risks with potent materials.

The term 'Life Writing' is taken broadly so as to reflect the academic, public and global reach of life writing, and to continue its democratic tradition. The series seeks contributions that address contexts beyond traditional territories – for instance, in the Middle East, Africa and Asia. It also aims to publish volumes addressing topics of general interest (such as food, drink, sport, gardening) with which life writing scholarship can engage in lively and original ways, as well as to further the political engagement of life writing especially in relation to human rights, migration, trauma and repression, sadly also persistently topical themes. The series looks for work that challenges and extends how life writing is understood and practised, especially in a world of rapidly changing digital media; that deepens and diversifies knowledge and perspectives on the subject, and which contributes to the intellectual excitement and the world relevance of life writing.

More information about this series at
http://www.springer.com/series/15200

Luke Seaber

# Incognito Social Investigation in British Literature

## Certainties in Degradation

Luke Seaber
Centre for Languages and International Education (CLIE)
University College London
London, United Kingdom

Palgrave Studies in Life Writing
ISBN 978-3-319-50961-7          ISBN 978-3-319-50962-4 (eBook)
DOI 10.1007/978-3-319-50962-4

Library of Congress Control Number: 2017935473

Cover illustration: Laurent Hamels/Getty Images

Printed on acid-free paper

This Palgrave Macmillan imprint is published by Springer Nature
The registered company is Springer International Publishing AG
The registered company address is: Gewerbestrasse 11, 6330 Cham, Switzerland

# ACKNOWLEDGEMENTS

This book began with a two-year Marie Curie project at University College London (the People Programme [Marie Curie Actions] of the European Union's Seventh Framework Programme [FP7/2007-2013] under REA Grant Agreement No 298208), and my first thanks must go to the Department of English Language and Literature at UCL for hosting me and to Neil Rennie for being my scientist-in-charge.

I must also thank Ben Doyle, Eva Hodgkin, Milly Davies and all at Palgrave Macmillan who have made publishing this book such a pleasurable experience, as well as the anonymous reader who made such useful suggestions, and Emma Caddy for preparing the index.

The book would have been impossible without conversations at conferences, pubs, the UCL English Department and the UCL UPCH office at CLIE, as well as without the help I received from various individuals. I need particularly to thank: Maurizio Ascari, Matthew Beaumont, Greta Borg-Corbett, Stephen Cadywold, James Cross, Eliza Cubitt, Greg Dart, Luke Davies, Anna Edwards, Lydia Fellgett, Jason Finch, David Fremlin, Pietro Gallina, Lis Hasted, Nick Hubble, Steve and Brenda Huettner, Les Hurst, Matthew Ingleby, Peter Jones, Richard Lance Keeble, Margaret Kettlewell, Dan Kilburn, Patrick Leary, Peter Marks, Michael McCluskey, Richard North, Chukwuma Okoye, Stephen Porter, George Potts, David Railton QC, John Redpath, Will Richards, Lisa Robertson, Michael Sayeau, Chris Stamatakis, Polly Toynbee, Tom Ue, Laura Vorachek.

I also profited from the help and expertise of staff from the following institutions: British Library, Bibliothèque nationale de France, Senate House Library, The London Library, UCL Library, University of Michigan

Special Collections Library, Imperial War Museum Collections, London Metropolitan Archives, British Film Institute, Mass Observation Archive at the University of Sussex.

I thank the Trustees of the Imperial War Museum for access to the Papers of David Railton.

Material from the Mass Observation Archive is reproduced with permission of Curtis Brown, London on behalf of The Trustees of the Mass Observation Archive.

Material from the archive of the Royal Literary Fund is reproduced with their permission.

A version of part of Chapter Two was published as 'Trust the Teller and Not the Tale: Reflections on Orwell's Hidden Rhetoric of Truthfulness in the London Section of *Down and Out in Paris and London*' in *George Orwell Now!*, ed. Richard Lance Keeble (New York: Peter Lang, 2015), and is reproduced with permission.

My parents too made this book possible, as does the person to whom I owe the most, Tiziana. This is for you, and Noemi.

# CONTENTS

# CHAPTER 1

# Certainties in Degradation: An Introduction to Incognito Social Investigation

This book is the first full critical history of what will be referred to as 'incognito social investigation texts' – in other words, works detailing their authors' experiences whilst pretending to be poor. There are few famous examples, the one great exception being *Down and Out in Paris and London*, but there has been a vast array of other books and articles in the genre since it was created in 1866 by James Greenwood's 'A Night in a Workhouse'.

The label given here to the texts under examination is not unproblematic, and is the first of two problems of terminology to be considered. The phenomenon that these works recount is simple enough to describe: disguising oneself as a member of a poorer social group in order to gather information about it. The reasons for choosing the admittedly rather unwieldy term 'incognito social investigation' need some justification. 'Slumming', as in the title of Seth Koven's important work on Victorian London, is also (and more accurately) employed to refer to visiting the poor or more generally spending time amongst them rather than endeavouring to pass as one of them.[1] In his work on American texts, Mark Pittenger recognizes the problem of nomenclature before deciding to call its practitioners 'down-and-outers', 'undercover investigators' and 'class passers' rather indiscriminately.[2] There are problems with all these labels. 'Down-and-outery' is too cumbersome a neologism; it also limits itself to description of only one subtype – in what way is someone who decides to work undercover in a factory pretending to be a 'down-and-out'?

© The Author(s) 2017
L. Seaber, *Incognito Social Investigation in British Literature*,
Palgrave Studies in Life Writing, DOI 10.1007/978-3-319-50962-4_1

'Undercover investigation' suffers from the opposite problem: it is too broad a label, and carries no suggestion of the economic specificity of these accounts. 'Class passing' is a useful term, modelled on the far more studied concept of racial passing;[3] it is better restricted, however, to one facet of the phenomenon – I understand it as referring specifically to (successful) disguise rather than the use made thereof. In other words, incognito social investigation is impossible without class passing, but class passing can be carried out for reasons other than that of incognito social investigation. There is also the anthropological or sociological terminology of 'complete participation', as described by Raymond L. Gold in his seminal 1958 classification of types of field observation in sociology.[4] This is the term used by Mark Freeman in an important article;[5] it has the disadvantage, however, of focusing overwhelmingly on methodology, and the wider scope of this book militates against its use here. The two most common terms are 'incognito social exploration' and 'incognito social investigation', and I have chosen the latter, chiefly for the reason that the former plays into the perception, amply documented by Mariana Valverde, of the 'poor' as akin to the 'savage'.[6]

The second terminological problem has to do with what we shall call the people who are the texts' object of study. These range from rough sleepers to respectable fishing families, taking in criminals, tramps, factory workers, domestic servants and many others. To talk of 'the working class' would often be inaccurate: many of those amongst whom our investigators go do not work, and perhaps never have, although it is a label that does have a certain use and will appear as required. Terms such as 'the proletariat' and 'lumpenproletariat' bespeak a theoretical *parti pris* that I wish to avoid suggesting, either on my part or on the part of the authors that I examine. What all those about whom our authors write have in common, regardless of when, where and how they are studied, is their poverty relative to those investigating them and those to whom reports of their lives are addressed. For this reason, and precisely *because* of its vagueness, we shall speak of 'the poor', as general a term as possible.

We shall see how a series of texts that might appear at first to be about subjective descriptions that attempt (or do not attempt) to seem objective are in fact far richer and more complex, offering subtle insights into questions of performativity and intersubjectivity that suggest the simple dichotomy of observer and observed is inadequate to describe the play of ontological and epistemological representations that these texts show. These are texts wherein authors' lives are written under the guise of describing the lives of others; these are texts wherein authors record themselves changing without their realizing it, and record other lives, the lives of 'the poor', sometimes better than they are perhaps aware that they are doing and sometimes far worse than they can understand.

Before we begin our journey through this forgotten tradition from its start in the cold January of 1866, however, let us look further back in the nineteenth century, to the near-forgotten figure of Charles Cochrane, and see what it is that we are *not* going to examine in the coming pages.

In the 1847 general election, those voting in the constituency of Westminster had to choose two representatives from three Liberal candidates and one Conservative. The Liberals won both seats, returning to Parliament Sir George De Lacy Evans, a Radical, and Charles Lushington, a Whig. The unsuccessful Liberal candidate was Charles Cochrane, also a Whig, who lost to Lushington by just twelve votes.[7] Lushington had been put up to stand against Cochrane by the local Reform Society, angry that Cochrane had been proposed by a group of some 150 voters who distrusted the connection between the Society and Lord John Russell's government, thus going against the customary procedure whereby the Society nominated candidates.[8] The campaign, as James Winter, the only person to have written on Charles Cochrane in any detail, says, 'had to do, and with a vengeance, with personalities, or, rather, a personality' – that of the eccentric Cochrane himself.[9]

Charles Cochrane was the illegitimate son of the Hon. Basil Cochrane, the younger brother of the ninth Earl of Dundonald. His father died in 1826, leaving him wealth and the possibility to live as a man of leisure. He lived in Marylebone, and in about 1840 was elected to the parish vestry; local London politics would soon become his overriding interest. He became an expert on street drainage and cleaning, and created the Street Orderly Brigades, uniformed bodies of men who cleaned the streets as a way to provide employment whilst providing a much-needed service. This came to the attention of Henry Mayhew, who devoted over twenty pages to it in the first volume of his monumental *London Labour and the London Poor*,[10] his encomiastic conclusion would be that 'the street-orderly system is incomparably the best mode of scavaging',[11] and Cochrane would be cited throughout the four volumes as an expert in street hygiene. He also founded, in 1841, the National Philanthropic Association, which notwithstanding its name was a purely London organization, and later the Poor Man's Guardian Society. Both of these aimed to alleviate the lot of the

London poor, the latter being perhaps the greatest of early Victorian soup kitchens. After his failure to be elected, Cochrane destroyed any future chances of re-election by announcing a demonstration against tax increases on 5 March 1848. Warned of the possibility of riot, Cochrane withdrew his support and announced his absence, but some 10,000 to 15,000 people attended, and the meeting indeed degenerated into a riot. His political hopes were ruined by this fiasco, and by 1853 his financial resources were depleted to the point that he left for a year's self-imposed exile in France, where he possibly suffered a nervous breakdown. After this, his energies, still considerable, turned to sabbatarianism. He returned to London, to die there in 1855.[12]

Cochrane at first sight appears to be just another early Victorian philanthropist and social reformer – more eccentric and firebrand than some and less paternalistic than others towards 'the poor' whom he helped, perhaps. Winter has very convincingly made the case for Cochrane's importance as an innovator in urban cleaning,[13] but his importance to us lies in an episode in his youth that became something of a minor scandal when he stood for Parliament. In February 1847 there appeared in the newspaper the *Sun* four letters, the publication of which led Cochrane to bring a successful 1848 libel suit against the editor, Murdo Young.[14] The first letter was dated from St James's on 17 February, and was given in the Law Report in *The Times* as follows:

> Sir, – As an elector of Westminster, allow me to ask whether Mr. Charles Cochrane, who now so ostentatiously parades his pretensions to represent Westminster, is the same person as one Senor [sic] Juan de Vega, who some few years back published a journal of a tour through Great Britain and Ireland, and who there paraded a series of adventures in various towns and places, at which modesty and decency felt ashamed, and whose public avowal signally proved the want of good taste and common propriety in the writer?[15]

Cochrane did not disavow this identification, and his victory in the libel case was based upon a frank admission of his erstwhile role as 'Juan de Vega', coupled with a denial of the character imputed to him in the letters. In a long pamphlet produced during the election, published as being by 'A Westminster Elector' but written by Cochrane himself, he said that he had been Juan de Vega, but that it had been a youthful folly and his motives had been innocent.[16]

Who, then, was the mysterious Señor Juan de Vega impersonated by Cochrane? His adventures had been published by Simpkin and Marshall in 1830 under the seemingly innocent title of *Journal of a Tour Made by Señor Juan de Vega, the Spanish Minstrel of 1828–9, through Great Britain and Ireland, a Character Assumed by an English Gentleman*. The form of the title, recalling as it does Boswell's book on the Hebrides as well as other, less well-known, travelogues, might at first suggest a work of travel literature distinguished only by the author's having carried out his tour in disguise. However, the two volumes detail little in the way of picturesque scenery and sights, and instead deal mostly with the anonymous traveller's romantic escapades and his experiences as a guitarist, and it was his amorous adventures that caused the furore.

If we examine Cochrane's motives for assuming the part of Juan de Vega, we will find his account of them almost comically mundane, as if his decision to act the role of a penniless itinerant refugee Spanish musician had been the most natural thing in the world. In the opening chapter of his book, he first claims that he had been planning to go to Paris after some long-planned project had fallen through, when his thoughts turned to his time in Columbia. We know from Winter's research that the mention of the South American country is a false clue to his identity. The project that he 'had for a long time ardently devoted [his] attention to',[17] and in which he had been disappointed, was the possibility of going to South America, in the pursuit of which aim he had devoted himself to studying Spanish. The Charles Cochrane who had been in Columbia was a homonymous relative who had published a book describing his experiences there.[18] This misdirection aside, his description of his thought processes seems straightforward:

During my stay in that country [Columbia], I had become well acquainted with the habits and manners of the Spaniards; – spoke their language with tolerable fluency; – had also known, and still knew, a great many Spanish emigrants personally, and many others by name. – What, thought I, if I assume the appearance, and personate one of those unfortunate characters, whose distress and persecutions have always found a sympathetic asylum in the breasts of my generous countrymen, and travel through these hospitable kingdoms? My acquaintance with the provincial habits of the English and Irish is very limited, and the idea of such a tour suggests many delightful opportunities of attaining that interesting information, in a manner not only unique in its method, and consequently gratifying from its novelty, but strictly calculated to lay before my observation the real character of all classes; for I entertain little doubt, under such a disguise, of being thrown into every variation of society.[19]

Cochrane presents his choice as one both easy and natural, but it is precisely the nonchalance with which he comes to his decision that makes his account of it so strange. There is nothing obvious about dressing as a wandering Spanish minstrel to take a ten-month holiday. Indeed, Cochrane seems so determined to hurry through his description of his motives that he even makes it more likely typographically that a reader will not pause at his reproduction of his thoughts. Whereas elsewhere the book uses the device, common at the time, of inverted commas at the beginning of every line of text denoting speech,[20] here Cochrane uses nothing but em dashes, far less visible within the text than a line of inverted commas down the margin. The eye moves more easily across Cochrane's thoughts, embedded as they are within his narrative with no visual detail to mark them out. By the time the reader reaches the punctuationally unmarked end of Cochrane's thoughts and the resumption of the narrative, only a change in tense is there to indicate the switch, and the break is made even less abrupt by the final part of his reflections being a list of characteristics that could, in fact, take the present tense without great difficulty even within a past-tense narrative.

Cochrane wishes to make his act seem normal, the decision underlying it being not worthy of any special reflection, and to which no attention need be called. That dressing up as a wandering minstrel to take an extended holiday was of course no more normal then than now can be seen in the fact that Cochrane's escapade was strange enough to inspire Henry Mayhew's highly popular 1834 farce *The Wandering Minstrel*. In this, the idea of a 'nobleman musician', the 'Wandering Minstrel' of the title (who never appears in the play) comes directly from Cochrane; that Mayhew knew Cochrane's book can also be seen by comparing the comic anti-hero of the play, Jem Bags, the Cockney street musician mistaken for the nobleman, with Jem, the man Juan de Vega meets who sings in the Cooper's Arms in Rochester.[21] If Cochrane's behaviour was outlandish enough to inspire a farce (or, for that matter, to merit being recorded in two volumes), why was he so keen to draw attention away from its strangeness?

We may speculate about psychological reasons: Cochrane's life was full of immoderacy, and we can never know to what extent this was caused by feelings of conflict, or betrayal, or guilt over his illegitimacy. Indeed, on 29 July 1847, *The Times* reported the husting speeches of the various candidates for Westminster. Cochrane's speech is notably livelier than those of his opponents, and one has the feeling of reading a genuinely impassioned oration rather than a necessary but dully formulaic speech. The one occasion on which Cochrane's fluency appears to desert him, given the way in which the report becomes confused, is not on the issue of Juan de Vega (he won applause and laughter by claiming that the 'whole amount of the charge was, that when he was a youth of 19 or 20 years of age he was fond of the girls'), but rather on an unnamed 'libel'; this was clearly his illegitimacy.[22] However, speculation over possible unknowable familial causes of his curious behaviour will not necessarily bring us any closer to the reasons for his attempt to draw attention away from it.

An explanation is to be sought, rather, in Cochrane's own published words. In the anonymous illeist defence of himself offered to the electors of Westminster, he first begs indulgence for his youthful folly.[23] The claimed nature of his experiences as mere boyish foolishness notwithstanding, he then goes on to imply that his tour of the British Isles was not only forgivable but beneficial. He first states an advantage implicit in his experiment: 'The whole of the book shows, that even in the brief period of ten months, the tourist amassed an amount of intelligence which, perhaps, would otherwise never have fallen to his lot';[24] he then says something clearly connected with pointing out his electability, in this case insofar as regards his knowledge of the poor: 'It was, however, upon this journey, and during the fatigues and trials which he underwent from the voluntary poverty which he then inflicted upon himself, that Mr. Cochrane first learnt the useful lesson of the sufferings and hardships of the poor'.[25] Although these two pieces of self-praise seem very similar, they have important differences. The latter, written for the context of the election, implies something contradicted by the 1830 book. The obvious sense of 'voluntary poverty [ ... ] inflicted upon himself' would be that Cochrane went amongst the poor as one of them. In Chapter 6 of the first volume of his travels, however, he details his earnings and expenditures, and states that he chooses to walk because of his small earnings (and thus far we may concur that he is sharing the privations of the poor); but there is another reason why he must economize. His outgoings include giving 'away a great deal of money to the lower orders for drink, into whose society I frequently entered, in order to learn their habits and modes of living'.[26] In other words, the experience Cochrane gained of the poor whilst disguised as Juan de Vega was far more similar in technique to that gained when acting as a philanthropist than his disingenuous statement in 1847 might suggest. The young man may have suffered privation, but it was in order to use the money to buy his way into acquiring knowledge of the poor; this, *mutatis mutandis*, is no different to the situation whereby when older he would almost bankrupt himself through his philanthropy. The former statement, on the other hand, that he learnt things whilst travelling as a Spaniard that otherwise he neither would nor could have learnt, is corroborated by his original book. The concept occurred in the hasty meditations that led him to abandon his idea of going to Paris ('calculated to lay before my observation the real character of all classes; for I entertain little doubt, under such a disguise, of being thrown into every variation of society');[27] it reappears in the peroration, where he contrasts the idea of mankind he had thitherto received 'from the artificial society [he] had always been accustomed to move in' to that which he received from moving amongst people of various stations in the role of Juan de Vega.[28]

Cochrane's 1847 defence of his book makes the case that his was a serious undertaking, a learning experience that made him fit for public office. In the book itself, however, although this may be hinted at in the peroration, the accent is on his amorous and picaresque adventures. In this, his critics had a point. I would argue that Cochrane's attempt at minimizing the importance given to his decision – written, we must remember, *after* he had returned to being Charles Cochrane, *after* he had returned to a more serious life – is a tactic aimed at having his experiences perceived as being a serious affair rather than merely a youthful folly. At first sight, this may seem paradoxical: if the Juan de Vega experiment is to be taken seriously as an attempt to learn things otherwise unlearnable, surely it would have made sense for more to have been made of the gravity of the decision to carry it out. This, though, would only hold true were Cochrane to have written a quite different book detailing his experience. As his book chiefly deals with light matters, had he prefaced it with an exposition of serious sociological aims, then the failure of those aims would have been clear. Doing as he does, conversely, and making the whole choice seem something taken lightly, he is able to portray himself as a victim of fortunate circumstances: precisely because he does not set out to learn with any real degree of seriousness, it is all the more praiseworthy that he *does* learn. He portrays himself as setting off not only ignorant of the things that he will learn, but also as taking the decision to set out in such a way as to show that he was ignorant of the fact that he would learn at all.

Cochrane's book may be ascribed to various currents: it is picaresque in its description of his adventures; it sometimes remembers to be the travel literature that its title suggests it might be; it may also appear to belong to the specific type of text the existence of which is posited by this book. As we have seen, Cochrane claims that his disguise was part of an attempt to learn about the manners of the poor in a way otherwise impossible. As we have equally seen, however, this version of Cochrane's has much about it of retrospective (self-)justification. Other than unknowable psychological motivations, there is no reason not to take Cochrane's escapades at face value as a young man's folly. The fact nonetheless remains that the kernel of Cochrane's experience, that of dressing as someone poorer than himself, could be considered as prefiguring all the other accounts that this volume will examine. If we accept this, however, we shall be opening the door to an endless study that can find precursors scattered throughout folklore, history and literature: James V of Scotland as the Goodman of Ballangeich,[29] and the stories of Harun al-Rashid's walks through Baghdad; *The Prince and the Pauper*; Zeus and Hermes when they were received by Baucis and Philemon; even, perhaps, the two angels who visited Lot in Sodom and, I am tempted to add, the very doctrine of the Incarnation itself.

Any approach to incognito social investigation that potentially considers all examples thereof from all sources risks missing the great sea-change that occurs in 1866 with James Greenwood and 'A Night in a Workhouse'. The world of texts to which Cochrane's book at least partially belongs is too homogeneous to be considered a single entity: we have stories of changing social roles that are folklore, history, picaresque, myth and a myriad other things beside, but the change in social role is never the key point; insofar as it ever becomes central, it is only important because of the discoveries it allows. Before Greenwood, the social change was never central; equally importantly, the texts dealt with personal, individual, transformations. To return to Cochrane, he has no sense that he is acting within a tradition. His motivations were private: even if we accept his retrospective explanation of his tour as being a form of instruction, it is still instruction solely for Charles Cochrane. His readers benefit from it, if at all, only indirectly.

It is with Greenwood that we see the creation of a twofold difference from works such as Cochrane's. The nature of this difference may be stated simply: after 'A Night in a Workhouse', incognito social investigation becomes *central* to the works in which it appears, and it is *non-individualistic*. The former concept is clear: social disguise before Greenwood was merely part of another structure, and not exactly a tradition in itself but rather a recurring detail in other traditions. From 1866 onwards it becomes a tradition in its own right, a tradition that authors are more or less conscious of writing in, and knowledge of which can be dissimulated or admitted. The latter concept requires perhaps a little more explanation. Incognito social investigators in the years following Greenwood were not acting solely for their own private reasons, but rather for reasons touching society. It might be argued that episodes such as Harun al-Rashid's anonymous night visits to Baghdad (whether folklore or history is of no importance here) are an example of a social investigator taking an interest in society. David Stevenson, in his work on the 'king in disguise' motif as it relates to James V of Scotland, divides it into three types: the political, the recreational and the accidental. The first of these is relevant here, as 'disguise could allow a king access to information that would not otherwise reach him, being filtered out by officials and court dignitaries'.[30] Nonetheless, Harun remained a caliph and James V remained a king: there is a difference between someone choosing to witness things so that they as a power-wielding individual can act in an informed manner and someone choosing to witness so that they can inform the wider community. These two key aspects of the genre Greenwood instituted, the centrality of disguise and an appeal to society, do of course differ quantitatively and qualitatively across the various authors that we shall examine, but it is in them that we see the true break from a book like Cochrane's.

What follows explores four subtypes of incognito social investigation. The focus will be on non-fiction accounts – or, more accurately, on texts that present themselves to the reader either as non-fiction or as fictionalized accounts of events experienced by the author. Exactly where any given individual text presents itself as being sited on the fiction/non-fiction continuum, and whether this positioning was generally accepted by readers, is an exceedingly difficult question; it will be dealt with where there is textual, paratextual and extra-textual evidence enough to justify a reasonable degree of certainty when discussing it. More generally, however, texts' self-presentation will be accepted, *faute de mieux*, as in the absence of other evidence it will be presumed that the superficial status is the 'true' one.

We shall begin by examining James Greenwood, the figure whose social investigation led to the publication of the work that may be considered the true onlie begetter of the genre of incognito social investigation. We shall examine those texts that followed most narrowly in its tradition of taking 'the poor' as their object of study, and meaning thereby the destitute, the outcast, the homeless. The next subtype is a rather nebulous one that shades into both the category exemplified by Greenwood and travel literature. This is the investigation of poverty through walking, for pedestrianism and poverty are linked in a number of heterogeneous texts, and the term 'tramping' is suitably bivalent. This is also a form with an ambiguous relationship with its own status as social investigation; indeed, whereas 'social investigation' *tout court* takes place when the investigator takes no pains to disguise his or her status as an investigator and incognito social investigation proper occurs when the investigator endeavours to pass unobserved, disguising him- or herself (or trying to, at least) as one of those being investigated, the particular subtype of the latter represented by tramping often shades into a third category: semi-incognito social investigation. This is what takes place when the investigator does not try deliberately to dissimulate his or her identity, but nonetheless because of various factors presents a face to the world that does not allow for easy social classification. In other words, this is dissimulation of one's status as a social investigator that is accidental and/or partial; as will be seen, the very ambiguity of its nature makes it of extreme interest and relevance to any discussion of the subject. With the third type, we shall focus on people looking at relative poverty rather than absolute, as we examine those who have taken on badly paid work in order to report on it. Of vital importance here is the fact that this is far and away the most common form of incognito social investigation carried out by women. We end with examination of a category looking at something that is on one level the opposite of tramping: those incognito social investigators who settled in the areas they explored.

As we shall see, not all incognito social investigation texts can be divided into these four categories (which should not themselves be thought of as mutually exclusive); classifying texts about 'the poor' is as problematic a venture as classifying the object of their study. The chief absence from the above classification and the present work is a movement that had roots stretching far further back than the 1860s, but nonetheless became a form of incognito social investigation over the years following as it was leavened by the social interests of the Greenwoodian tradition. This is an interest in the life of Gypsies and a sharing thereof.[31] Gypsying stands alone, although it may have points in common with all of the other categories – Romanis can be extremely poor and their world can on occasion touch that of the homeless; incognito social investigation amongst them can mean having to tramp; amongst them one can work as they do; they may be settled rather than nomadic (and nomadism, oxymoronically but obviously, is a form of peripatetic settlement). Far more than the other four categories, however, this was also in many ways an inheritor of pre-Greenwood concepts and traditions; this, and the near-total impossibility of disguising one's non-Romani status places it apart.

A further important (sub)type that is not examined in this work is the phenomenon of middle-class writers enlisting in the armed forces in the ranks, even though this can produce texts of great interest.[32] On the one hand, writers' motivations are often too individual and specific to be of use in drawing conclusions about overarching phenomena; on the other, the regimentation of military life is necessarily such that those living it must to a great extent be limited in their choice of action, and this is anathemic to that central part of incognito social investigation, which concerns how the disguised individual tailors his or her actions and reactions to situations encountered.[33]

The four subtypes described above are still not the complete story. They can never be so. The corpus of texts examined here is necessarily incomplete: an approach to a full corpus deserving of the name would imply hunting for accounts of incognito social investigation in every issue of every newspaper and magazine ever published in the United Kingdom over a century and a half and every biography and autobiography of the period; it would also imply, as we shall see, a similarly comprehensive – and therefore impossible – approach to travel literature, and, indeed, literature *tout court*. Such completeness is not of this world. The body of texts studied in this work is the largest grouping yet examined, but there should be no illusions about the fact that more examples may remain to be unearthed in a parish magazine from Thurso or a short-lived newspaper from Truro...

Although many accounts of incognito social investigation are formulaic and, quite frankly, dull, this does not mean that there may not still be somewhere gathering dust in some provincial newspaper's archives a text offering more than just information about conditions in the local work-house, but rather insight into the text form as a whole. Indeed, it should be pointed out here that the texts analysed here are chosen not because of the interest of their contents vis-à-vis what they describe (the beds in this lodging house; the food in that workhouse; the argot of the unemployed here; the sumptuary rules of wandering workers there), however much interest such details may have to the historian. Rather, the choice of texts upon which analysis is focused is dictated by the insights they offer into the history of incognito social investigation accounts as a text form and the degree to which they contain valuable points regarding the theoretical questions that this work examines. For all that one may hope to have found all the texts whence more overarching conclusions can be drawn, such a hope must always remain unfounded in reality. An example of this is the article from the *Craven Herald* discussed in Chapter 1: this short piece, not much more, in fact, than filler, contains the only example yet found of an incognito social investigator for whom incognito social investigation *is part of a tramp's lifestyle*. Even more importantly, this is a text that raises the fascinating possibility that it is in fact a destabilizing appropriation of the text form by one of the class that would usually be studied by it. This is clearly an important text; it is also a text that was discovered very late in the writing of the current study, and its inclusion is, in that sense, fortuitous.

The title of this book is deliberately bivalent. Incognito social investigators often sought certainty, whether socially epistemological or personally psychological, in the relative degradation that their field allowed; equally, however, the ambiguities and contradictions of the texts that they produced degrade those same certainties. This book is a first attempt to chart a whole textual world that, with all its richness and strangeness, has too long been invisible.[34]

# NOTES

1. See Koven, Seth. 2004. *Slumming: Sexual and Social Politics in Victorian London*. Princeton and Oxford: Princeton University Press. This is a major study and of great importance, but its very choice of 'slumming' as a name for the phenomenon in question points to its problem: it does not distinguish enough between different types of slumming, and analyses settlements of the Toynbee Hall type alongside accounts such as that of Greenwood as if disguise and an incognito status were mere details.
2. Pittenger, Mark. 2012. *Class Unknown: Undercover Investigations of American Work and Poverty from the Progressive Era to the Present*. New York and London: New York University Press, p. 4.
3. For an excellent overview of passing of all types, see Sánchez, María Carla and Linda Schlossberg (eds.). 2001. *Passing: Identity and Interpretation in*

*Sexuality, Race, and Religion*. New York and London: New York University Press.

4.  Gold, Raymond L. 1958. 'Roles in Sociological Field Observations'. *Social Forces* 36:3, pp. 217–23, pp. 219–20.

5.  Freeman, Mark. 2001. '"Journeys into Poverty Kingdom": Complete Participation and the British Vagrant, 1866–1914'. *History Workshop Journal* 52, pp. 99–121.

6.  Valverde, Mariana. 1996. 'The Dialectic of the Familiar and Unfamiliar: "The Jungle" in Early Slum Travel Writing'. *Sociology* 30:3, pp. 493–509.

7.  Stooks Smith, Henry. 1973. *The Parliaments of England: From 1715 to 1847*, ed. F.W.S. Craig. Chichester: Political Reference Publications, p. 470.

8.  Winter, James. 1989. 'The "Agitator of the Metropolis": Charles Cochrane and Early-Victorian Street Reform'. *London Journal* 14:1, pp. 29–42, p. 36.

9.  Ibid.

10. Mayhew, Henry. 2009 [1861–1862]. *London Labour and the London Poor: A Cyclopædia of the Condition and Earnings of Those That Will Work, Those That Cannot Work, and Those That Will Not Work*. New York: Cosimo, vol. II, pp. 253–75.

11. Ibid., p. 275. Mayhew uses the term 'scavaging' to refer to street cleaning.

12. All biographical information taken from Winter, 'The "Agitator of the Metropolis"', except the year of Basil Cochrane's death, taken from *Burke's Peerage*.

13. Winter, 'The "Agitator of the Metropolis"', pp. 39–41.

14. 'Law Report: Cochrane v. Young', *The Times* 22/06/1848, p. 7.

15. Ibid.

16. 'A Westminster Elector' [Charles Cochrane]. n.d. [1847]. *An Address to the Business-Like Men of Westminster on Their Present Candidates with a Review of Mr. Cochrane's Work 'Juan de Vega'*. London: Longman and Co., pp. 9–11.

17. Anon [Charles Cochrane]. 1830. *Journal of a Tour Made by Señor Juan de Vega, the Spanish Minstrel of 1828–9, through Great Britain and Ireland, a Character Assumed by an English Gentleman*. London: Simpkin and Marshall, vol. I, p. 1.

18. Winter, 'The "Agitator of the Metropolis"', p. 30.

19. Cochrane, *Journal*, vol. I, pp. 3–4.

20. See Finnegan, Ruth. 2011. *Why Do We Quote?: The Culture and History of Quotation*. Cambridge: Open Book, pp. 91–2 for details of this practice.

21. Cochrane, *Journal*, vol. I, p. 28.

22. 'The General Election: Westminster', *The Times* 29/07/1847, p. 2.

23. Cochrane, *Address*, pp. 9–11.

24. Ibid., p. 19.

25. Ibid., p. 20.

26. Cochrane, *Journal*, vol. I, p. 126.

27. Ibid., vol. I, p. 3.

28. Ibid., vol. II, p. 399.

29. See Stevenson, David. 2004. '"The Gudeman of Ballangeich": Rambles in the Afterlife of James V'. *Folklore* 115:2, pp. 187–200.

30. Stevenson, '"The Gudeman of Ballangeich", p. 289. The type that Stevenson classifies as 'recreational' covers Cochrane's experiences rather well.

31. The exonym 'Gypsies' is used to mark the fact that many of the social investigators in question were interested in a romantic construction of the 'Gypsy' rather than 'real' Romanis.

32. Above all Lawrence, T.E. 1955. *The Mint: A Day-Book of the R.A.F. Depot between August and December 1922 with Later Notes by 352087 A/c Ross*. London: Jonathan Cape.

33. Although I have not looked at texts of this sort, the title of this book nonetheless draws on a work related to them. See Lawrence, T.E. 1962 [1926]. *Seven Pillars of Wisdom: A Triumph*. Harmondsworth: Penguin, p. 581.

34. The field of incognito social investigation has hitherto received only partial attention from critics and historians. The most important work published so far is an anthology (Freeman, Mark and Gillian Nelson (eds.). 2008. *Vicarious Vagrants: Incognito Social Explorers and the Homeless in England, 1860–1910*. Lambertville: The True Bill Press), examining only the Victorian and Edwardian periods; its introduction is to date the only serious academic overview of the field. However, it refers to a far smaller corpus than that examined here, and offers only a historical survey, with no analysis of the texts themselves. There are also two important anthologies including (with some very basic commentary) incognito social investigation texts alongside other types of journalism. These (Keating, Peter (ed.). 1976. *Into Unknown England 1866–1913: Selections from the Social Explorers*. N.p.: Fontana; Donovan, Stephen and Matthew Rubery (eds.). 2012. *Secret Commissions: An Anthology of Victorian Investigative Journalism*. Peterborough: Broadview Press) have on the one hand a wider focus than incognito social investigation alone and on the other a narrower focus in time, thus limiting their usefulness. The only serious attention paid to post-Edwardian texts regards 1930s texts: see Cunningham, Valentine. 1988. *British Writers of the Thirties*. Oxford: Oxford University Press, passim.

# CHAPTER 2

# Learning by Actual Experience: James Greenwood and the Birth of a Genre

In 1886, W.T. Stead, one of the fathers of modern journalism, published a lengthy piece in the *Contemporary Review* dealing with the power journalists and newspapers held over government. He gives as an example of 'a piece of sensationalism of the best kind' the 'Amateur Casual', James Greenwood, who spared no pains 'to make every detail stand out in as life-like and real a fashion as was possible, and the object of [whose narrative] was the attainment of a definite improvement in the treatment of the poorest of the poor'.[1] 'Sensationalism' for Stead here is clearly similar to what would now be called investigative journalism, and the Amateur Casual was famous enough a figure to require no further explanation for readers. A year earlier, Chatto & Windus had published a well-received anonymous account of life in a workhouse for an indoor pauper 'by One of Them'. This too contains a reference to the Amateur Casual, but here the presumption of reader familiarity with the text is such that only the slightest information is given: 'Among the casuals themselves, there was none of that intense eagerness for ribald anecdote and narrative with which they have been credited ever since the publication, years ago, of a certain clever and highly coloured sketch of a night in such a place.'[2]

These references, which serve to underline the long-lasting cultural familiarity of Greenwood's work, refer to three articles published two decades earlier in the *Pall Mall Gazette* under the title 'A Night in a Workhouse', and soon republished in *The Times* and elsewhere, as well as in various pamphlets.[3] What was 'A Night in a Workhouse', that it could

© The Author(s) 2017
L. Seaber, *Incognito Social Investigation in British Literature*,
Palgrave Studies in Life Writing, DOI 10.1007/978-3-319-50962-4_2

be so easily referenced and recognized twenty years later? This, after all, is not usually the case with brief pieces of journalism, as Stead noted ('The day before yesterday is as the date of the deluge') in the same article,[4] seemingly not noticing the contradiction.

'A Night in a Workhouse' recounts the anonymous narrator's experiences when he asks for admission to the casual ward of a workhouse in Princes Road, Lambeth.[5] It details the squalid conditions that he (soon known to be James Greenwood) found there and the 'horrors' of some of the behaviour that he witnessed. He is surreptitiously dropped off by a carriage near the workhouse, and, presenting himself to the admissions clerk, is placed into the care of 'Daddy', a trusty. He is made to strip and wash, and is given a shirt and rug and sent to a room full of casuals to sleep. He describes those whom he sees there, as well as the various activities that disturb his sleep, although when these cease he sleeps no better thanks to cold and discomfort. The morning sees breakfast and the work that the paupers in the casual ward have to do, turning cranks to grind corn for a miller. This over, Greenwood leaves the workhouse to find the carriage waiting to pick him up.

Greenwood had been asked to carry out his experiment by his brother Frederick, editor of the *Pall Mall Gazette*. It was a very topical issue: the previous summer had seen *The Lancet* highlight bad conditions in workhouses; it had not, however, been able to stir up any great public feeling about the matter, and this was what the Greenwoods set out to do.[6] James Greenwood was to go to Lambeth workhouse accompanied by a friend named Bittlestone, whose presence was passed over in silence, thus magnifying the 'heroism' of the journalistic act.[7]

It was, quite simply, the first work of its type. Thitherto, there had of course been descriptions of 'the poor', the most famous being Henry Mayhew's massive *London Labour and the London Poor: A Cyclopædia of the Condition and Earnings of Those That Will Work, Those That Cannot Work, and Those That Will Not Work*, composed through the 1840s and published in its final four-volume collaborative form in 1861. However, as the subtitle of Mayhew's work suggests, already offering as it does three categories of the poor, such texts present views of the poor that claim an objectivity based upon observation recognized as such. None of Mayhew's informants and interviewees could ever have concluded that the man to whom they were talking was anything but someone from outside their world interested in representing them to other members of the class to which he belonged. Information about the poor is not only mediated through Mayhew, but also through his informants' relationship with him. What Greenwood was attempting was a way to offer his readers 'the truth'; a truth necessarily mediated through him, but that had reached him unadorned by any further mediation between him and the objects of his study. We may say that Mayhew's was an openly etic account of the poor, whereas Greenwood aimed at an emic account.

These terms of art borrowed from anthropology will be of great importance in what follows, and some explanation is necessary. In 1954, the American linguist and anthropologist Kenneth L. Pike coined the terms 'etic' and 'emic' by giving an autonomous life to the terminations of the words 'phonemic' and 'phonetic', defining an etic approach as one where there are 'generalized statements about [ ... ] data' without reference to any particular cultures and 'emic' as one 'in essence valid for only one language (or culture) at a time'.[8] They have been used in various ways over the years,[9] but I shall be using something similar to what Thomas N. Headland has called the 'heuristically helpful' 'simplest and most common definition':[10] an etic description is one made from outside the system being described; an emic description is one made from within the system being described. However, I wish to specify usage in this volume a little more precisely: in what follows, 'etic' refers to descriptions and analyses that are based on criteria belonging to the person or group describing and 'emic' to descriptions and analyses based on criteria belonging to the person or group described. In this usage, the key detail is not whether one *belongs* to a system but whether one is willing or able to work within the conceptual framework of that system. This is not the same as choosing between subjectivity or objectivity, as Marvin Harris has pointed out.[11] Let us take a hypothetical example to show how this distinction is to be understood. An incognito social investigator says that a particular tramp is dirty. This may be objective (according to a generally accepted scale of cleanliness the tramp is dirty) or it may be subjective (according to the writer's own personal standards the tramp is dirty). Analysis of this objective or subjective fact may then be etic (the writer freights 'dirtiness' with meaning applicable to the observer and not the observed) or emic (the writer examines what this 'dirtiness' means in terms of the tramp's criteria).

Critical attention to Greenwood has been limited. He is an important figure in the history of investigative journalism, as the primacy of 'A Night in a Workhouse' is rightly recognized. The only sustained examination, however, of Greenwood's text is in Seth Koven's seminal 2004 *Slumming*.

Here the focus lies on the unspoken 'horrors' at which Greenwood hints, and Koven places questions about male homosexuality at the centre of his discussion.[12] Koven also examines other analogous cases of the nexus between sexual questions and social investigation, but his focus is always on this nexus rather than the phenomenon of social investigation itself. What is of interest to us here, though, is neither phenomena *related* to incognito social investigation nor incognito social investigation as part of the history of journalism: it is incognito social investigation itself, which is in turn part of the history of how social class has been constructed and interpreted.

'A Night in a Workhouse' opens with a novelistic third-person narration of a carriage depositing its occupant:

At about nine o'clock on the evening of Monday, the 8th inst., a neat but unpretentious carriage might have been seen turning cautiously from the Kennington-road into Princes-road, Lambeth. The curtains were closely drawn, and the coachman wore an unusually responsible air. Approaching a public-house which retreated a little from the street, he pulled up; but not so close that the lights should fall upon the carriage door, nor so distant as to unsettle the mind of any one who chose to imagine that he had halted to drink beer before proceeding to call for the children at a juvenile party. He did not dismount, nor did any one alight in the usual way; but any keen observer who happened to watch his intelligent countenance might have seen a furtive glance directed to the wrong door: that is to say, to the door of the carriage which opened into the dark and muddy road. From that door merged a sly and ruffianly figure, marked with every sign of squalor. He was dressed in what had once been a snuff-brown coat, but which was faded to the hue of bricks imperfectly baked. It was not strictly a ragged coat, though it had lost its cuffs – a bereavement which obliged the wearer's arms to project through the sleeves two long inelegant inches. The coat altogether was too small, and was only made to meet over the chest by means of a bit of twine. This wretched garment was surmounted by a 'birdseye' pocket handkerchief of cotton, wisped about the throat hangman fashion; above all was a battered billy-cock hat, with a dissolute drooping brim. Between the neckerchief and the lowering brim of the hat appeared part of a face, unshaven and not scrupulously clean. The man's hands were plunged into his pockets, and he shuffled hastily along in boots, which were the boots of a tramp indifferent to miry ways. In a moment he was [out] of sight; and the brougham, after waiting a little while, turned about and comfortably departed.[13]

The following paragraph opens with the revelation that the 'mysterious figure was that of the present writer,[14] and the third drops the third person in favour of the first. To the reader who has yet to reach the second paragraph, however, there are two clear categories here: the coachman, a respectable working man with a responsible air and intelligent countenance, and the disreputable pauper, one of what would soon come to be known as the residuum, the unrespectable and unhelpable poor.[15] Once the reader knows that the mystery tramp is in fact a journalist, these categories must necessarily be put into question. Koven rightly points out that this would have raised questions about the reliability of clothing as an indicator of social status or economic need: if one so clearly a tramp can be a journalist in disguise, then how can we know whether the object of charity is deserving or not?[16] This would immediately suggest that Greenwood is subverting any facile characterization and categorization of the poor, but I would like to suggest that what is happening is in fact rather more complex.

Greenwood's opening paragraph presents two figures, the pauper and the coachman, but briefly calls into a shadowy semi-existence a third: the implicitly counterfactual 'keen observer'. This figure stands in stead of the reader, with the task of observing the scene and drawing conclusions from it. The scene is curious: the coachman has an *unusually* responsible air and the implied praise of his intelligence is complicated by his 'furtive' glance (is perhaps a crime of some sort about to take place?). Why is a man so clearly poor and disreputable getting out of this middle-class carriage (there is also an air of contrastive hypallage about its departing 'comfortably')? The hypothetical keen observer, and thence the reader, is given a mystery to unravel, one insoluble until the second paragraph is reached. The problem of interpretation lies not in visual categories per se, for immediately we know that the 'pauper' is a journalist the problems resolve themselves: there is no conceptual difficulty in understanding that a man can be in disguise. Rather, Greenwood's opening paragraph challenges a method of interpretation: the observer (and implicitly the reader) is misled not because he or she relies upon visual criteria, but because he or she relies *solely* upon visual criteria. Had it been possible for the hypothetical observer to speak to the pauper or the coachman and ask what was taking place, or somehow to know their thoughts, then of course the implied erroneous acceptance of appearances would not have occurred. There is buried here a methodological criticism that prefigures the whole of Greenwood's experiment: by 'becoming', however briefly, a casual,

Greenwood attempts to avoid the trap into which the 'keen observer' may fall through too great a dependence on external observation. This is not to say that observation of externals is without use: Greenwood observes and describes the visible features of many of those whom he meets in the workhouse. However, he is able to distinguish between 'blackguards' and 'decent men' later on because he has not limited himself to judging by externals (one would imagine anyway that the two categories are indistinguishable in the dark of a workhouse dormitory, even supposing that they have any unambiguous external identifiers) because he has left off being an observer and become a participant, and therefore able to judge and categorize with more information than would have been available to anyone trying to do the same thing that night in a Lambeth street.

The second paragraph solves the mystery posed in the first paragraph and reveals the purpose of the masquerade. It also provides an explanation of Greenwood's motivation: 'Much has been said on the subject – on behalf of the paupers – on behalf of the officials; but nothing by any one who, with no motive but to learn and make known the truth, had ventured the experiment of passing a night in a workhouse, and trying what it actually is to be a "casual".'[17] There is a clear contrast between previous attempts to speak on people's behalf and the current case where actually 'being' a casual will mean not speaking *for* others but rather speaking on one's own behalf and thereby avoiding such possible errors of interpretation as the opening paragraph prepares us for. The implied statement of intent is that Greenwood will have access to knowledge otherwise inaccessible, which he will then be able to communicate to his readers, thus avoiding a superficial and erroneous level of interpretation. This is also shown by a sly detail in the sentence preceding that just quoted. Greenwood speaks of his desire to learn 'by actual experience [ ... ] how the night passes with the outcasts whom we have all seen crowding about workhouse doors on rainy nights'.[18] 'Whom *we* have all seen': Greenwood sites himself within the observing, non-pauper class in the very moment that he disassociates himself from its methodology of pure, at-a-remove, observation.

The prominence Greenwood gives to implying the inadequacy of observation alone continues in the next paragraph. The only person whom he encounters also waiting is 'a decently dressed woman', an external observation that anyone might make; he only '*afterwards* learned' (my italics) that she was being refused admittance until she had recovered from her drunkenness.[19] Once again, this clearly shows that observation such as his readers might usually use is not enough: the woman cannot be visibly intoxicated, as this would remove the need for specifying that it was only afterwards that he learnt of her condition. More significantly, Greenwood then describes his first impressions of the workhouse. For anyone expecting an immediate denunciation of horrific treatment of the poor, these were perhaps a disappointment. Greenwood knocks, and the door is opened 'promptly' (it is significant that the adverb is positive): 'Just within a comfortable-looking clerk sat at a comfortable desk, ledger before him. Indeed the spacious hall in every way was as comfortable as cleanliness and great mats and plenty of gaslight could make it.'[20] Greenwood is doubly on the threshold: he stands quite literally between the outside world known to him and his readers and the inside one thitherto known only to its inhabitants; he stands figuratively between an erroneous and incomplete form of knowledge based upon observation that would take this 'comfortable' scene (the adjective picks up the adverb at the end of the first paragraph to underline how the surface belongs to the world being left behind) at face value and a more complete form of knowledge that will attempt to no longer base itself purely upon a privileged observer's visual classification.

Once in the workhouse and entrusted to the care of 'Daddy', Greenwood is led into a room 'where were ranged three great baths, each one containing a liquid so disgustingly like weak mutton broth that my worst apprehensions crowded back'.[21] Having stripped and made his belongings up into a bundle, he screws up his courage and plunges into one of the baths. Koven reads Greenwood's bath as 'a parodic baptism, not into a community of Christian brothers, but rather into an atavistic fraternity of casuals', adumbrating 'an even more disorderly mingling of male bodies awaiting him in the sleeping shed';[22] however, what happens is more complex than Koven suggests. Greenwood immerges himself when Daddy's back is turned; when the pauper trusty hears the splash he exclaims, '"Lor now! there was no occasion for that; you look a clean and decent sort of man. It's them filthy beggars" (only he used a word more specific than "filthy",) that want washing. Don't use that towel – here's a clean one."'[23] Koven reads this as Daddy's recognition of Greenwood's superior social status, reproducing the social distinctions found outside the workhouse walls.[24] However, Koven neither quotes nor discusses the authorial aside contained between parentheses. If Daddy did not really say 'filthy', which term did he use that Greenwood euphemizes? Given that Greenwood describes it as 'specific', we should not think of some general taboo intensifier such as 'bloody', but rather a taboo term with a very precise meaning. Confirmation of what this is comes in Greenwood's description of some of his fellow-casuals' morning toilet, when they 'commenced an investigation for certain little animals which shall be nameless'.[25] These animals are lice, and the adjective is of course 'lousy'. In light of this, we may read Daddy's statement that Greenwood (or rather 'Joshua Mason', his pseudonym in the casual ward) in fact need not have bathed himself and looks 'a clean and decent sort of man' not as points about class but rather as statements of fact: quite simply, Greenwood is not louse-infested and therefore does not need to wash. Equally, whereas Koven reads the detail of Daddy giving Greenwood a clean towel as corroboration of a recognition of his social status, in this reading it is merely to further avoid any possibility of Greenwood's contracting lice.

The care Daddy takes over his charge is not owing to any class question but is rather a matter of hygienic practicality. The true focus of this episode is not the bath itself, but Greenwood's relationship thereto. He does not mistakenly bathe because Daddy has yet to recognize his social status; he mistakenly bathes because of his ignorance of the situation. Greenwood does not know that the bath is only required from those who are dirty: he, unlike Daddy, is presuming all casuals are treated equally and all must use the filthy water. He is once again showing the limitation of interpretation based upon incomplete knowledge. Furthermore, he is undermining his own authority: although he is willing to experiment and his methodological status is therefore better than his readers', he is nonetheless not (yet) expert in what he is doing.

Another example of Greenwood's willingness to show his ignorance of the rules of the society in which he finds himself is more interesting yet. Whilst Greenwood is trying to settle for the night, Daddy returns 'to do me a further kindness, and point out a stupid blunder I had committed' – Greenwood had forgotten his bread. This is once again an example of an incognito social investigator recognizing his or her relative lack of ability to play a role; in Greenwood's case, it also points out the sheer novelty of his undertaking – unlike Orwell, London and a host of others, the genre's onlie begetter could not rely on previous reports to help him. However, the real fascination of Greenwood's faux pas lies in what it leads to, and the questions this raises about homosexuality in 'A Night in a Workhouse'. Having been returned his bread, Greenwood mulls over the problem of how to avoid eating it, but his problem is soon solved:

> By good luck, however, I presently got half way over my difficulty very neatly. Just behind me, so close indeed that their feet came within half a yard of my head, three lads were sleeping together.
> 'Did you 'ear that, Punch?' one of them asked.
> ''Ear what?' answered Punch, sleepy and snappish.
> 'Why, a cove forgot his toke! Gordstruth! you wouldn't ketch me a forgettin mine.'
> 'You may have half of it, old pal, if you're hungry', I observed, leaning up on my elbows.[26]

Greenwood here is obviously attempting to kill two birds with one stone: he avoids having to eat bread that disgusts him, whilst also trying to ingratiate himself with those whom he would study. His choice of address is particularly interesting: when Greenwood first entered the dormitory, one of the men there asked him to pass him some water, addressing him as 'old pal'. That this was not a form of address to which Greenwood was accustomed is made clear by his immediate authorial repetition of the phrase, this time in scare quotes: 'Such an appeal of course no "old pal" could withstand.'[27]

The problem with Greenwood's attempt at camouflage is that it perhaps leads him into a view of the casual ward coloured by his own actions. Seth Koven has strongly argued for reading 'A Night in a Workhouse' as shocking its readers with its suggestion that male homosexuality was widespread in the Lambeth casual ward. The key individual in this, the only detailed critical analysis of the piece, is 'Kay':

> Soon afterwards the ruffian majority was strengthened by the arrival of a lanky boy of about fifteen, who evidently recognized many acquaintances, and was recognized by them as 'Kay', or perhaps I should write it 'K'. He was a very remarkable-looking lad, and his appearance pleased me much. Short as his hair was cropped, it still looked soft and silky; he had large blue eyes, set wide apart, and a mouth that would have been faultless but for its great width; and his voice was as soft and sweet as any woman's. Lightly as a woman, too, he picked his way over the stones towards the place where the beds lay, carefully hugging his cap beneath his arm.
> 'What cheer, Kay?' 'Out again, then, old son!' 'What yer got in yer cap, Kay?' cried his friends; to which the sweet voice replied, 'Who'll give me part

of his doss (bed)? — my — eyes and limbs if I ain't perishin'! Who'll let me turn in with him for half my toke' (bread)? I feared how it would be! The hungry young fellow who had so readily availed himself of half my 'toke' snapped at Kay's offer, and after a little rearrangement and bed-making, four young fellows instead of three reposed upon the hay-bags at my head.[28]

The description of Kay's appearance, Koven says, bespeaks a certain suggestion of effeminacy and, concomitant therewith, of homosexual activity pointed up by his eagerness to share a bed.[29] More interestingly, however, is the parallel between Kay's actions and Greenwood's. Both offer to share bread, but whilst (in this reading) Kay knows that this is a prelude to some sort of sexual activity, Greenwood does not. We may suggest that if Koven's interpretation is correct and the true scandal putatively uncovered by 'A Night in a Workhouse' is that of the prevalence of homosexuality in the casual ward, then the centrality Greenwood gave to it was thanks to his ignorance of its social codes in offering bread to one sleeping next to him and thus suggesting *his* interest in initiating bartering for sex. In this interpretation, the centrality of homosexuality becomes another problem of Greenwood's methodology: his attempt at mimicry and improvisation causing him to be taken for one interested in sharing his bed, and thus giving a distorted view of 'normal' events in the casual ward of Lambeth workhouse.

We should also consider, though, the possibility that Koven is mistaken in his making 'sodomy' so central to 'A Night in a Workhouse'. Koven is almost certainly right that the description given of Kay, and the various hints at 'horrors [ . . . ] infinitely more revolting than anything that appears in these papers',[30] should be taken to refer to some form of sexual activity, although given contemporary views on the subject this could well have been masturbation;[31] however, his case for the *centrality* of such activity is less strong than it might appear. He does recognize the possibility that Kay may wish to share a bed for warmth rather than sex, but treats the possibility rather cursorily. He quotes the 'Real Casual', an unemployed draughtsman and sleeper in casual wards who wrote a response to Greenwood's piece.[32] In the Real Casual's account of the Gray's Inn Road casual ward, he states that he had been extremely cold, but had preferred not to avail himself of the possibilities for warmth found there: 'I might have been a little warmer if I had chosen to cling up to my companions, as they wanted me to; but I would sooner have borne more than I did than do so, for two dirtier or more repulsive men I never saw.'[33] Koven's commentary on this is that it admits of two interpretations. The first is that the Real Casual was not disgusted by 'men sharing their bodies with one another' in itself, but rather by the dirtiness of these particular examples; the other is that 'physical contact that a gentleman observer might choose to construe as sexual may well be merely an undesirable but sexless survival strategy from the perspective of a naked, freezing pauper. Whether acts *are* sexual rests not in the eye of the beholder, but rather in the minds of those involved.'[34] There is a refusal here to engage with any of the questions of epistemology that Greenwood implies, and as it is for his methodological pioneering that he is still remembered today, we should surely examine what these possible contradictions may mean considered in such a light. The contention that whether an act is to be considered sexual is solely to be decided by its participants is problematic. If society judges an act to be sexual – and the incognito social investigator and observer ('the eye of the beholder') is, so to speak, here standing *pars pro toto* for society – then that act *is* sexual. Koven is of course right in implying that different groups within a society may reach different conclusions; but this problem of etics and emics (Greenwood as an etic observer may consider acts sexual that he would not so consider were he a more emic observer) is so central to 'A Night in a Workhouse' and the tensions it creates so complex that it requires more careful examination.

Perhaps the most important point to be made about the question of homosexuality in 'A Night in a Workhouse' from this point of view is an almost banally simple practical one. The weather was cold, and Kay's complaint upon arriving is that he is 'perishin''. Quite simply, when two or more people huddle together for warmth under blankets, it is warmer if they are naked. If we add to this the literal lousiness of workhouse clothes, then sleeping naked when not in bed alone appears as a physical practicality rather than an erotic choice. Koven reads the situation described etically, and we now have to ask ourselves whether he is misreading Greenwood or reading Greenwood correctly, but accepting Greenwood's (etic) misreading of the situation.[35]

A good demonstration of the fact that naked sleeping need not automatically be associated with sex comes in the work of a later incognito social investigator, Stephen Graham.[36] In his *London Nights* (1925) he recounts having slept in a doss-house:

> I noticed there were far more middle-aged and old men than young ones. They slept stark naked with their clothes under their pillow. [ . . . ] The reason some of them slept naked may have been because they had no

underclothes. One explained to me afterwards that they did not sleep in their clothes because they did not wish to gather insects from the beds. Another said he did not wish to wear out his shirt sleeping in it. [37]

It is significant that Graham is here talking chiefly about older generations, the oldest members of which could even have slept in workhouses in the mid-1860s: there is no cause to believe that the reasons Graham and his informants give were not also present when Greenwood was laying the genre's foundation-stone (indeed, given that those observed by Greenwood were sleeping in even less hygienic conditions than those observed by Graham, the motivations may be held to be relevant a fortiori). Whence, then, this change in explanation from Greenwood's implications of sexual activity to Graham's practicality? The physical characteristics of sleeping in a doss-house or casual ward are unlikely to have changed enough over the half-century separating the accounts to make us look for the reason there; rather, the cause lies in the observer. Greenwood created the genre; he had no prior accounts to look back on, nor is there any particular reason in his own personal history for which he should have been especially knowledgeable about the practicalities of sleeping in difficult and dirty conditions. Graham, on the other hand, not only had fifty years of accounts from authors following in Greenwood's footsteps to look back at, but he had also himself slept in such conditions many times, for example whilst travelling (in another example of (semi-)incognito social investigation) with poor immigrants to New York.[38]

Graham's counter-example notwithstanding, we can never know with full certainty whether Greenwood associated naked sharing of sleeping quarters with sex or with survival, although the greater awareness of problems of heat conservation that the Victorian context would have instilled does make it more feasible that he did not misread the situation. A more suggestive indication that Greenwood understood the physicalities of sleeping in an unheated room in January comes from something that Koven uses as a clue to Greenwood having, quite literally, 'sodomy' in mind. Greenwood writes that after an argument occasioned by 'decent men' in the ward upbraiding the 'blackguards' for telling 'abominable' 'autobiographical anecdotes', 'I could not help thinking of the fate of Sodom; as, indeed, I did several times during the night'.[39] Koven admits that 'Greenwood's allusion to Sodom need not necessarily carry with it sexual connotations; in the 1860s, Sodom represented vice and deviant behavior in many forms', but goes on to claim that the arrival of Kay shows that Greenwood thought 'several times during the night' of Sodom with reference to eponymous sexual practices.[40] I would like to suggest that 'Sodom' has a *third* possible interpretation that is neither 'sodomy' nor vice in general, but rather something specifically relevant to Greenwood's situation. References to Sodom are usually presumed to refer to Genesis 19, the story of Lot. However, there is another important Old Testament reference to Sodom, where her sins are categorized differently. This is Ezekiel 16:48–50. Of crucial importance to us here is 16:49, where God bids Ezekiel address Jerusalem as follows: 'Behold, this was the iniquity of thy sister Sodom; pride, fulness of bread, and abundance of idleness was in her and in her daughters, neither did she strengthen the hand of the poor and needy.' We have here an explicit linkage of Sodom and mistreatment of the poor; we even have 'fulness of bread', which suggests the contrast between Greenwood and his companions with their 'toke' and those who have good bread and full bellies. This is surely a simpler explanation for Greenwood's thoughts repeatedly turning to Sodom than that given by Koven.[41] Furthermore, Greenwood does not in fact state that his thoughts turned to Sodom; they turned rather to the *fate* of Sodom. This is not mere pedantic quibbling: if what he was observing made Greenwood think himself somewhere analogous to Sodom, then he need only have stated that that city came to his mind as he observed. Instead, he took care to say that it was of Sodom's fate that he thought. To think of the city's fate is to think of its punishment, but with reference to the future of the analogous situation. This is a form of thought that focuses more on the wider system than on the individual: one speaks of places or institutions suffering the fate of Sodom, not individuals. With this being the case, then is it not more likely that the Sodom that Greenwood was thinking off was *not* the local reality of the casual ward of Lambeth workhouse but rather the system so well described in Ezekiel whereby those who have 'fulness of bread' allow such ill treatment of the 'poor and needy'? The punishment was not for the individuals in the workhouse, but for the society that created such places.

After the horrors of the night and the epistemological issues raised by them came the morning, when Greenwood had to do the work required from each casual in order for them to be allowed to leave. This consisted of turning cranks to grind a certain measure of corn. It is here that Greenwood's attempt at emicity starts to falter. He describes the system whereby the casuals have to work blind, insofar as they turn the cranks to grind the corn, but cannot see what they are grinding; they have to grind four measures, and a mechanical system informs them via a ringing bell when a measure has been completed. The taskmaster, Greenwood says, soon leaves, and the men are checked on only once or twice by the miller. The paupers' disinclination to work infuriates the journalist: whereas whatever he had witnessed the night before may have disgusted him, it had been disgust in the visceral sense, not an intellectual disgust born of anger. His tone when describing the casuals' labour is quite different from that he uses to describe their activities at night:

> [T]he grinders are as lazy as obscene. [ ... ] The result of this laxity of overseeing would have disgusted me at any time, and was intensely disgusting then. [ ... ] I am convinced that had the work been properly superintended the four measures of corn might have been ground in the space of an hour and a half. As it was, when the little bell tinkled for the fourth time, and the yard gate was opened and we were free to depart, the clock had struck eleven.[42]

His anger is palpable. He makes no pretence of an emic approach; he is the superior outside observer who would make those inferior to him work as he desired. His *parti pris* is clear from the fact that he includes amongst the 'half the gang' that do not work four men who are certainly working: two who are mending their clothes; one who is mending a friend's clothes; one who is cutting another's hair. In other words, 'work' in Greenwood's mind is only construed as that which is ordered by more respectable classes, classes with which he now sides more openly than at any other point in his account. Why might it be that it is in the question of many of the men's refusal to work as he is tacitly desiring that Greenwood so abruptly changes character? The answer, I suspect, lies in his refusing to allow any conscious recognition of the possibility that it might not be sheer idleness alone preventing some half of the men from working as hard as he might like or at what he might desire. Syed Hussein Alatas's great study *The Myth of the Lazy Native* has shown that 'laziness' is a possible form of resistance:[43] the casuals find themselves having to work on trust, as they cannot know how much they have in fact ground, only how much they are *told* that they have ground; equally, there is no incentive to work well, with no rewards given for finishing quickly other than leaving earlier. Greenwood interprets this etically: 'the paupers by profession taking matters quite easy' whereas the 'honest fellows' wish to finish quickly and leave earlier,[44] but surely emically the 'professional' paupers know that finishing sooner means being out on the cold January streets sooner. As Alatas says, 'An absence of the will to work conditioned by circumstances can hardly be called indolence.'[45] Greenwood finds it easier to have a more emic approach when he is dealing with the paupers' personal lives than when with their working lives, as to allow himself to be aware of their resistance against the work imposed upon would imply recognizing in them a level of agency that he is loath to consider.

Greenwood, as we have seen, does attempt to be emic, and up to a point succeeds, or at least is honest about his ignorance and inability to interpret. His great failure is when it comes to the work required of the paupers. Here he is quite clearly etic in the sense that Pike defined in a letter to Harris, a definition key to any understanding of incognito social investigation: 'etics' denotes 'an approach by an outsider to an inside system, in which the outsider brings his own structure – his own emics – and partly superimposes his observations on the inside view, interpreting the inside in reference to his outside starting point'.[46] The reason, I would suggest, for Greenwood's volte-face lies in the situation into which emically recognizing the casuals' agency would lead him. Greenwood is a reformist not a revolutionary: he is willing to attempt to be emic over matters that he considers could be ameliorated through reform, such as conditions within the casual ward or even the very existence of the workhouse system itself. However, reform means agency remains with the class that he represents. Were he to accept the possibility that the 'idleness' exhibited whilst turning the cranks cannot be solved through reform, but only by the overthrow of a system allowing that some may dictate and others can only be dictated to, then he would also have to accept that such an overthrow would mean the loss of his privilege – the very privilege that allows him to be a reformist and observer. His unconscious unwillingness to be emic here is self-protection against recognizing that he is only the most 'important' person in the casual ward thanks to the wider social system that recognizes him as such.

'A Night in a Workhouse' not only stands as the founding text of incognito social investigation in Britain, but it also manages to be in itself a plurality of text forms. There followed close on the heels of its initial publication in the *Pall Mall Gazette* two pamphlets selling in their thousands.[47] One, the shilling edition, was a soberly presented opuscule with a plain cover consisting of simply the title, the fact that it is a reprint from the *Pall Mall Gazette* and the publisher's details, all in a sober serif typeface. The other, priced at only a penny, a twelfth of the price, lacks any such restraint: its cover is a riot of multiple exclamation marks, different typefaces, italics and bold. These two pamphlets have the same contents, but it is nonetheless the case that they should be counted as different texts inspiring different strands within the genre.

To see what is meant by this, we may consider something of a paradox in the most important anthology of incognito social investigation texts, Mark Freeman and Gillian Nelson's *Vicarious Vagabonds* (2008), which collects ten texts from 1866 to 1910.[48] These texts taken together, presented together, clearly appear a genre. However, as Rosalind Crone noted in an extremely perceptive review, such a collection has a particular problem when 'the sources have been literally "reproduced" so that surrounding literary and decorative features have been eliminated'.[49] The removal of paratextual features creates a false impression of uniformity. Depriving these accounts of incognito social investigation of their paratexts is to deprive them of much of their identity. Herein lies a paradox: it is *variety* that unifies in this case rather than uniformity. If accounts of incognito social investigation were to differ solely at the level of contents (that is, text rather than paratext) then we would merely have the same thing repeating itself in different guises – these texts would share subject matter, but be a subgenre of investigative journalism, or the political tract, or autobiography, or some other text form. Recognition of the paratextual variety of accounts of incognito social investigation allows us to recognize the real similarities in otherwise disparate pieces; dismissal of paratextual variety, on the other hand, leads the reader to see superficial similarities that are significantly less complex and rewarding than the complicated web of similarities and differences in tension that the original texts hold. Accounts of incognito social investigation have in common a methodology: they are a single genre (or rather, perhaps, collection of subgenres) insofar as they detail a series of similar methodological approach to an epistemological problem, but the presentation of these attempts at solving the problem, and the uses to which the accounts are put, span a huge range.

J.H. Stallard's *The Female Casual and Her Lodging* (1866) opens with an avowal of the importance of Greenwood's work: 'Until the publication of "A Night in a Workhouse" there was a very general ignorance both of the character of the vagrant poor and the treatment they receive in the casual wards.'[50] One might therefore legitimately imagine that Stallard's book represents an attempt to do for female casuals what Greenwood did in his for male; this interpretation, however, would miss three key points.

The first is that whereas Greenwood's experiences were first reported as newspaper articles and then as pamphlets, and were originally attributed to the anonymous 'Amateur Casual', Stallard's work appears as a true book. This is not just a difference of physical medium. The title page of *The Female Casual* contains a description of its author that is as far from Greenwood's anonymity as is possible. The book is given as being by:

J.H. STALLARD, M.B. Lond.,
AUTHOR OF 'LONDON PAUPERISM;'
Member of the Royal College of Physicians, London; formerly Physician to the Great Northern Hospital, the St. George's and St. James's Dispensary, and for some years Surgeon of the Leicester-shire Militia, and Medical Officer of the Leicester Union Workhouse; Author of 'Work-house Hospitals,' etc. etc.[51]

This array of titles academical and professional is in stark contrast with the bare descriptiveness of 'Amateur Casual'; equally, the professionalism implied in this list contrasts with Greenwood's self-declared amateur status. Stallard may be taking his inspiration from the journalist, but he and his publishers are in no way associating themselves with him. The one-sentence recognition of the debt that Stallard owes to Greenwood with which the book opens paradoxically serves to minimize Greenwood's importance: the more seminal author's name or pseudonym goes unmentioned, and the suggestion is that Greenwood has merely a chronological importance. He may be the first, but the whole paratext of Stallard's work indicates a level of seriousness and thoroughness that the damning of Greenwood with faint praise hints is lacking in the earlier work. The stated, advertised, seriousness of *The Female Casual* would in turn add to paratextual praise of Stallard's standing: later books of his include it amongst the various titles appended to his name on title pages.

The second point of difference between Stallard's work and Greenwood's can be seen in *The Female Casual*'s subtitle: '*With a Complete Regulation of Workhouse Infirmaries*'. Stallard was a doctor and workhouse medical official: his book is in fact two books published as one. Besides the account of incognito social investigation into female casual wards, it also contains a long second part detailing proposals for work-house infirmaries entering into such minutiae as the exact amounts of different types of food and drink various types of patient should receive.

This practical aspect of Stallard's volume makes it a near-unique piece amongst the texts considered here. Stallard is not only interested in knowing what life in a casual ward is like; nor is his goal the description of that life for an audience belonging to classes unlikely ever to be reduced to indigent homelessness. Rather, he is a reformer, but one who uses the information that he has gained to bolster his arguments for the changes that he thinks should be made to the system that he is investigating. That part of *The Female Casual* that recounts incognito social investigation has above all a function as evidence: this goes a long way towards explaining Stallard's stress on the level of his achievement and his dismissal of Greenwood.

Stallard's insistence on his book's ground-breaking nature in looking at *female* casuals is closely tied to the third point wherein Stallard's book shows itself as being in no way a simple equivalent of Greenwood's work that focuses on female casuals rather than male. Quite simply, Stallard himself is *not* the social investigator: this role he deputes to another. His discussion of this is of great interest:

> Now, if the difficulties were great in ascertaining the character of the male casual and the treatment he receives, how much greater will they be when the females are in question! A gentleman, having dressed to the part, descended from his brougham to the dirty gruel, and assuming the air and character of the casual himself, passed safely through the wards with little chance of insult; but no lady could be found to imitate the act, and if the attempt were made, no rags would disguise her character, no acting would conceal her disgust; discovery would be all but certain, and no one can scarcely tell where the disagreeables [sic] would end.[52]

The first point to observe here is that we have Stallard's second and last reference to Greenwood, albeit in a form that does not specify that it is to the journalist that reference is being made. There is in fact something rather odd about Stallard's summary of Greenwood's actions: the indefiniteness of 'a gentleman', coupled with the curious syntax, which suggests that the 'gentleman' (and the reference to a brougham makes it clear that he is Greenwood) first dressed the part, then entered the workhouse to eat his gruel (Greenwood in fact missed his as he arrived too late), *then* assumed the air of a pauper! The impossibility of a 'lady' carrying out what Greenwood had is a further indication of Stallard's implied refusal to acknowledge any debt to his journalist precursor: Stallard's achievement is greater than Greenwood's as the latter only achieved the possible, whereas the former is setting out to achieve the impossible. Stallard himself obviously cannot pass as a female pauper, but no female of his class could either.

Of course, Stallard here is begging the question: a lady cannot perform this role and carry out this investigation because a lady would not be able to do so ... Stallard sees a gendered impossibility, yet his solution is not one of gender, but one of class. He simply sends a working-class woman as an incognito social investigator. Stallard's account of his reasoning behind choosing this course of action for carrying out his social investigation by incognito proxy is detailed, and affords the reader various insights into the prejudices that he brings to his task. He rules out the casuals as a source of information on their own condition, as they are 'suspicious' and unwilling to give confidence to those from other classes;[53] workhouse officials, on the other hand, are too biased against their charges, whom they will paint in the blackest colours possible in order to justify their ill treatment, as well as saying whatever they think will profit them the most vis-à-vis the workhouse authorities who employ them.[54] Stallard then gives a list of criteria for one 'qualified to visit the haunts of these female Bohemians':

[S]he must be accustomed to dirt and rags, and hardships must be no novelty to her. She should be one who has slept without a bed upon the floor, who has dined upon a crust of bread, and by a course of suffering has prepared to endure misery of the very lowest kind without a murmur of complaint. Yet with all this she must be sufficiently familiar with cleanliness, honesty, and plenty, to be able to contrast the condition of the vagrant with that of the industrious poor. Cleverness, courage, and tact will be required, moreover [ ... ] and besides this, there must be a real good nature, which is the only passport to the hearts even of the most abandoned, and the only means of ascertaining the true character of these most degraded specimens of their sex.[55]

The first thing to leap out here is that Stallard is once again very much begging the question: he knows what characteristics are needed of an investigator, because he knows what she will find – 'these most degraded specimens' – and that there is a difference between the residuum ('the vagrant') and 'the industrious poor'. When we consider that this comes before we are presented with the reports of Stallard's proxy investigator, we realize that *The Female Casual* will be the mediation of these accounts of workhouse conditions by the nominal author of the book, who is in fact for much of it a highly prejudiced editor.

The underlying tension between Stallard, the 'author' of the volume and the woman who in fact wrote much of it is clear before he even lets her speak for herself. Having given his list of criteria, he continues with the observation that '[s]ome of these qualifications are evidently possessed by the person who made the following narration'.[56] '*Some* of these qualifications': Stallard is introducing the person who makes possible the whole volume that he is 'writing' by indicating that she does not fully meet the standards that he would like. Equally, the adverb leaves it unclear as to whether the 'evident' qualifications that she possesses are the less respectable ones of a knowledge of indigence or the more positive moral ones. Stallard goes on to explain that his informant is a 'pauper widow' who 'volunteered, as an act of gratitude' to carry out this research as a way of paying back 'some slight assistance' given her 'in a period of great distress':[57] he immediately places his source as being in a position of debt towards him; any possibility of collaboration as equals in any sense is denied before it can be raised. This pre-emptive dismissal of the authority of a working-class woman as opposed to a man from the professional classes is hammered home by how Stallard continues. He states that his proxy investigator's character 'has been vouched for by persons who have known her for many years' and that 'every effort has been made to confirm the truthfulness of the descriptions by visits to the wards themselves and other means'.[58] In other words, whereas he, presumably like Greenwood, whom he does not criticize for a lack of reliability, can say what he will with his name and authority as guarantee enough, his 'pauper widow', who is not even granted the dignity of having her real name made known, must have her word checked at every turn.

This leads to a dilemma regarding analysis of the parts of *The Female Casual* written by Stallard's informant. To what degree are we justified in presuming that she is an incognito social investigator to be analysed in the same manner as the others examined here? Is it right to include a genuine pauper amongst an array of other incognito social investigators somewhere on the middle-class continuum? I would contend that what is central in what is being examined here is its *incognito* nature: Stallard's investigator may be a 'pauper' in her own right, but to presume from this that she is therefore genuinely one of those whom she investigates, that she is only pretending to pass and merely reporting on the social grouping to which she already belongs, is to fall into the same *petitio principii* as

Stallard. It would be to assume that, although 'we' may discern different groupings within 'the poor', there still exists an insurmountable barrier separating 'them' (who must be reported or, at the very least, have their reports mediated) and 'us' (who can report with no need for mediation). Treating the anonymous author of much of *The Female Casual* as an incognito social investigator in her own right is simply to do her the courtesy of accepting her accounts, a courtesy her principal was loath to afford her without hedging it with caveats. Indeed, it should be pointed out that notwithstanding any question over her 'genuineness', she states that she felt that every time she asked for admittance to a workhouse she was at risk of being recognized as a social investigator, and believed that she passed only because of the state of her boots, which she had taken care to make sure were worn out.[59]

We do not know the real name of the incognito social investigator who contributed Chapters 2 to 5 of *The Female Casual*. She does give the names under which she registered (Ellen Stanley, Jane Wood, Ellen Smith and Ellen Taylor); these, however, are not enough for us to say anything with certainty, except to note that there is a possibility that her real first name may indeed have been Ellen, given the overwhelming proportion with which she gives this as her forename, and in what follows 'Ellen' will be used to refer to Stallard's source. Although Freeman and Nelson state that Ellen's first-person narratives are 'Stallard's written version of his accomplice's accounts [ ... ], which were presumably given to him verbally'[60] (though, as we have seen, 'accomplice' is a singularly inappropriate term) and Stallard points out that he has had to 'soften down much of the language',[61] we shall take these reports to be Ellen's work rather than Stallard's.

The reason for which I think it justified to posit Ellen's authorship rather than Stallard's lies in the degree to which the reports from casual wards in *The Female Casual* differ from the commentary on them. Put simply, Ellen does not make negative judgements. Her descriptions of the four workhouses she visits – Newington, Lambeth, Whitechapel and St George in the East – describe what she sees and detail her (negative) physical responses thereto; they also describe those whom she meets, but at no point is she truly judgemental. When he introduces Ellen's texts, Stallard speaks of 'the hardiest and most impudent vagrants in the Metropolis' and their 'idleness', 'dreadful language' and 'disgusting habits';[62] Ellen, however, at no point has recourse to such an intemperate tone. Even when she is mistaken for a prostitute,[63] or jeered at by policemen,[64] she does not presume to judge those insulting her and speak of them in such terms as Stallard uses. The one seeming exception to her refusal to stop observing her fellows and begin judging them is when she says of 'Cranky Sal', whom she meets in Lambeth, that she came to the conclusion that she was 'more rogue than fool';[65] but even here the use of the set phrase suggests at most mild condemnation, a view supported by Ellen's going on to say that '[Sal] boasted that she was so'.[66] Indeed, when she by chance meets Sal again, this time in St George in the East, Ellen says of her: 'Poor Sally! I am convinced she is not vicious, and is to be greatly pitied'.[67]

Ellen's focus – and here we see what truly sets her apart – is not on the people she meets but on the places she visits. She is not concerned with moral judgements, but rather with practical ones. She describes the quality of food, the heat and lack of fresh air, the type of fabric used for the beds and their degree of comfort, the level of insect infestation. This accords with Stallard's role as a practical reformer, but whereas he cannot forbear from adding moral judgement, Ellen can. She describes what she finds and her responses to it: she lacks the arrogance necessary to move from describing what she can know to what she must presume. She has an epistemological humility that is hugely rare in the genre: she is the only working-class social investigator of this type, and almost the only one to recognize that one's ability to gather physical information gives one neither an automatic ability to see into others' minds nor the right to judge their moral status at the same level as one judges the comfort or otherwise of a workhouse bed.

As this suggests, Ellen is also strongly emic, and the contrast with the far more etic Greenwood can be seen in their respective responses to the labour that is required of them before they can leave the workhouse. Whereas Greenwood is disgusted by the casuals' shirking, Ellen reacts quite differently. In the Whitechapel ward, the women are set to pick oakum:

It was very old and hard, and quite unfit for women to pick. I was nearly four hours doing mine, although I worked very hard, and my hands were quite sore when I had finished. There were four women who, after doing a little bit, refused to go on. I observed that none of them troubled themselves to do it; and when I had nearly finished mine I said to a woman, 'Why don't you get on? you will never be let out to-day'. 'Oh no,' said she, 'they cannot keep you in after twelve o'clock'. I said if I had known I would not have done mine.[68]

Here there is no condemnation. She recognizes the unsuitability of the work, but does it because she believes it a requisite for being allowed to leave, and there is no reason not to believe her statement that had she known otherwise she, like those whom Greenwood (and, one suspects, Stallard) would condemn, would also have done as little as possible. She shares the other women's view of this labour as something to avoid; she sees through the rhetoric of making the workhouse experience 'unpleasant' so that the residuum not be tempted to see casual wards as an easier choice than actual work. The workhouses that she visits are already dreadful; *pace* Greenwood's implication, no dignity is to be gained by doing hard physical labour after a night in which it is nigh on impossible to sleep.

Ellen's account of the four workhouses that she has visited ends, and Stallard begins his commentary. Unfortunately, he does not recognize the uniqueness of his informant as the only female working-class incognito social investigator, nor do his conclusions do justice to the woman who suffered so that he could have another publication to his name. His findings are of a quite different nature to the reports that occasioned them. He states that the 'evidence derived from the foregoing narrative shows that two distinct classes are admitted to the casual wards'.[69] One is that of 'old stagers', 'idle vagabonds' who 'wallow in filth';[70] the other 'the distressed poor who are really destitute'.[71] The latter, Stallard proposes, should be given 'bed and breakfast at the public cost' (with the caveat that mechanisms be set up to assure that responsible figures such as magistrates can assess the genuineness of such cases); the former should be detained for at least a month and made to work (he generously allows that the work should be 'somewhat less severe' than that required from a convict).[72] This conclusion is quite unjustified. Ellen's narrative deals with the physical discomforts of extremely badly run workhouses: nothing suggests that she is carrying out such a division into sheep and goats. Equally, Stallard concludes the need for more paperwork, to identify the '*bonâ fide* traveller, destitute of means':[73] many of Ellen's most unpleasant moments, however, come precisely from her having to adhere to the bureaucratic rules already in place and be interrogated by the police – she even decides to visit Whitechapel and St George in the East because there was no requirement in either to pass first through the hands of the police and she would thus be able to 'escape the ordeal of the station'.[74] Whereas Ellen's focus is on the physical practicalities (by way of example, when she is first sent, from Newington workhouse, to Kennington Lane to ask for an order at the police station, it takes her three-quarters of an hour to find it; time and energy casuals could clearly ill afford with night approaching),[75] Stallard pays no attention to the valuable mass of information that he has been given, but quite simply continues with outlining a project that is clearly the result of his lucubrations rather than of the data for which Ellen suffered.

The 1880s saw a recrudescence of accounts of workhouse life by incognito social investigators. An interesting example of the further ramifications of the fame of Greenwood's experiment two decades after is C.W Craven's 'A Night in the Workhouse', from 1887. The near-identical title immediately suggests Greenwood's ground-breaking work, which is also clearly invoked in the piece's final words, 'nor shall I forget for a long time to come, my experience in the Vagrants' Ward of the Keighley Union as an "Amateur Casual"'.[76] The degree to which Greenwood's experiences had become a model may be seen in Craven's peripherality. He was a bookseller from the West Yorkshire town of Keighley, whose work – a mixture of local journalism, verse and short stories of local interest – was self-published. He was not only an amateur as a casual, but, more importantly, he was an *amateur* Amateur Casual. He lacked any journalistic or sociological imperative such as Greenwood or Stallard might profess. His was purely local writing for a local readership; at no point does he describe Oakworth Road, where the workhouse was situated, and his references thereto have an air of easy familiarity bespeaking an expectation of an audience as well versed in local topography as he is himself. Greenwood's example is now being followed outside the metropolitan centre not only in geographical terms, but also in terms of distance from levels of rhetorical power. One need not even have any presumption of rhetorical authority in order to become an amateur casual: it is enough to have 'had a desire for a long time to obtain an insight into the vicissitudes of a vagrant's life'.[77]

Craven's account opens with his putting himself at centre stage: his actions, he claims, exist to satisfy his curiosity, and no wider purpose is being served. We have once again an indication of Craven's distance from his model(s): there is no sense of this being an exposé or an attempt to change conditions. He does, it is true, conclude with a condemnation of workhouse food and an appreciation of workhouse cleanliness, but this ends with a return to the importance of this being *his* experience, *his* adventure, which he will never forget. However, notwithstanding the framing of his narrative between these two examples of naïve self-aggrandizement, 'A Night in the Workhouse' is in many respects curiously impersonal. Craven details what he observes, but his personal involvement in commentary is severely limited. The only dramatization of the rather flat presentation of things observed comes in the headings with which the text is interlarded, headings that in fact are normally part of the text before and/or after them (for example: 'I was then furnished with a couple of rugs and ordered into/THE INNER OR SLEEPING ROOM,/and the lock turned on me').[78] This relative lack of authorial presence suggests some interesting points. We have seen how in Greenwood the incognito social investigator's ignorance of certain workhouse forms is a question of some importance; Craven, however, when he understands the demand 'Pipe and matches?' as asking whether he would like to be given said items rather than being a question of whether he has any to confiscate, sees no value in dwelling on the matter.[79]

The most detailed incursion of the author into the text is when he describes the physicalities of sleeping on cold hard boards; but he is also explicitly present in passing in his application of such adjectives as 'contemptuous' when referring to the attitude of the pauper who delivers the casuals' breakfasts.[80] His judgement, however, is emic: he takes issue with the man's tone towards him and his temporary companions in misfortune – in other words, he is not complaining etically of the contemptuous tone in the abstract, but rather emically of its use in this case. A further, more significant example of his emicity comes when he describes the work that the casuals have to do, and once again his personality briefly makes itself explicitly known in the flat descriptiveness of the text. The casuals have to grind corn using handles attached to a wall; they must grind four bushels but have no way of observing how far they have progressed towards their goal. This is the same situation as that described by Greenwood, but whereas the professional Amateur Casual uses the experience to criticize the work ethic of those turning the cranks, Craven first limits himself to describing without comment the behaviour of his companions, before allowing us a rare sight of a personal response: 'The most aggravating part of the affair was that none of us could observe how much work had been accomplished.'[81] This granting of an importance to the purely psychological side of forced labour, the recognition of autonomous thought and feeling on the part of the casuals is a strong indicator of emicity, and marks Craven out from other incognito social investigators of the time, however much more literarily gifted, socially important or metropolitanly central they may have been. Paradoxically, the relative impersonality of Craven's text also allows us to observe the degree to which his own emicity is present. As has been said, he reports most of what he sees and hears without any commentary, reporting casuals' conversations and copying down pieces of poetry that had been written on a newly whitewashed wall. This is done in a spirit of pure observation, but the removal, insofar as possible, of the observer from observation means an emic observer here, as Craven allows the casuals to speak for themselves, whether it be the 'tramp with diarrhoea' who says that he prefers to spend Sundays incarcerated in a workhouse as it prevents him being exposed to unfriendly stares by those (we may infer) in their Sunday best,[82] or the casuals whose conversations, ranging from the possibility of finding work to an appreciation of the ballad 'The Workhouse Door', he reports.[83] Although the Keighley bookseller was of higher social standing than Ellen the London pauper widow, they share a degree of removal from positions of authority that differentiates them from the great majority of the other incognito social investigators who visited workhouses and are examined here.

Another figure whose account of a night spent in a workhouse shows certain differences from the Greenwoodian model is F.G. Wallace-Goodbody, whose 1883 'The Tramp's Haven' is one of the more curious texts that we shall examine here. It details a night spent by its narrator in an unnamed workhouse casual ward somewhere in London, but this superficial description does not do justice to its particularity. The first is that the narrator states that he finds himself in the casual ward not through journalistic curiosity but through a mixture of misfortune, poverty and chance. He has found himself reduced to poverty for reasons not explained; ill, he has been given papers to go to a workhouse infirmary, but owing to various muddles and misunderstandings finds himself for one night in the casual ward. No real description of himself is given, but we learn that he has recently returned from the Colonies, where he served as a soldier in what he describes as 'the Austral Brigands',[84] a piece of facetiousness similar to his reporting of the name that he gave as 'Slitcoat Downatheel'.[85] 'The Tramp's Haven' was originally published in the *Gentleman's Magazine,* and the whole tone of the piece, as well as the French and Latin tags Wallace-Goodbody scatters throughout it, suggests that the author is upper middle class; he even says of himself that when faced with the tramp-master he tries to 'maintain the bearing of a man who had once been possessed of considerable advantages in a mundane sense'.[86] Freeman and Nelson in their introduction to their anthology speak of his 'idiosyncratic description';[87] in fact, such is the overall tone of Wallace-Goodbody's article that the legitimate suspicion may arise that it is a pure fabrication: the workhouse is unnamed (although its address is given as the fictitious 'Sinai Avenue');[88] nothing is known of the author; the tone is quite unlike any other description of incognito social investigation. Two brief extracts will suffice. The first is from his description of the bullying 'tramp-master': 'This agreeable physiognomy was illuminated at the upper extremities by a pair of greenish-hued, baleful optics, whilst the lower was decorated by a full dark beard.'[89] The affected vocabulary and convoluted construction just to say that the man had green eyes is typical of Wallace-Goodbody, but it is a far cry from the more sober and less belle-lettristic style employed by other investigators of workhouses. The second is from when the tramp master returns the casuals their possessions. That bully appears 'bearing the *pot-[à]-salade* before alluded to, containing, to use the language of Gil Blas, the *hardes* and the *nippes* of the assembled company.'[90] Wallace-Goodbody has already glossed *pot-à-salade* at its first mention ('the basket into which the head fell after having been severed from the trunk by the guillotine'),[91] but leaves the other (far from obvious) French terms unexplained. This intellectual affectation is once again quite unlike the normal run of accounts of incognito social investigation.

Although its peculiarities undoubtedly cause 'The Tramp's Haven' to have an air of spuriousness or even perhaps falsification about it, if we look in some detail at the few indications scattered through it, then we shall find that it is possible to identify the workhouse in which Wallace-Goodbody stayed; a workhouse, furthermore, described with a level of incidental detail that indicates a personal knowledge of it, and further research into the forgotten figure of Wallace-Goodbody himself suggests that he was indeed in such a situation as he describes. The chief clue given is the definition of the area in which the workhouse is found:

> Sinai Avenue is *not* situated in a quarter of the capital by any means in keeping with the character of this charitable and hospitable institution, nor [ ... ] is the entertainment there to be met with administered at all in the manner in which it is lavished in mansions situated but a few yards off. Sinai Avenue is *not* surrounded on all sides by a labyrinth of filthy alleys and lanes teeming and seething with vagabond turbidity; but, on the contrary, reposes at a stone's throw from one of London's best-known squares.[92]

We may also presume that this is not in the City itself, as the workhouse bath is compared to those of 'a similar establishment that I once had occasion to visit in the City',[93] a contrast that makes little sense if the workhouse in 'The Tramp's Haven' is also found there. This places us in West London, and the most obvious contender is the workhouse belonging to the parish of St George's Hanover Square, which lies in the heart of Mayfair, between Grosvenor Square and Berkeley Square.[94] This was on Mount Street, and 'Sinai' is of course extremely plausible as a pseudonym for 'Mount'. Conclusive evidence that the Mount Street workhouse is that described by Wallace-Goodbody comes if we examine three pieces of information given the reader. The first is that as he waits for admission, 'at length eight o'clock sounded from a neighbouring church'.[95] Still today the bell at Grosvenor Chapel strikes the hours from a bell that was already installed and tolling the hours in the early 1880s.[96] Before he is released, Wallace-Goodbody has to pick oakum in a shed off the workhouse yard. Here he describes what he can see as he works: 'the shed [ ... ] opened upon a small paved court, bounded by a row of iron railings, that served to separate the precincts of the workhouse from what struck me as being perfectly in consonance with my situation, namely, a graveyard, over which protruded the irregular backs of the houses of a London street'.[97] Contemporary maps show that the Mount Street workhouse did indeed back onto a graveyard surrounded by the backs of houses, and from any point within the yard or in a building opening on to it this would have been visible.[98] Finally, whilst in the yard, Wallace-Goodbody hears a bell ring, and asks a fellow-casual what it is. He is told by an old tramp that it is 'for the morning service of a Roman Catholic chapel [ ... ] and it's generally very fashionably attended'.[99] The workhouse backed onto Farm Street, home to a Catholic chapel, opened in 1849, and certainly a place frequented by highly placed Catholics. The bell was almost certainly already installed when the chapel opened, and besides being used for the Angelus and Sunday Benediction was also used to give warning of the Elevation of the Host.[100] Wallace-Goodbody heard the bell at some point before eleven in the morning and presumably after ten:[101] Mass at the time was celebrated at ten o'clock on weekdays, so the time would agree perfectly for his having heard the Elevation bell during Mass.[102] St George's Hanover Square workhouse meets all of the conditions described by Wallace-Goodbody, and must be that described in 'The Tramp's Haven'.

Although hitherto very little has been known about F.G. Wallace-Goodbody, research in the archives of the Royal Literary Fund, to which he applied for assistance, has discovered new biographical details.[103] He was born Frederick George Goodbody in London on 25 July 1852 (later adding his mother's maiden name to become Wallace-Goodbody); his father was one of the Serjeants-at-Arms of the House of Lords, where Wallace-Goodbody would himself be given a post in 1872. He served with Baker's Horse in South Africa, although whether he served in that troop's first incarnation before the Anglo-Zulu War or in its second during the war itself is unknown.[104] After his return to England he tried to become a writer, publishing a novel entitled *Rosalba: A Story of the Apennines* in 1891, before moving to Florence where he eked out an extremely precarious living putting his ability to write in English at the service of a local hotelier in return for very basic board and lodging. In 1894 he applied for support from the Royal Literary Fund; this was refused, as he had published but five articles in various publications and one novel, and this was considered insufficient to allow him to be considered an author deserving of the Fund's help.[105]

Of Wallace-Goodbody's five articles, three were on military matters and two on the poor. One of these latter was 'The Tramp's Haven'; the other was published in *L'Indépendant du Var*, a local newspaper published in Hyères in the south-west of France.[106] The article, entitled 'Le Paupérisme en France et en Angleterre', appeared in two parts on successive Fridays, on 2 and 9 September 1883. It is a general overview of the differences between legal approaches to paupers in the two countries; it also – in a remarkable coincidence – recalls Orwell's three articles for *Le Progrès Civique* in 1928 on the 'grande misère de l'ouvrier britannique'.[107] It includes, in the second part, a description of workhouses (glossed as *'maisons de travail'*) and, finally, a note on casual wards (*'asiles de nuit'*). His brief comment is interesting: *'Les asiles de nuit ne sont pas toujours des établissements dignes d'être appelés humanitaires. La presse anglaise révèle de temps en temps des actes de brutalité révoltante commis dans ces asiles.'*[108] His articles were published in September, after he had had first-hand experience of casual-ward life as described in 'The Tramp's Haven', a description that itself contains an account of brutality in its recounting of the scene witnessed in which an ex-soldier suffering from consumption is boxed around the ears by the tramp-master.[109] Is this mention of newspaper exposés a coded reference to his own article in the *Gentleman's Magazine*? We should not dismiss the possibility out of hand, as a certain sly humour elsewhere in the article (see, for example, the description of members of workhouse Boards of Guardians as *'des messieurs honorables et fortunés'*,[110] where the second adjective is not without an ironic charge that undercuts the first) suggests that Wallace-Goodbody is consciously writing something somewhat more complex – or at least more subtle in its contents – than it might at first sight appear.

I would argue, however, that Wallace-Goodbody's modesty about his having penned a denunciation of brutality in a casual ward is not a knowing wink, as it were, to himself (and himself alone, as we may presume the overlap in audience between the *Gentleman's Magazine* and *L'Indépendant du Var* to be vanishingly small). Rather, it is of a piece with the simple fact that he is only an incognito social investigator by accident. He experienced poverty through no choice of his own, and when in the casual ward was there with no design to report on it. However, report on it he did, and his curious style allows us an important insight. Wallace-Goodbody's belle-lettristic style resembles no other account of incognito social investigation known to me; crucially, though, it does have similarities with another account of workhouse life, *Indoor Paupers: Life inside a London Workhouse* by John Rutherford, which was published in 1885.[111] I would argue that this literarization is conscious: Wallace-Goodbody is distancing himself (as Rutherford does) from those unfortunates amongst whom he finds himself. Greenwood and those examined here who followed the path he had blazed attempted emicity to a greater or lesser extent, yet remained fundamentally etic observers. Wallace-Goodbody, on the other hand, uses distancing literarization to suggest his eticity; this eticity, however, remains as elusive as the emicity sought by Greenwood and others: Wallace-Goodbody *is* giving his readers an insider's view, however much he may stylistically try to suggest that he is no real insider.

The half-century Golden Age of Greenwoodian incognito social investigation drew to an end as the Edwardian era closed, but its final period saw the appearance of one of the most curious of all the texts that the tradition produced. This appeared in a local newspaper in Yorkshire, the *Craven Herald*, on 1 July 1910. It was included in the 'Odds and Ends' collection of various articles of local interest not attaining to the status of 'news', a gallimaufry published under the byline 'Phil-Up'. The great majority of the first piece, headed 'Peripatetic Journalist's Experience at Skipton', is not by the anonymous Yorkshire complier, as Phil-Up's preamble makes clear:

A peripatetic journalist called at the 'Herald' Office on Monday morning with some 'copy' that for a consideration he was prepared to surrender, and which, he urged, would be of interest to 'Herald' readers. The consideration was given, and the 'copy' became the property of the editor. The writer shows how easy it is to live on a half-penny a day for nine days, finishing up with a 33 miles' walk from Leeds to Skipton, and crowning it with a night in the Skipton tramp ward. The problem the journalist set himself was: Could he live for a week on a threepenny loaf. It was practically living on nothing, but, the narrative avers, the deed was done.

Setting off last Sunday morning with no money and only a three-half-penny loaf to go on with, the journey was commenced, the objective being Westmorland where some work awaited him. He intended staying at Keighley, to which point his bread had lasted out, but disappointed at not finding a friend at home, he decided to tramp the extra ten miles to Skipton.[112]

This is followed by the 'copy' regarding a night in Skipton workhouse. The description itself is not of any real interest considered as a description of a night in a casual ward; its interest lies in the bizarre circumstances related regarding its genesis.

This episode in the life of the Peripatetic Journalist (hereafter 'P.J.') may be summarized thus: for reasons unstated he decides to spend nine days with almost no money or food; unable to be hosted by a friend he sleeps in a workhouse; he makes money by writing up his experiences; he continues on his way for some days to reach a workplace in Westmorland. The oddities in the presentation of P.J., however, mean that to accept him simply as a 'peripatetic journalist' looking for an experience for copy is difficult. After all, why would a journalist walk for nine days in order to reach a job? Keighley had a workhouse, so why did he not stay there? Why did he undertake to prove that he could survive on so little?

Two possible explanations may be offered, and both, in a text from the end of the great period of this text type, raise rather remarkable questions about incognito social investigation, at least of the Greenwoodian type.

The first bases itself upon the article's conclusion, P.J.'s dreams in the workhouse and the fact that he speaks proudly of having walked 33 miles in nine hours. He dreams of strange women, windows, children and railway engines, and takes up a long paragraph describing his nocturnal visions; his conclusion – 'the moral I wish to draw' – is that 'we all eat three times as much as is good for us. I have never felt stronger than I do at this moment after living on a halfpenny a day for nine days.'[113] The oddness of the dreams and the emphasis put upon them, the pride in what would appear to be unnecessary walking and the fixation with fasting

(P.J. does recognize that the Skipton workhouse breakfast, although fine for one such as him, who has been on such a diet for nine days, may not be enough for those who have to break stones to pay for their lodging; however, he gives it to be understood that he was spared this owing to its being his first time there): all these, coupled with his story's inconsistency and oddity, suggest that one solution to the problem of P.J.'s motivations is that he was, at the very least, eccentric. This in itself is not the key point: a journalist has as much right to be eccentric as anyone else; and eccentricity is no bar from also being an incognito social investigator.

In this reading, however, where P.J. is a genuine incognito social investigator, albeit an unconventional one, the interest lies in the very fact of his publishing in the *Craven Herald*. This was not part of his original plan, for he says that he was still quite fresh upon his arrival in Skipton, and 'was capable of another twenty miles, and if it were not for the necessity of earning a few shillings by means of this article, I should have walked on through the night'.[114] Incognito social investigation, it is suggested here, is by now so much part of the journalistic landscape that this route-marching eccentric could count upon a local newspaper, necessarily chosen purely by proximity, paying him for an unrequested example of the genre.

At this point, incognito social investigation almost begins to appear as if it were itself part of the subject of its own study: P.J. is an incognito social investigator, but one of the things that he does whilst playing the role of a tramp is to play the role of an incognito social investigator... Fasting, walking and sleeping in a workhouse: to these are added writing a report on them for publication. No better instance of how in fifty years incognito social investigation had woven itself into the fabric of journalism could be found than this.

The above argument takes P.J. as not being genuinely poor. However, the point about the ubiquity of incognito social investigation also holds if we do not accept this. Indeed, it is strengthened, and a reading emerges of quite remarkable interest. If P.J.'s inconstancies and oddities are taken to mean that he was not in fact a journalist, peripatetic or otherwise, what in fact was he? The clear answer is that he was a tramp. In this interpretation, incognito social investigation had become so well known a concept that a tramp wishing to make some extra money could, in an astonishing game of appropriation, pass himself off as a journalist passing himself off as a tramp...

Ambiguity is at the heart of the most interesting examples of incognito social investigation, those instances where it is not merely the repetition of an increasingly hackneyed cliché of journalistic methodology; it is a form, or set of forms, that has at its heart the ambiguities of how we recognize and identify people and experience, and the degree to which a text shows this, whether implicitly or explicitly, is the degree to which it is of interest not solely to the historian of the conditions of the poor, but is instead of wider interest to the student of their representation, and even of representation *tout court*. No better example of this could be sought, perhaps, than the possibility of a tramp pretending to be a journalist pretending to be a tramp. With what authority does P.J. speak? What authority may his readers have attributed to him? How does one recognize 'authority' when reading?

This is the epistemological question of authors' 'truthfulness': that is, to what extent can the reader (whether the most superficial and naïve of casual browsers or the most acute and profound of critics matters not) recognize a description of lived experience as 'truthful'? The common answer (and most useful) is of course insofar as that description tallies with the reader's own experience. Whilst this is reasonably unproblematic both for descriptions that one may fairly presume to be common to author and reader, at least when they both come from the same or similar cultures (certain emotional states, certain situations purportedly universal within that culture) and for descriptions of things so alien (cultural specificities that cannot legitimately be expected to be shared by the reader, experiences recorded only because they are so outré as to make them putatively unique) that one must simply either accept the author's reliability or deny it, in the case of descriptions of the lives of the poor we find ourselves in a grey area vis-à-vis our acceptance or otherwise of authors' reliability. Rare would be the reader who had never experienced poverty in some way, whether through personal experience or simple observation: the difficulty in gauging the veracity of incognito social investigators' reports lies in the high degree of specificity of the reader's personal history allowing recognition of a detail's being true to life or not. This is a problem that concerns not so much the reader as the critic. The degree to which an individual reader recognizes a description as accurate or false may be interesting, but when that individual reader is a critic basing parts of his or her argument upon that recognition of veracity, then the problem is clear. Modern academic practice rather frowns upon the intrusion of the critic's biography, but in this case it is useful, I think, to bear in mind that my, Luke Seaber's, reaction to certain incognito social investigation texts and the problem of their veracity can only ever be a result of my own lived experience with regard to the questions of poverty treated therein.

P.J., the tramp-journalist or journalist-tramp, offers one of the best examples for discussion regarding this issue. He describes the problems caused by the lack of width of the bed in Skipton workhouse:

> For a man who has done a long walk the best way of resting is to lie on the side and draw up the knees. But the bed was not wide enough for this, and the only way I could get any comfort was by lying on my back, drawing up my legs, and letting my feet rest flat. But this was not the position my feet needed. They were blazing hot, and the touch of the rug made them worse.[115]

I – the personal, autobiographical I and not the relatively anonymous critical voice – recognize this as 'true'. If you have walked a long way on hard roads and eaten little, the first position described is the most comfortable and restorative; if this is impossible, one tends to adopt the second. The anonymous incognito social investigator does not say it – he may not even consciously know it – but drawing up one's knees tends to assuage hunger to some extent, whence it is reasonable to assume the second position described as better for one's overall comfort although not for that of one's feet. I – or rather, 'one' or 'we'; the critical, anonymizing voice – cannot know whether the journalist is telling the truth: we cannot trace the bed into which he was put; we cannot even trace the reality of his existence outside this one column in the *Craven Herald*. However, I – the autobiographical voice – can at least recognize that his description of his experience agrees with certain analogous experiences that I have had. We cannot presume that those reading this recognize the accuracy of my recognition of the journalist's accuracy any more than we can presume that his original readers recognized his accuracy. This problem in itself is far from new, and usually one can safely pass over it silence. In this case, however, where we have to deal with questions of reliability as well as presumptions regarding experience, and where, above all, the great selling point of incognito social investigation is to communicate secret experience, as it were, experiences otherwise unknowable to the investigators' readerships, then this problem is crucial.

This is not a problem that can be solved in the normal academic manner. As an example of why this is, let us consider a detail from a book that some years after the heyday of the Greenwoodian tradition would become the most important work in it. In Paris, at his lowest ebb, Orwell notes a discovery about what happened to his saliva when he had not eaten for three days:

> Complete inertia is my chief memory of hunger; that, and being obliged to spit very frequently, and the spittle being curiously white and flocculent, like cuckoo-spit. I do not know the reason for this, but everyone who has gone hungry several days has noticed it.[116]

It is possible to make an appeal to authority here regarding the 'accuracy' of Orwell's observation: although there is a certain dearth in the scientific literature of studies on the effects of fasting on saliva, that which there is agrees that it causes a decrease in production.[117] It is also the case that fasting, like a similar drop in liquid intake, would tend to make spittle thicker and gummier – more 'flocculent', therefore.[118] This, at first sight, would suggest that Orwell is partially 'right': one's spittle when one fasts does undergo the changes in texture that he notes, but its production decreases, which might suggest that he is wrong about being obliged to spit more frequently. However, fasting spittle, being thicker, is less easy to spit – therefore leading (in my own experience) to the impression of having to spit more often, even when one is in fact spitting less in terms of volume. The 'truth' of this in Orwell's case can only ever be conjecture: Orwell says that this is how things are; whether the reader believes him hinges on the twin poles of previous experience of fasting that matches or does not match Orwell's and previous experience of Orwell and the degree to which one finds him and has found him reliable – where one's conviction or lack of it in his reliability comes from (personal experience, analysis of his writings, the secondary literature ... ) matters not.

Once again we reach the insoluble problem of readers' recognition of 'the truth'; we can only ever speak truly for ourselves and our reactions: although it is possible in many cases to compare incognito social investigators' reports against the thing reported, which is valuable and offers much insight into the various mechanisms, spoken and unspoken, conscious and unconscious, through which the authors' experiences were filtered, what cannot be explored is readers' reactions to those reports. We can in many cases know what people said about their reading; we cannot know how many people reading Orwell, say, had fasted enough to experience what he experienced regarding spittle. Indeed, more importantly, *I* cannot know how general the experience that I share with Orwell of having observed the same changes in one's spittle is amongst those who have fasted to the same point. This unknowability of readers' reactions to investigators' reports has, of course, one exception: my reactions. This only shifts the problem: I cannot speak for my readers' reactions to my report of my reaction to investigators' reports...This is a philosophical problem, admitting of no solution and beyond the present work's remit; it only remains to say that this question must be borne constantly in mind at some level whilst all the other issues explored are being discussed.

*Down and Out in Paris and London* belongs to the period after 1910, which we may conveniently take to be the approximate end of the Greenwoodian tradition in the narrow sense. The next chapter will explore the slow death of James Greenwood's creation, and how it was paradoxically accompanied by its appeal to the intelligentsia reaching its maximum spread.

## NOTES

1. Stead, W.T. 1886. 'Government by Journalism'. *Contemporary Review* 49, pp. 653–74, p. 672.
2. 'One of Them' [John Rutherford]. 2013 [1885]. *Indoor Paupers: Life inside a London Workhouse*. N.p.: Workhouse Press, p. 15.
3. First published in the *Pall Mall Gazette*, 12, 13 and 15 January 1866 and thereafter in *The Times*, 13, 15 and 16 January. Also published shortly afterwards in abridged or amended forms in several other British and Irish newspapers (*Birmingham Daily Post, Belfast News-Letter*, etc.). The text used here is Greenwood, James. 2008 [1866]. 'A Night in a Workhouse'. In Freeman, Mark and Gillian Nelson (eds.). *Vicarious Vagrants: Incognito Social Explorers and the Homeless in England, 1860–1910*. Lambertville: The True Bill Press, pp. 53–75.
4. Stead, 'Government by Journalism', p. 655.
5. Now Black Prince Road.
6. Koven, Seth. 2004. *Slumming: Sexual and Social Politics in Victorian London*. Princeton and Oxford: Princeton University Press, p. 25.
7. See Ibid., p. 36.
8. Pike, Kenneth L. 1954. *Language in Relation to a Unified Theory of the Structure of Human Behavior*. Glendale: Summer Institute of Linguistics, pp. 8–12.
9. See Headland, Thomas N. 1990. 'Introduction: A Dialogue between Kenneth Pike and Marvin Harris on Emics and Etics'. In Headland, Thomas N., Kenneth L. Pike and Marvin Harris (eds.). *Emics and Etics: The Insider/Outsider Debate*. Newbury Park, London and New Delhi: Sage, pp. 13–27, pp. 20–1.
10. Ibid., p. 22.

11. Harris, Marvin. 1990. 'Emics and Etics Revisited'. In Headland, Thomas N., Kenneth L. Pike and Marvin Harris (eds.). *Emics and Etics: The Insider/ Outsider Debate*. Newbury Park, London and New Delhi: Sage, pp. 48–61, pp. 50–1.
12. See Koven, *Slumming*, pp. 25–87.
13. Greenwood, 'A Night in a Workhouse', pp. 53–4.
14. Ibid., p. 45.
15. On the 'residuum', see Harris, José. 1998. 'Between Civic Virtue and Social Darwinism: The Concept of the Residuum'. In Englander, David and Rosemary O'Day (eds.). *Retrieved Riches: Social Investigation in Britain 1840–1914*. Aldershot and Brookfield: Ashgate, pp. 67–87, and Welshman, John. 2006. *Underclass: A History of the Excluded, 1880–2000*. London and New York: Hambledon Continuum, pp. 1–20. The term was first used, by the MP John Bright, in 1867, a year after Greenwood's experiences (José Harris, 'Between Civic Virtue and Social Darwinism', p. 74).
16. Koven, *Slumming*, p. 37. Cf. Jaffe, Audrey. 1990. 'Detecting the Beggar: Arthur Conan Doyle, Henry Mayhew, and "The Man with the Twisted Lip"'. *Representations* 31, pp. 96–117, pp. 99–102.
17. Greenwood, 'A Night in a Workhouse', p. 54.
18. Ibid.
19. Ibid.
20. Ibid., p. 55.
21. Ibid., p. 56.
22. Koven, *Slumming*, pp. 39–40.
23. Greenwood, 'A Night in a Workhouse', p. 56.
24. Koven, *Slumming*, p. 41.
25. Greenwood, 'A Night in a Workhouse', p. 68.
26. Ibid., p. 59.
27. Ibid., p. 58.
28. Ibid., p. 61.
29. Koven, *Slumming*, p. 44.
30. Greenwood, 'A Night in a Workhouse', p. 68.
31. For the level of stigmatization of masturbation, which would certainly warrant Greenwood's talk of 'horrors' as much as homosexuality, see Hall, Lesley A. 1992. 'Forbidden by God, Despised by Men: Masturbation, Medical Warnings, Moral Panic, and Manhood in Great Britain, 1850–1950'. *Journal of the History of Sexuality* 2:3, pp. 365–87, especially pp. 374–5.
32. See Koven, *Slumming*, pp. 66–68 and notes.
33. Quoted in ibid., p. 68.
34. Ibid.
35. It should be noted that there were at least some contemporary readers who read 'A Night in a Workhouse' with Koven's homoerotic subtext. It was

discussed in the editorial meetings of *Punch* in terms such as 'that blood on the blanket! Had a sodomite taken a maidenhead?', but given the atmosphere of male homosociality and joking characterizing these meetings, we should not presume this to be a factually accurate reading of the account. I am indebted to Patrick Leary for sharing material from his forthcoming annotated edition of the Henry Silver diary of *Punch* table-talk.

36. See Hughes, Michael. 2014. *Beyond Holy Russia: The Life and Times of Stephen Graham*. Cambridge: Open Book.
37. Graham, Stephen. n.d. [1925]. *London Nights: A Series of Sketches of London at Night*. London: Hurst and Blackett Limited, p. 48.
38. Graham, Stephen. 1914. *With Poor Immigrants to America*. London: Macmillan and Co.
39. Greenwood, 'A Night in a Workhouse', p. 60.
40. Koven, *Slumming*, pp. 43–4.
41. It is worth noting that the early 1860s saw new editions of the most important English-language work on Ezekiel, William Greenhill's monumentally exhaustive *Exposition*, increasing the possibility that Greenwood had this book of the Bible in mind.
42. Greenwood, 'A Night in a Workhouse', pp. 71–2.
43. Alatas, Syed Hussein. 1977. *The Myth of the Lazy Native: A Study of the Image of the Malays, Filipinos and Javanese from the 16th to the 20th Century and Its Function in the Ideology of Colonial Capitalism*. London: Frank Cass. See for example pp. 66 and 103.
44. Greenwood, 'A Night in a Workhouse', p. 72.
45. Alatas, *The Myth of the Lazy Native*, p. 106.
46. Quoted in Marvin Harris, 'Emics and Etics Revisited', p. 49.
47. See Koven, *Slumming*, p. 25.
48. Freeman, Mark and Gillian Nelson (eds.). 2008. *Vicarious Vagrants: Incognito Social Explorers and the Homeless in England, 1860–1910*. Lambertville: The True Bill Press. It is curious that 1860 is given as the starting year rather than 1866.
49. Crone, Rosalind. 2010. 'Reading the Victorian Underworld'. *Crime, Histoire & Sociétés/Crime, History & Societies* 14:1, pp. 95–101, p. 95.
50. Stallard, J.H. 1866. *The Female Casual and Her Lodging: With a Complete Regulation of Workhouse Infirmaries*. London: Saunders, Otley and Co., p. 1.
51. Ibid., unnumbered title page.
52. Ibid., p. 2.
53. Ibid.
54. Ibid., pp. 2–3.
55. Ibid., pp. 3–4.
56. Ibid., p. 4.

57. Ibid.
58. Ibid.
59. Ibid., p. 6.
60. Freeman and Nelson, *Vicarious Vagrants*, p. 84, n. 4.
61. Stallard, *The Female Casual and Her Lodging*, p. 4.
62. Ibid., p. 5.
63. Ibid., p. 20.
64. Ibid., p. 7.
65. Ibid., p. 28.
66. Ibid.
67. Ibid., p. 56.
68. Ibid., pp. 39–40.
69. Ibid., p. 63.
70. Ibid., p. 63–4.
71. Ibid., p. 65.
72. Ibid., pp. 69–74.
73. Ibid., p. 69.
74. Ibid., p. 29.
75. Ibid., p. 7.
76. Craven, C.W. 2008 [1887]. 'A Night in the Workhouse'. In Freeman, Mark and Gillian Nelson (eds.). 2008. *Vicarious Vagrants: Incognito Social Explorers and the Homeless in England, 1860–1910*. Lambertville: The True Bill Press, pp. 181–8, p. 188.
77. Ibid., p. 181.
78. Ibid., p. 183.
79. Ibid., p. 182.
80. Ibid., pp. 186–7.
81. Ibid., p. 187.
82. Ibid., pp. 184–5.
83. Ibid., p. 184.
84. Wallace-Goodbody, F.G. 2008 [1883]. 'The Tramp's Haven'. In Freeman, Mark and Gillian Nelson (eds.). 2008. *Vicarious Vagrants: Incognito Social Explorers and the Homeless in England, 1860–1910*. Lambertville: The True Bill Press, pp. 119–140, p. 130.
85. Ibid., p. 129.
86. Ibid., pp. 127–128. This goes against what Rachel Vorspan says in her important 1977 article on the New Poor Laws when she speaks of Wallace-Goodbody as a 'self-proclaimed "respectable unemployed working-man"' (Vorspan, Rachel. 1977. 'Vagrancy and the New Poor Law in Late-Victorian and Edwardian England'. *English Historical Review* 92, pp. 59–81, p. 67); nowhere, in fact, does Wallace-Goodbody use this expression of himself.

87. Freeman, Mark and Gillian Nelson (eds.). 2008. Editors' Introduction. *Vicarious Vagrants: Incognito Social Explorers and the Homeless in England, 1860–1910*. Lambertville: The True Bill Press, pp. 7–47, p. 30.

88. Freeman and Nelson note that this name is not be found in the *Post Office London Directory* for either 1882 or 1895 (Wallace-Goodbody, 'The Tramp's Haven', p. 120, n. 2).

89. Ibid., p. 123.

90. Ibid., p. 138–9.

91. Ibid., p. 125, n. 11.

92. Ibid., p. 121.

93. Ibid., p. 133.

94. All information regarding individual workhouses, unless otherwise noted, comes from Peter Higginbotham's remarkable site, workhouses.org.

95. Ibid., p. 121.

96. Personal correspondence with Lis Hasted, Administrator, The Grosvenor Chapel.

97. Ibid., pp. 137–8.

98. I verified this with a site visit in June 2013.

99. Ibid., p. 138.

100. Personal correspondence with Anna Edwards, Assistant Archivist at the Jesuit Archives (British Province).

101. Wallace-Goodbody is interrupted in the reveries that hearing the bell occasions by the tramp-master, who doles out the casuals' belongings that he had confiscated the night before; this is over by eleven o'clock (ibid., pp. 138–9). Ten o'clock as a *terminus post quem* is slightly less certain, but is probable, based on the fact that before talking about the bell Wallace-Goodbody recounts the scene of an old soldier mistreated by the task-master set to watch over the oakum-pickers, stating that the sick man was summoned to the doctor at ten (ibid., p. 137).

102. Mass times are from the *Catholic Directory* for 1883. I owe this information to Anna Edwards.

103. I owe knowledge of the fact that Wallace-Goodbody had applied to the Royal Literary Fund to Cross, Nigel. 1980. *A Select Catalogue of Applicants to the Royal Literary Fund 1790–1870 with a Historical Introduction*. Unpublished PhD thesis, University College London, no page number.

104. See Castle, Ian. 2003. *Zulu War – Volunteers, Irregulars & Auxiliaries*. Oxford: Osprey, p. 36.

105. London, British Library, Loan 96 RLF 1/2440.

106. The fragile state of the copies held in the Bibliothèque nationale de France mean that I have been able to see copies of these articles only, and cannot provide further bibliographical information.

107. 'great poverty amongst British workers'. All translations are my own.

108. 'Casual wards are not always establishments that are worthy of being called humanitarian. Every so often, the English press reveals acts of revolting brutality committed in them.'
109. Wallace-Goodbody, 'The Tramp's Haven', pp. 136–7.
110. 'gentlemen who are honourable and lucky'.
111. The book was attributed to 'One of Them' when published, but the author has been identified by Peter Higginbotham (Higginbotham, Peter. 2013. Preface to 'One of Them' [John Rutherford]. *Indoor Paupers: Life inside a London Workhouse*. N.p.: Workhouse Press, pp. 1–3, p. 2).
112. 'Phil-Up'. 1910. 'Odds and Ends: Peripatetic Journalist's Experience at Skipton'. *Craven Herald*, 1 July 1910, p. 2.
113. Ibid.
114. Ibid.
115. Ibid.
116. Orwell, George. 1997 [1933]. *Down and Out in Paris and London* [*The Complete Works of George Orwell*, ed. Peter Davison, vol. 1]. London: Secker & Warburg, p. 36.
117. See Rahim, Z.H.A. and H.B. Yaacob. 1991. 'Effects of Fasting on Saliva Composition'. *The Journal of Nihon University School of Dentistry* 33:4, pp. 205–10, p. 207 ('salivary flow rate decreased by almost 50% on fasting').
118. Personal communication with Professor Stephen Porter of the UCL Eastman Dental Institute, whom I thank.

# CHAPTER 3

# Down and Out: George Orwell and the Death of a Genre

Anyone reading the *Thanet Advertiser and Echo* for 19 November 1921 may have had their eye struck by a headline on page 7 announcing **'VICAR'S ORDEAL'**, but any hopes of a story that would satisfy prurience or ghoulish curiosity would immediately have been dashed by the line below, 'as unemployed tramp'. The story is a report of a talk given to Margate Rotary Club by the Vicar of Margate, the Reverend David Railton, describing his recent experiences 'tramp[ing] across Cumberland simulating the accents of a Scotsman looking for work, begging his way from town to town'.[1] At first sight, Railton's experiences of tramping to look for work and sleeping in doss-houses makes him another, albeit late, provincial example à la Craven of those who followed in Greenwood's wake. This is not the case, however.[2]

The report begins as follows: 'An astonishing story, reminiscent of the days when it was almost a custom in social circles for a man to disguise himself as a tramp for the sake of experiencing the woes of others, was told yesterday to the members of the Margate Rotary Club.' This is one of the very few times that an account of incognito social investigation recognizes the existence of a tradition of such a thing, and perhaps the only time that the very commonness of the phenomenon is stated within an example of it. Furthermore, this sites a certain tradition of incognito social investigation in the past, and it may not be a coincidence that this rarity is not found in a more up-to-date metropolitan publication, but rather in one where fashions – in journalism, in

© The Author(s) 2017
L. Seaber, *Incognito Social Investigation in British Literature*,
Palgrave Studies in Life Writing, DOI 10.1007/978-3-319-50962-4_3

this case – would to a certain degree have lagged, and memories of their heyday were less distant.

This implicit suggestion that Railton's exploits are noteworthy not because they are unique, but because they belong to a phenomenon that is rare *now*, brings us to the other reason why I think this column-and-a-half, local news story is of such interest. In order to look at this, we have to examine the career of the Vicar of Margate, of whom the *Advertiser* says merely that he holds the Military Cross, had been an Army chaplain and 'took a place of honour at Westminster Abbey last week when the Ypres-flag was installed in its prominent position on Armistice Day'. This rather underplays Railton's role in the proceedings.[3] Armistice Day, 11 November 1921, had seen the interment of the Unknown Warrior in Westminster Abbey, and his pall had been the 'Ypres-flag', a Union Jack given to Railton by his mother and used by him as an altar cloth at the Front. The pall used was Railton's flag because it had been the Vicar of Margate who had suggested the whole idea of burying an unknown warrior in the Abbey to its Dean, Herbert Edward Ryle. Railton is celebrated now for having been the originator of the idea, and thus commands a minor but important role in British history.

The seeds for his 'tramping', we may surmise, were sown much earlier than the 1920s. His father was George Scott Railton, an influential early commissioner in the Salvation Army, and we may presume that his son grew up with a keen interest in the poor. It is, however, in the selection of extracts from his letters home from the Front during the First World War preserved in the Imperial War Museum that we see the depth of his interest in social questions, continuing as it did even under horrific conditions.[4] In one letter he talks of a storm in which the Colonel had given up his tent for soldiers, and laments the fact that similar self-sacrifices are not to be seen amongst the moneyed classes outside of a war context;[5] in another he exclaims how his contact with working-class troops has created in him a desire to help them as a class, 'Later on, please GOD, we can help our England. Now, we experiment on the Army – by and by we may be used in England or abroad'; this in a letter where he also notes that when all the men wash together social barriers are broken down as the men are equal in their God-created nakedness.[6] The winter cold at the beginning of 1917 focused him not only on the problems of the poor but also on his epistemological position with regard to them: 'I never knew the terrors of winter before. Even when I used to appeal for the poor I did not know how fearful it was for them. I thought I did. I did not. Never properly dry, never really warm.'[7] We may posit that it was this awareness of a need to experience the physical suffering of the poor oneself in order to be able to understand it, coupled with his desire to 'spend half my life in getting their rights for the men who fought out here',[8] that led him, in the *Thanet Advertiser*'s words, to 'study the difficulties of the ex-service man seeking employment'.

The anonymous local journalist who reported Railton's talk was right: the Greenwoodian tradition belonged to an earlier generation, and was an increasingly rare phenomenon. The most celebrated work of incognito social investigation in English, *Down and Out in Paris and London*, was still to appear, and the tradition that had started in 1866 had begun to look old-fashioned. I would argue that 'The Ramble of a Rotarian' may be taken as the first occasion in which we see the stirrings of the sea-change that profoundly altered incognito social investigation between the wars. Thitherto, those following in the tradition created by Greenwood, like that tradition's onlie begetter himself, had presented themselves as being motivated impersonally. At most, they speak of vague longings and desires,[9] but at no point is there the articulation of anything more detailed. These are practical accounts, with practical aims, even if it only be making the plight of the destitute better known. They are obviously part of their historical context, but there is no avowed mixing of this with the personal: the presentation of these works is that they are pieces created to engage with an immediate problem exterior to the writer.

The little that we know of Railton's talk, however, coupled with what is said in his wartime letters, allows us to see his motivation as something quite different from the various shades of philanthropy, campaigning and journalism (mercenary to a greater or lesser extent) that characterize the Greenwoodian tradition before him. As is clear from his letters quoted, he felt a very strong *personal* drive to explore this question; it is also the case that some of the details of how he carried out his plan indicate personal involvement.[10] His daughter recalls that the name he used in his tramping was 'Lionart'; this was also the name that he used when playing football (an activity of which his wife disapproved). Furthermore, the *Thanet Advertiser* reports that he called at one house where a 'gorgeously-attired chauffeur' 'looked at the tramp with withering scorn and contempt', but goes on to say that he was there offered half-a-crown; what it does not report is that he also called on his in-laws' house, where the servants (who had never seen him before in any guise) turned him away empty-handed. This mixing of the personal and the social marks Railton out as an unheralded pioneer, for the 1920s and '30s would see this become dominant, reaching its apotheosis in Orwell's life and work.

In his encyclopaedic *British Writers of the Thirties* Valentine Cunningham charted bourgeois intellectuals' 'going over' to the proletariat in Britain in the 1930s;[11] one sometimes has the impression that all those of Auden's generation – and not just 'the Auden generation' of MacSpaunday itself – at certain points in their careers became social investigators of one sort or another. Orwell, of course, is the most celebrated, whether as the incognito dishwasher and tramp of *Down and Out in Paris and London* or the declared observer of *The Road to Wigan Pier*, but he is only the tip of the iceberg. Henry Green worked in his family's Birmingham factory;[12] Christopher Isherwood adopted 'a slight Cockney twang' on holiday amongst working-class boatmen;[13] Tom Driberg slept on the Embankment and wore the ragged and dirty clothes of a young down-and-out whom he picked up.[14] These examples may be multiplied from amongst the famous and forgotten intelligentsia of the years leading up to the outbreak of war; and who knows how many other unrecorded members of the middle classes played at being poor when it was so fashionable a pastime?

On some levels, however, we should be chary of over-exceptionalizing the period from the end of the 1920s up to the Second World War. On the one hand, we have the whole fraught question of bohemianism and its relation with social investigation; on the other, the more complicated and ultimately unknowable web of personal urges and epochal drives. As an example of this latter problem: Auden's 1920s slumming in Berlin was clearly of a different, more joyous, nature to the later squalor in which he lived in New York, when the doorman to Hannah Arendt's building could mistake him for a tramp;[15] the former may be to some extent be viewed as social investigation whereas the latter obviously may not. Such examples complicate any simple reading of the 1930s as an unambiguously unique period in which social investigation, incognito or otherwise, flourished in a way not seen before or after.

Indeed, the putative cultural shift away from the concerns of Modernism towards those of the 1930s is less clear cut if what interests us is social investigation in these relatively broad terms. Modernist works also show flashes of a similar undercurrent of interest in taking on the attributes of the working classes. David Seabrook was nominally speaking of David Railton when he reached the ambiguous and intertextual conclusion that he 'do the Poor in different voices',[16] but the context of his discussion of the vicar-tramp was the genesis of *The Waste Land*. The sly bon mot could also refer to *Ulysses*, where the voices of the poor are similarly heard. Edy Boardman's speech early on in the Circe section is strikingly reminiscent of Ellen Kellond as channelled through Eliot in 'A Game of Chess':[17] 'Did you, says I. That's not for you to say, says I'.[18] One also begins to wonder whether Pound was being in any way disingenuous when he implicitly distanced himself and his love of Villon from the 'experimenters [and] searchers for sensation' who saw in the Frenchman a poet of 'taverns and whores' and sought to emulate him by plunging themselves into that world.[19]

These are deep waters. I have no wish here to offer a reheated *olla podrida* of cases of literary class mimicry and representation of the poor in the early twentieth century; I want merely to append the caveat that any over-precise attempts to generalize about the presence or absence of certain themes and preoccupations in given periods are always going at some level to fail. With this in mind, we can nonetheless acknowledge that the British 1930s saw an unarguable increase in social investigation; in light of what at times can seem almost the ubiquity of the phenomenon, the fact that the decade saw the publication of the one incognito social investigation text that may be uncontroversially described as canonical, *Down and Out in Paris and London* (1933), should come as no surprise.

The title of Orwell's first book is misleading. Banally enough, it suggests that it deals with the experience of being down and out in two cities; such differences as one may expect to find will lie in the differences between French and English cities. This is not the case: Orwell's experiences in Paris are methodologically quite distinct from those in London. This can be seen emblematically in the use of the two cities' names in the title, even though only one of them is the sole site of his poverty in the country in question. Orwell is certainly down and out in Paris, but it would be more precise, although less euphonious, to speak of 'London and surrounding areas'. In France, he stays within the city; in England, he travels from casual ward to casual ward. This is more than just a reflection of the fact that Orwell investigated more than one type of poverty. Living and working in a place on the one hand and living the wandering life of the homeless on the other are two quite different methodologies in incognito social investigation: the latter is the Greenwoodian type, and it is that which we shall analyse here. We should note here that it is not the presence or absence of movement per se that changes the methodology. Greenwood did not move about to research the piece that founded the genre; nor did many of the other early incognito social investigators feel the need to sample more than one casual ward. Equally, not all those who have wandered in assumed poverty have therefore been following the Greenwoodian tradition. Indeed, as Chapter 3 argues, 'tramping' is a form of incognito social investigation with its own history and rules. The identifying factor of incognito social investigation in the Greenwoodian tradition is, rather, its focus on the homeless. However, 'homeless' here should not be given the connotations it currently holds. At no point in the Greenwoodian tradition is 'homeless' used as a key classifying category with its modern importance: on those occasions when homelessness does not go quite unmentioned, it is merely a given, something inextricably intermingled with, but of manifestly lesser interest than, questions of moral status (deserving versus undeserving poor), or whether drink is to blame, or whether those investigated are urban or rural. An excellent example of how 'homelessness', when it is mentioned, is not the central point about 'tramps' comes in Frank Gray's *The Tramp: His Meaning and Being* (1931). Gray, an eccentric former Liberal MP for Oxford, begins his book taking about the 'homeless poor', or 'vagrants', or 'tramps', but the chief meaning of 'homeless' here is 'wandering': what matters to Gray is movement rather than homelessness. Indeed, when he offers a chapter-long classification of tramps and their lodgings, the question of homelessness in the recognizable modern understanding of that word is limited to saying of 'by far the largest class', that of 'the habitual drunkard', that they 'sink lower in the social scale till they are no longer able to sustain themselves in homes or lodgings'.[20] No more is said: even for Gray, perhaps the most classificatory and 'scientific' of incognito social investigators, the whys and wherefores of homelessness are simply not a productive category. To avoid the connotations that now accompany talk of the 'homeless', we may more accurately say that the identifying factor of the Greenwoodian tradition is its focus on those without homes. This may be combined with an interest in tramping *stricto sensu*, but the difference is one of the relative importance given to the different experiences. In this, the 'London' section of *Down and Out in Paris and London* belongs firmly in the Greenwoodian tradition, and is indeed in many respects both that the *nec plus ultra* and swansong of that form.

George Orwell had his first experience as a down-and-out long before he was George Orwell; he was still Eric Blair when in August 1920 he wrote to his Eton friend Steven Runciman about his 'first adventure as an amateur tramp'.[21] This was not social investigation of any type; Blair was not showing a precocious interest in the poor. As he says, like most tramps he was driven to it.[22] Blair was travelling down to Polperro in Cornwall on holiday, when a failed attempt to change train compartments at Seaton Junction led to his arriving too late at Plymouth to catch a train to Looe that night, and he found himself faced with having to choose whether to sleep at the YMCA and not eat, or eat something but sleep rough. He chose the latter, sleeping in a field corner, and notwithstanding the cold and discomfort in the end managed to oversleep and miss the first train out. His conclusion, ironically enough, was 'I am very proud of this adventure, but I would not repeat it.'[23] Reading too much significance into this episode would be anachronistic – Orwell himself never mentioned this experience when discussing his forays amongst the poor, whether as a first spark kindling his interest in such things or merely as a curious coincidence. However, this very reticence is not without meaning. *Down and Out in Paris and London* is presented not as an experiment but as an account of experiences lived through chance; the most cursory knowledge of his correspondence and biography shows that this is false (at least for 'London'): Orwell set out quite deliberately to hunt for new experiences – hop-picking, rough-sleeping, imprisonment, lodging houses, workhouses . . . Reference, even knowing, ironic, reference, to this previous event would have given rise to various problems. Any reference to this would only surely have been worth including if the coincidence of such an incident happening to one who would later write a whole book putatively based around such things were highlighted, but this would have meant a more explicit admission of Orwell's privileged background than can be found at any point in his 1933 book. Orwell's book is not presented as deliberate incognito social investigation, and any attempts at seeking motivation would of course have run up against the quite false narrative framework of poverty experienced through necessity that Orwell sets up for the English section.

Orwell's text is strongly fictionalized, and this in terms of the genre of incognito social investigation texts is rather rare. One of the *raisons d'être* of the tradition lies not in what it investigates but in the very act of investigation itself: the London section of Orwell's book is undoubtedly the most famous text in the Greenwoodian tradition, but it also departs significantly from it in this central point. Orwell does not wish to appear a brave explorer of unknown realms and social depths: he wishes, rather, to be taken for one plunged *nolens volens* unprepared into a life of poverty. Let us look at the completely fictional moment when Orwell finds himself back in England and, learning from 'B.' that he has to wait a month before his promised employment materializes, faces the prospect of being a pauper:

> There was a month to wait, and I had exactly nineteen and sixpence in hand. The news had taken my breath away. For a long time I could not make my mind up what to do. I loafed the day in the streets, and at night, not having the slightest notion of how to get a cheap bed in London, I went to a 'family' hotel, where the charge was seven and sixpence. After paying the bill I had ten and twopence in hand.
>
> By the morning I had made my plans. Sooner or later I should have to go to B. for more money, but it seemed hardly decent to do so yet, and in the meantime I must exist in some hole-and-corner way. Past experience set me against pawning my best suit. I would leave all my things at the station cloakroom, except my second-best suit, which I could exchange for some cheap clothes and perhaps a pound. If I was going to live a month on thirty shillings I must have bad clothes – indeed, the worse the better. Whether thirty shillings could be made to last a month I had no idea, not knowing London as I knew Paris.[24]

Whereas previous incognito social explorers had made much of their expertise (Greenwood's willingness to make his ignorance known was a practice rarely adopted by those that followed him), Orwell here is making himself seem far *less* expert than was in fact the case. He is falsely naïve, falsely ignorant. He was fully aware of how to get a cheap bed in London; indeed, he is here making himself out to be not only less knowledgeable than he was, but also less knowledgeable than was likely: the existence of lodging houses for those not yet reduced to casual wards, Salvation Army shelters or Embankment sleeping was common knowledge, as was the existence of the Rowton Houses, created by Lord Rowton at the end of the nineteenth century to provide working men with a better option for accommodation than that provided by the common lodging houses. It would perhaps be useful to distinguish between author and narrator here. The former was far more knowledgeable than the latter, but the narrator too was not without *some* expertise: he knew better than to pawn his best suit. Why might the narrator here in a scene aimed at presenting himself as an innocent abroad in London in many respects be allowed this one flash of pre-existing wisdom regarding poverty? The answer, I suspect, lies in the book's two-part structure. The pseudo-documentary nature of the text means that, structured as it is, when we read the above passage not only does the assumed ignorance of how to deal with poverty in London prepare us for the presentation of the narrator's coming adventures, but the nod to his knowledge about not pawning his best suit, an awareness that can only have come from his Paris experiences, also reinforces the 'veracity' of the French section of the book. The little detail of not pawning the best suit is in some ways the true link between the 'Paris' and 'London' sections: it underscores both the narrator's ignorance of London poverty and his hard-earned knowledge of its Parisian equivalent – and in doing so subliminally suggests to the reader that the end result of his experiences will be a gain in awareness; the detail of not pawning the suit adumbrates the final chapter and the 'one or two things I have definitely learned by being hard up'.[25]

The strange situation whereby Orwell sought to make his text, the importance of which lay in his being a middle-class observer of poverty and not in his being simply middle class and poor, deny that it in any way appertained to the text tradition initiated by Greenwood is something that commands our attention. In the terms that this study is using, what can be said about emicity and eticity in relation to the *two* stories being told by *Down and Out in Paris and London* – the fictionalized one contained within its narrative and the historical one contained not only within the text but also within a whole host of extra-textual material regarding Orwell?

Our focus here will be above all on a technique that I believe Orwell uses to muddle questions of eticity and emicity, a technique I shall call, at risk of oxymoron, 'typicalizing individualization'. This is the seemingly paradoxical situation whereby individualizing oneself makes one seem more typical of a group. It is in fact no paradox, but almost a truism. If one only wishes to suggest that one can pass for belonging to a group, then it is indeed enough to take on all that group's attributes, to the point of stereotypicality. However, if one wishes to suggest that one *is* part of a group, then it is better to present oneself as individually as possible. Self-individualization, in this sense, suggests that one belongs to a group despite those characteristics that one has that are not (stereo) typical thereof. This is of course more realistic, for the truly typical is in fact untypical: however rare a public-school-educated tramp interested in making notes on slang may be, he is more likely to be accepted as a 'real' tramp than someone who is absolutely typical – and yet is able to write up his experiences and have them published. The narrator's story in *Down and Out in Paris in London* may be accepted as true *because* he is not a 'typical' tramp (any more than anyone else is: the more emic the observer, the less what they see is an undifferentiated group) rather than in spite of this fact.

A good starting point for an example of this, and the uneasy relationship between Orwell's desire for fact-finding and his role play more generally, comes when he meets a crowd on Tower Hill assembled to listen to the preaching of two Mormons. The combined heckles of an atheist and someone denouncing the Mormons for their presumed polygamy make it impossible to hear anything other than a confusion of voices. Orwell's conclusion is worth noting: 'I listened for twenty minutes, anxious to learn something about Mormonism, but the meeting never got beyond shouts. It is the general fate of street meetings.'[26] On the one hand, it may be read as Orwell at his most short-sightedly etic. He seems to regret the fact that the East End crowd will not allow him to listen as he would like; that they have as much – or rather *more* – right to speak than two uninvited preachers is not taken into account. This is in sharp contrast with his judgement on the 'slumming-party' that 'invades' (the verb is deliberately pejorative) one of the lodging houses where he stays, when he concludes that it 'is curious how people take it for granted that they have a right to preach at you and pray over you as soon as your income falls below a certain level'.[27] Orwell, though, may be doing something rather more complex in the scene with the Mormon preachers than merely regretting poorer Londoners' lack of middle-class silence when listening to public speakers. I would suggest that Orwell is here in fact trying to do is to strengthen his claim to being *truly* down and out rather than what he in fact is, an incognito social investigator. This works on two levels. First, paradoxically, the very fact of his not following the crowd insofar as he wishes to listen to the Mormons and is clearly irritated by his inability to do so can be read as making him belong *more* to the crowd, not less. By showing his readers his desire to hear the Mormons' talk, Orwell is individualizing himself, standing out from the crowd. The crowd in this case is not a single entity, but rather a clear collection of individuals – the lame, bearded atheist, the anti-polygamist, the man who continually shouts out to everyone not to 'get on the argue'. The members of the crowd do not feel any need to hide their individuality. Had Orwell been more superficially emic and not mentioned his impatience with the lack of reactive silence, then he would in fact have been much more an external observer, wanting above all to fit in. Instead, by standing out, he is merely doing what everybody else whose voice in the crowd we hear is doing. In other words, Orwell is showing that his priority is not observation of the East End crowd: he is there not through choice to observe but through necessity, and has therefore no need to *pretend*. This stance of Orwell's is disingenuous pretence, but still a very subtle way of asserting his authority as one who has *truly* known poverty rather than another mere investigator in a long tradition. In this interpretation, the contrast between the scene with the Mormons and Orwell's reaction to it and that with the slumming party does not show inconsistency or hypocrisy. Rather, it shows that *Orwell has learnt something*. Again, this is a distancing of himself from those who have come before him and were openly investigating: the very fact that he does not notice the change suggests that it is 'real'; it is not something he has consciously learnt, with the implication that he has set out to learn it, as is the case with the things he lists in the concluding chapter. Orwell learns things without noticing it because, he is suggesting, he is not an incognito social investigator but simply one whom poverty has forced into certain situations.

Orwell is always reminding us that he is an individual, with all an individual's contradictions. He is deliberately unprofessional, so to speak, in order to underline how much deeper he has gone into the down-and-out world than those more expert and more professional incognito social investigators who observed with a clearer eye and endeavoured to stop their individuality from intruding between them and the object of their gaze. He is inconsistent because he is real. As an example, it is instructive to look at Chapter 26, in which Orwell goes to 'Romton' (almost certainly Romford), meets an old Irish tramp and goes with him to a chapel that hands out tea to tramps after prayer. The degree of inconsistency in this chapter, I would suggest, is too great to be casual or attributable to inability on the author's part: it is a deliberate ploy to have the reader accept Orwell's version of his account as a true story of an unlooked-for descent into poverty. This is not to say that Orwell's mask does not always slip, as we shall see.

When he arrives in the marketplace in Romton, Orwell meets an old Irish tramp, whom he offers tobacco. The ensuing conversation is curious:

> 'By God,' he said, 'dere's sixpennorth o' good baccy here! Where de hell d'you get hold o' dat? *You* ain't been on de road long.'
> 'What, don't you have tobacco on the road?' I said.
> [ ... ]
> 'D'you come out o' one o' de London spikes [casual wards], eh?' he asked me.

> I said yes, thinking this would make him accept me as a fellow tramp, and asked what the spike at Romton was like.[28]

Orwell distances himself from the tramp on the one hand – the second-person pronoun in his bizarrely incredulous question is anything but inclusive. Notwithstanding this, the tramp's question would appear to mean that he remains of his first opinion, that the man in front of him is newly on the road rather than simply not being a tramp. In other words, Orwell is once again playing up his naïveté to underscore his genuineness. In the interpretation here of Orwell's technique, the strangeness is in fact not in his question, nor in his later ones about different types of work-house or what 'skilly' is, as all of these fit into his strategy. The mask of poverty does slip here to show us a glimpse of the incognito social investigator beneath, but it is in his aside to the reader about his motivation in saying that he had come from a London casual ward: 'thinking this would make him accept me as a fellow tramp'. What is the point of his adding this? He has otherwise presented himself to the reader as he is presenting himself to the Irish tramp: as one honestly in need. If what Orwell has been recounting up to this point has been true, then he quite simply *is* a tramp, albeit an inexperienced one lucky enough to know that his state is temporary. Orwell's ingenuous questions to the tramp have shown his lack of experience; this he has already seen does not make the Irishman doubt him. To include such an aside to the reader can only risk sowing a seed of doubt regarding the veracity of Orwell's account. It is because the inclusion of this aside can be read as a genuine error of judgement on Orwell's part that we may read his other inconsistencies as deliberate, as they can be fitted into a structure of strategy, which this cannot.

Remaining within this chapter, we can find other excellent examples of Orwell's deliberate 'carelessness'. When describing the prayer meeting, he says that 'We hated it. We sat around fingering our caps',[29] and the inclusive pronouns are significant. He is now one of the tramps; but there follows another parenthetical statement addressed to the reader, 'a tramp feels indecently exposed with his cap off',[30] that might once again suggest a slipping of the mask as he suddenly and briefly switches voice and assumes that of an anthropologist noting an interesting detail of some savage tribe. I would of course argue that this, included as it is in the same sentence where the repetition of 'we' makes it seem a particularly glaring piece of authorial carelessness, is in fact another declaration of Orwell's individuality and thence his genuineness. He can allow himself this flash of pseudo-scientific interest, just as he allows himself the luxury of a non-narrative chapter of 'notes, as short as possible, on London slang and swearing',[31] because it is personal interest, personal curiosity, personal pleasure and even, if you will, astonishment, that causes him to blurt out these observations. He can afford to be personal because he is (he wants us to believe) living, not observing: he observes such things through passion and intellectual curiosity, not because he is seeking them out.

The same sleight-of-hand may be seen in two comparisons that Orwell makes a few sentences later in the chapter. He talks of a 'spry, red-nosed fellow looking like a corporal who had lost his stripe for drunkenness',[32] and extols the qualities of the chapel tea by saying that it is 'as different from coffee-shop tea as good Bordeaux is from the muck called colonial claret'.[33] These comedically *de haut en bas* phrases, stereotypically reminiscent of the sort of people who would never find themselves in a suburban chapel dressed as a tramp in order to drink free tea before a casual ward opened for the night, are another variation on the technique already identified. They allow Orwell to assert his strangeness to the situation in which he finds himself, and thus, paradoxically, his right to be there as an inhabitant, albeit temporary, of that world rather than as a visitor.

This examination of how Orwell increases his authority and concomitantly his readers' faith in the claim that what they are reading is reportage rather than fiction leads us to a question that has never been settled: to what extent is this true, and what parts (if any) of Orwell's incognito social investigation texts are fiction(alized)? This situation is exacerbated by his relative vagueness (partially prompted by an understandable fear of libel proceedings) regarding the practical details of his forays into the world of tramps and dishwashers; this, combined with the disappearance of such documents as the admissions books for the casual wards of Romford and Edmonton (almost certainly the spikes hidden behind the names of Romton and Edbury in *Down and Out in Paris and London*),[34] has meant that Orwell's most important work where there are issues of interplay between fact and fiction has remained stubbornly resistant to informed analysis in these terms. However, documentary evidence regarding one of his incognito social investigation exhibitions has now been found. This is Orwell's failed attempt in December 1931 to be sent to prison, given the title 'Clink' but not published, the writing of which Davison dates to August 1932. His plan was to be arrested for being drunk and incapable, and, he says, after four or five pints and the best part of a bottle of whisky he was picked up and taken to Bethnal Green police station. As he was arrested on a Saturday, he had to wait until Monday to be taken to Old Street Police Court to be seen by a magistrate. He describes those whom he saw there waiting to go in front of the judge, as well as his relative disappointment that even though he was unable to pay his six shilling fine, his time in custody during the Monday was enough to spare him further incarceration.

The discovery of the Register of the Court of Summary Jurisdiction sitting at Old Street Police Court for December 1931 shows that in this,[35] the only case as yet for which we can compare his account against documentary evidence, Orwell was consistently accurate.[36] We know that Orwell's account of why and how he found himself reduced to penury in London is fiction, but the evidence from 'Clink' suggests that the reportage itself may be relied upon as an accurate account of what he experienced and witnessed.

Before moving on to discussion of the effect *Down and Out in Paris and London* had on the Greenwoodian tradition, it is worth our while to pause to look at Orwell's statements about his book and his status as described therein. In a November 1932 letter (that in which the name 'George Orwell' first appears) to his agent, Leonard Moore, written whilst the details of publication were being finalized, he wrote a PS suggesting *The Confessions of a Dishwasher* as a title, as 'I would *rather* answer to "dishwasher" than "down & out"'.[37] The day before, he had written to Eleanor Jaques with the same message: 'I don't answer to the name of down & out.'[38] This was certainly private honesty; but had Orwell had his way and seen his first book published under a different title, then it would have been a form of public honesty as well, as Orwell's dishwashing truly was through necessity in a way that his down-and-outery was not. The only instance known to me where Orwell in any way *publicly* made this point, however, was in the 'About the Author' paragraph on the dust jacket of the Harper & Brothers American edition of *Down and Out in Paris and London*, published in June or July 1933, of which Davison rightly says that it was 'almost certainly based on material supplied by Orwell'.[39] This brief biographical note mentions Orwell's career up to his resignation from the police in Burma, going on to conclude:

> Subsequently he has earned his living by schoolmastering and private tutoring, and he has also worked in a Paris hotel, picked hops, pushed a barrow in

Billingsgate and done other varied jobs. Soon after he came home from Burma he became interested in the lives of destitute people and began to make expeditions among tramps. It was only after he had done this a number of times that it occurred to him that his experiences could be used for literary purposes. Later on when he was genuinely hard up he was glad to know the ropes in the world of the destitute.[40]

Here, uniquely, Orwell recognizes that it was not mere misfortune that took him to the casual wards. However (and in this, I think, we can see Orwell's hand in the writing of the note), the details are presented in such a way as to suggest a chain of events resembling that described in the book rather than what biographically occurred; this, though, is done in such a way that at no point can one accuse Orwell (or whoever was the note's author) of falsehood. The obvious reading is that the various jobs done by Orwell are unrelated to his 'expeditions among tramps'; we know that this was not the case, and he picked hops and ported fish in order to have the experiences of doing so, not through need. Nonetheless, this still stands as the only admission that Orwell was indeed at certain points an incognito social investigator.

I said earlier that we may consider *Down and Out in Paris and London* the *nec plus ultra* of the Greenwoodian tradition. I would argue that it has in many ways become that which cannot be surpassed, the masterpiece of the form. However, it also became that which could not be passed: a boundary stone marking the genre's end, after which this form of incognito social investigation text would no longer be productive. There is a stark contrast between the steady flow of material from 1866 up to 1933 and its near-total disappearance thereafter. One of the two reasons for which the Greenwoodian tradition softly and suddenly vanished away lies, I believe, precisely in its relative ubiquity amongst the 1930s intelligentsia. The Second World War may be viewed as an interregnum insofar as incognito social investigation was to all intents impossible: this being the case, the post-war literary and cultural world, when Greenwoodian social investigation had become practically possible again, found itself viewing the phenomenon as something inextricably linked to that low, dishonest decade. Furthermore, there was the looming presence of its inescapable link with the controversial figure of the archetypal one-man awkward squad that was Orwell. Raymond Williams described this very well in an interview with the *New Left Review* in the 1970s: 'In the Britain of the fifties, along every road that you moved, the figure of Orwell seemed to be waiting. If you tried to develop a new kind of popular cultural analysis, there was Orwell; if you wanted to report on work or ordinary life, there was Orwell.'[41] Greenwoodian social investigation was either old-fashioned, a view that could only be strengthened by the passing of time, or it was a territory that had been claimed by Orwell. This works both for those who appreciated Orwell's work and those who disliked it or disagreed with it. Given the relatively rapid rise, to social canonicity,[42] of Orwell as an anthropologist of the poor,[43] to write a piece on one's night in a casual ward, say, meant for the former attempting to out-do the master; for the latter, it meant recognizing Orwell's primacy in the field. Both were situations to be avoided.

The other cause, I would argue, for the rapid decline that the Greenwoodian tradition experienced is a more practical one. This lies in the changing nature of the spaces in which Greenwood and those who came after him very much tended to work: casual wards and common lodging-houses. After the end of the workhouse system in 1930, some casual wards continued on into the 1960s and beyond, normally becoming known as Reception Centres. Common lodging-houses (often known as doss-houses) were cheap (and usually nasty) lodging in dormitories with shared kitchens, regulated by law. These in London after 1894 were licensed and controlled by London County Council; an idea of just how many people slept in their dormitories can be seen in the fact that in London in 1927, 165 common lodging-houses offered 17,045 places, which was already a marked descent from when the law had changed in 1894, when 625 offered 29,574.[44] The nearest equivalent to the common lodging-house today would now be the hostel on the one hand (although the modern version is much less likely to be used as reasonably long-term lodgings for itinerant or newly arrived workers, a function that has rather been taken over by bed-and-breakfasts and pubs) and the night shelter on the other.

The existence of these two spaces meant that those working in the Greenwoodian tradition had, as it were, half their job done for them. They did not have to gain the trust of the people they were studying and reporting on in the same way that would have been necessary had they been investigating rough sleepers; they were in spaces where it was usual for there to be a transient population, where one could observe without it being necessary to gain – laboriously, perhaps – the trust of individuals. The whole Greenwoodian tradition was partially made possible by the existence of safe spaces in which to go hunting, so to speak; the increasing absence of these spaces after the 1930s is clearly an important motive for the weakening of the genre.

Under the combined weight of these two factors, the cultural and the practical, in the years following Orwell almost no texts in the Greenwood tradition were produced. There are two important partial exceptions, however: Jeremy Sandford's *Down and Out in Britain* and Robin Page's *Down among the Dossers*. Both of these late flowerings deserve attention. Sandford, like Orwell, was an Old Etonian; his fame lies in his two television plays from the 1960s and '70s, both of which deal with home-lessness: *Cathy Come Home* and *Edna the Inebriate Woman*. The title of his book is a clear reference to Orwell's work, but other than that he avoids Orwell's overshadowing presence by the simple but disingenuous proce-dure of never mentioning him or his text. There is only one reference in the book to the most important, famous and canonical work of incognito social investigation ever produced in Britain, but it is significantly not made by Sandford's narrative voice, but by one of the people whom he interviews, and even this reference does not involve Orwell's investigation per se, but rather one of the things that he describes: 'Those boarding houses described by George Orwell, where a rope is hung across the wall and the men lean across it.'[45] Not only is Orwell otherwise absent from the text, but there is a tacit assumption of his absence from the reader's mind, as it were – 'spike', a word one may presume a reader of *Down and Out in Paris and London* to know, is glossed by a note to the first paragraph of the introduction as 'a Reception Centre'.[46]

This refusal to name the author whose presence is evoked by his book's title is not the only example of Sandford's less than honest dealings with his readers. The introduction begins thus: 'For a while I descended into the bilges of our society. Wearing boots that gaped at the seams and an ancient great-coat, I allowed my beard to grow and my hair to become matted with dirt. I wanted to meet and talk with down and outs, dossers, tramps, the inhabitants of kiphouses, derries, Spikes.'[47] This mirrors the blurb on the front flap of the dust jacket, which repeats, in the third person, the opening of the introduction, concluding, however, with the addendum 'He also mingled among down-and-outs in psychiatric hospi-tals and prisons, and talked with unmarried mothers and social workers.' The suggestion is very clear: the book that you are about to read is an account of incognito social investigation. This is not wholly false. There are indeed a few pages in which Sandford (mostly or entirely in Glasgow) does don a tramp's garb, but these incidences are rare. The overwhelming majority of the book is taken up with interviews with social workers of various types, the author's socio-political musings and guided tours amongst the homeless. The book begins in Waterloo Station, but what at first glance may appear to be experience gleaned whilst posing as one of the homeless soon reveals itself to be the author's experience whilst accompanying a nun who runs a soup kitchen. Notwithstanding the book's presentation, both textual and paratextual, *Down and Out in Britain* is not really an incognito social investigation text. It does contain some first-hand experience whilst in disguise, but it is but a very small fraction of the text.

The bulk of Sandford's book is in fact an undigested mix of stories involving those whom society has in one way or another mistreated: those in prison and in mental hospitals; single mothers; drug addicts and alcoholics...This may be read as compassion, which would suggest a certain level of emicity and empathy; I would argue, however, that such undifferentiated caring is strongly etic. All is grist to Sandford's mill, and he is interested in the cases rather than the individuals: including on the same level the arrested protester, the mentally ill artist, the 'persecuted' experimental dance group commune and the unemployed homeless ex-cowman is implicitly etic insofar as to do so means not considering individuals' own view of their statuses. They have in common nothing except as objects of Sandford's levelling pity.

Sandford carried out his experiments in the mid- to late 1960s; the early 1970s saw another late example of Greenwoodian incognito social investigation. This was a book published in 1973 under the title *Down among the Dossers*, and its author could not have been more different from Sandford. Sandford was an Oxford-educated left-wing Old Etonian with a strong interest in counter-culture; Page was a right-of-centre former civil servant who would later become famous as the presenter of *One Man and His Dog* and writer of the *Daily Telegraph*'s Country Diary, and it is clear throughout his book that he is anything but counter-cultural in the usual sense of that word. These differences aside, there are a few seemingly salient points in common between the two men. Just as Sandford's text is far from being pure incognito investigation, but rather an undifferentiated mix of different types of reportage with social comment and suggestions for how to ameliorate people's lot, Page's book (although comprising far more incognito social investigation *stricto sensu*) also contains his suggestions for resolving the problem of 'dossers' and a (faintly hilarious) report on his experiences at the Weeley rock festival. At first sight, the comments made regarding Sandford's near-total refusal to mention Orwell also hold true for Page. There is only one open reference to him: when Page is endeavouring to classify the homeless and categorize some of them as belonging to that group that Mayhew described as 'those that will not work', he says that 'George Orwell, when he lived rough in the early thirties, came across "swindlers" and the workshy.'[48] Furthermore, 'spike' is also glossed here, which *prima facie* would suggest that Page too is avoiding the comparisons with the by then recognized and undisputed master of the genre. However, three points stand out against this interpretation: the reference to Orwell is buttressed by a footnote directing the reader to *Down and Out in Paris and London*; 'spike' is glossed not as '*a* Reception Centre' (my italics) as in Sandford (a generic usage implying the reader's total ignorance of the term) but as '*Brighton* Reception Centre' (my italics),[49] which is a much less presumptuous piece of elucidation, telling the reader as it does exactly where is being talked about; finally, when Page realizes that his tramping (as in Orwell's book, this form of investigation is also found; once again, though, it is the *focus* that makes this a text in the Greenwoodian tradition) has already brought him nearer the centre of London than he had planned, he states that 'Whether I liked it or not it seemed that I was already down and out in London',[50] and the reference to the 1930s model is clear. Orwell is far less absent from *Down among the Dossers* than he is from *Down and Out in Britain*, for all that the latter's title is a clear reference to his book.

These similarities, such as they are, pale into insignificance when compared with the two men's almost diametrical political and cultural opposition. We encounter here, however, something that is perhaps rather unexpected. Given the respective political stances of Sandford and Page, one might expect the former to be a more emic, sympathetic and empathic observer than the latter. This supposition (based though it may be to various degrees, depending on one's own political views, on prejudice and stereotyping) is borne out if we limit ourselves to the authors' analyses of the problems that they have witnessed and their suggestions for alleviating them. Sandford advocates the 'provision of small permissive hostels with a resident father figure';[51] his counter-cultural *parti pris* is clear, and the great fault lies with state and society, which between them have created the problems described. Permissiveness is key to Sandford's analysis, but Page, on the other hand, advocates such measures as the possible introduction of ID cards and compulsory detoxification of drug addicts and alcoholics,[52] and he criticizes the Cyrenians for their 'inexperienced helpers and over-permissive hostels',[53] the very reasons, almost, for which Sandford praises other, similar, organizations.[54] Indeed, Page's description of 'do-gooders' who write 'as if they wished to be remembered as compassionate and farsighted intellectuals, rather than recorders of the actual facts' that 'every dosser is a downtrodden victim of the capitalist system and a reject of the affluent society',[55] could almost be taken as a caricature of Sandford.

The great difference between Page's text and Sandford's is that the latter is in fact clearly the text of one who wishes to teach, the former is one of a person who wishes to learn. One need not agree with Page's conclusions to see that they *are* conclusions: the fruit of his experiences as an incognito social investigator. This is not the case with Sandford. He learns of individual cases, but – as the barrage of stories to which he subjects his readers attests – his conclusions do not grow out of them. They are merely examples of the things that he wishes to fight. In other words, the right-wing writer has an approach that is distinctly more respectful of the agency and individuality of the poor. The reason for this, I suspect, is to be sought in the two authors' differing stances vis-à-vis counter-culture and the dominant system. Sandford, a far more intellectualizing figure than Page, has the certainty of a convert that the alternatives he proposes are part of a better system than the one currently prevailing: this very certainty that he is helping those with whom he sympathizes prevents him from using forms of observation that do not, ultimately, revolve around the observer rather than the observed. Page, on the other hand, is a far simpler figure: he is willing to show his ignorance, to admit that 'many of my illusions on down and out life have been broken, and even some comparatively recently held views or prejudices have been modified'.[56] *Down among the Dossers* is a manifestly lesser book than Orwell's, but in its account of what one man learnt through observation as an incognito social investigator it is a fitting end to the main body of the tradition that Greenwood started and Orwell made great.

## NOTES

1. 'Vicar's Ordeal: As Unemployed Tramp'. *Thanet Advertiser and Echo*, 19 November 1921, p. 7.
2. I owe knowledge of Railton's talk to Seabrook, David. 2002. *All the Devils Are Here*. London: Granta, p. 10, and it was this reference that first awoke my interest in the topic.
3. Unless otherwise noted, all information regarding Railton comes from Baigent, Elizabeth. 2004. *Oxford Dictionary of National Biography*, s.v. 'Railton, David (1884–1955)'.

4. London, Documents and Sound Section, Imperial War Museum Collections, The Private Papers of Reverend D Railton, ref. Documents.4760. Extracts only from the letters are available, and there is little information regarding recipients.

5. 30 August 1916.

6. London, Documents and Sound Section, Imperial War Museum Collections, The Private Papers of Reverend D Railton, ref. Documents.4760, 7 March 1917.

7. London, Documents and Sound Section, Imperial War Museum Collections, The Private Papers of Reverend D Railton, ref. Documents.4760, 19 January 1917.

8. London, Documents and Sound Section, Imperial War Museum Collections, The Private Papers of Reverend D Railton, ref. Documents.4760, 9 January 1917.

9. For example: 'having had a desire for a long time to obtain an insight into the vicissitudes of a vagrant's life' (Craven, C.W. 2008 [1887]. 'A Night in the Workhouse'. In Freeman, Mark and Gillian Nelson (eds.). 2008. *Vicarious Vagrants: Incognito Social Explorers and the Homeless in England, 1860–1910*. Lambertville: The True Bill Press, pp. 181–8, p. 181).

10. All information that follows regarding Railton's tramping comes from personal correspondence with his grandson, David Railton QC, to whom I am extremely grateful.

11. Cunningham, Valentine. 1988. *British Writers of the Thirties*. Oxford: Oxford University Press, passim, but especially pp. 241–55.

12. Treglown, Jeremy. 2000. *Romancing: The Life and Work of Henry Green*. London: Faber and Faber, pp. 68–72.

13. Isherwood, Christopher. 1996 [1938]. *Lions and Shadows: An Education in the Twenties*. London: Minerva, p. 153.

14. Driberg, Tom. 1977. *Ruling Passions*. London: Jonathan Cape, pp. 75–8.

15. Davenport-Hines, Richard. 1995. *Auden*. London: Heinemann, p. 334.

16. Seabrook, *All the Devils Are Here*, p. 10.

17. See Eliot, T.S. 1971. *The Waste Land: A Facsimile and Transcript of the Original Drafts Including the Annotations of Ezra Pound* (ed. Valerie Eliot). London: Faber and Faber, p. 13, n. 5.

18. Joyce, James. 1992 [1922]. *Ulysses*. London: Penguin, p. 564.

19. Pound, Ezra. 1970 [1910]. *The Spirit of Romance*. London: Peter Owen, p. 176. It is also worth noting that Pound (p. 171) singles out for praise the line 'Ne voient pan qu'aux fenestres'; the same line would inspire Orwell to muse on the ignorance of 'real' poverty amongst 'educated people' (Orwell, George. 1997 [1933]. *Down and Out in Paris and London* [*The Complete Works of George Orwell*, ed. Peter Davison, vol. 1]. London: Secker & Warburg, p. 121). On Orwell and Villon, see Davison, Peter. 1991.

'George Orwell: Dates and Origins'. *Library* s6-13:2, pp. 137–50, pp. 137–9.

20. Gray, Frank. 1931. *The Tramp: His Meaning and Being.* London and Toronto: J.M. Dent and Sons Ltd., p. 78.

21. Orwell, George. 2000. Letter to Steven Runciman, August 1920. In *A Kind of Compulsion: 1903–1936* [*The Complete Works of George Orwell,* ed. Peter Davison, vol. 10]. London: Secker & Warburg, pp. 76–7, p. 76.

22. Ibid.

23. Ibid., p. 77.

24. Orwell, *Down and Out,* pp. 128–9.

25. Ibid., pp. 215–16.

26. Ibid., p. 137.

27. Ibid., p. 183.

28. Ibid., p. 140. The parenthesis translating 'spike' is Orwell's.

29. Ibid., p. 142.

30. Ibid.

31. Ibid., p. 176.

32. Ibid., p. 142.

33. Ibid., p. 143.

34. See http://www.workhouses.org.uk/Romford/ and http://www.workhouses.org.uk/Edmonton/, accessed 16 October 2013.

35. London, London Metropolitan Archives, PS.OLD/A/01/090.

36. Seaber, Luke. 2014. 'Edward Burton, Fish Porter, Drunk and Incapable: New Evidence on Orwell's "Honesty" from the Records of his 1931 Conviction'. *Notes and Queries* 61:4, pp. 597–602.

37. Orwell, George. 2000. Letter to Leonard Moore [19/11/1932]. In *A Kind of Compulsion: 1903–1936* [*The Complete Works of George Orwell,* ed. Peter Davison, vol. 10]. London: Secker & Warburg, p. 274.

38. Orwell, George. 2000. Letter to Eleanor Jaques 18 November 1932. In *A Kind of Compulsion: 1903–1936* [*The Complete Works of George Orwell,* ed. Peter Davison, vol. 10]. London: Secker & Warburg, pp. 272–3, p. 273.

39. Davison, Peter. 2000. 'Publication of *Down and Out in Paris and London* in the United States'. In *A Kind of Compulsion: 1903–1936* [*The Complete Works of George Orwell,* ed. Peter Davison, vol. 10]. London: Secker & Warburg, pp. 318–19, p. 318.

40. Ibid., pp. 318–9.

41. Williams, Raymond. 1979. *Politics and Letters: Interviews with New Left Review.* London: NLB, p. 384. Christopher Hitchens has polemically but convincingly shown up Williams's bad faith when dealing with Orwell (Hitchens, Christopher. 2002. *Why Orwell Matters.* New York: Basic Books, pp. 46–58); this does not disqualify his judgement, not of Orwell, but of Orwell's *reputation.*

42. See Moretti, Franco. 2000. 'The Slaughterhouse of Literature'. *Modern Language Quarterly* 61:1, pp. 207–27, p. 209.
43. See Rodden, John. 1989. *The Politics of Literary Reputation: The Making and Claiming of 'St. George' Orwell*. New York and Oxford: Oxford University Press, pp. 177 and 228.
44. http://www.workhouses.org.uk/lodging/, accessed 3 June 2014.
45. Sandford, Jeremy. 1971. *Down and Out in Britain*. London: Peter Owen, p. 34.
46. Ibid., note * to p. 9.
47. Ibid., p. 9.
48. Page, Robin. 1973. *Down among the Dossers*. London: Davis-Poynter, pp. 110–11.
49. Ibid., p. 14.
50. Ibid., p. 60.
51. Sandford, *Down and Out in Britain*, p. 163.
52. Page, *Down among the Dossers*, pp. 135–43.
53. Ibid., p. 133.
54. Sandford, *Down and Out in Britain*, note * to p. 163 and p. 174).
55. Page, *Down among the Dossers*, p. 111.
56. Ibid., p. 144.

# CHAPTER 4

# Tramping Ambiguities: On the Road with Harry A. Franck, Hilaire Belloc and James Greenwood

Incognito social investigation in the strictly Greenwoodian tradition is marked by its staticity. There may be some description of the travels and travails necessary to reach the workhouse or lodging-house, but once the narrator reaches the site and focus of his or her investigation, movement is curtailed, for the workhouse investigation narrative is at base a narrative of stasis and stagnation. This chapter, however, examines something else: 'tramping'. The bivalency of the term is deliberate: to tramp is to walk, but it is also used here in the sense of 'to pass as a tramp'. It is that form of incognito social investigation that sees those who recount it walking through the world to experience poverty. At times it may relate stays in workhouses or lodging-houses; at others, periods of casual labour. Nonetheless, in its focus on the dynamic interstitiality of the 'road' rather than the workhouse or workplace, neither of which is interstitial or dynamic, tramping is clearly a distinct subtype of incognito social investigation.[1] The term will be used below to refer both to walking and social investigation; it should, however, always be clear which of the meanings is the desired one – except, of course, on those occasions when the ambiguity is desirable.

Tramping in both its senses was above all a phenomenon of the very late Victorian age and the years ending with the outbreak of the First World War. It was not limited to this period, of course; and, unlike the other subgenres examined, a full understanding of it requires reference to sources from outside the British Isles. Furthermore, although this study

© The Author(s) 2017
L. Seaber, *Incognito Social Investigation in British Literature*,
Palgrave Studies in Life Writing, DOI 10.1007/978-3-319-50962-4_4

is explicitly not about accounts of social passing or class movement in fiction, the cultural reach of tramping does mean that a certain attention to sources other than the purely non-fictional (or more accurately to sources other than those that *present* themselves as non-fiction) is necessary. Equally, whereas elsewhere the subject of our study are those who change class in order to report on their experiences, and do so quite deliberately and knowingly, here we shall also have to do with people who were not incognito social investigators in this sense. The reason for this too lies in tramping's particular nature: although we wish to seek insight into those who were social investigators *stricto sensu*, some of the most fruitful material is nonetheless to be found in those whose motives were different, though their actions similar.

A useful starting point for discussions of tramping in the wider cultural consciousness is *The History of Mr Polly*. At a certain point, the narrative breaks off to include a long quotation from an imaginary intellectual combining the physique of Sidney Webb with the views of Wells himself. This composite figure, of 'a gifted if unpleasant contemporary',[2] classifies Mr Polly as one of 'that vast mass of useless, uncomfortable, under-educated, under-trained, and altogether pitiable people we contemplate when we use that inaccurate and misleading term, the Lower Middle Class';[3] notwithstanding the terminological caveat and the obvious satire, the categorization is accurate. Mr Polly is certainly an Edwardian Everyman, but a distinctly lower-middle-class one. We might therefore read his escape from respectability and marriage to the open road and the wayside pub as a flight from a class straitjacketed by its own mores into another, freer, one. This would not be a false reading in itself, but it would miss the great paradox of the freedom Polly finds in exchanging one social class for another. In terms of vertical class stratification, he escapes not downwards, but upwards.

To explain this, the key passage is not to be found in descriptions of Polly's tramping itself, but rather in the moment when he decides to take to the road. His escape from Fishbourne, after his catastrophic success as an arsonist and failure as a suicide, begins with his nocturnal realization that all that it takes for him to leave is the decision to do so:

> And he would go off along the white road that led to Garchester, and on to Crogate and so to Tunbridge Wells [ ... ] And so to other towns and cities. He would walk and loiter by the way, and sleep in inns at nights, and get an odd job here and there, and talk to strange people.[4]

This is what he does, and a month suffices to transform him into 'a leisurely and dusty tramp',[5] who has gone further, in class terms, then his initial musings had suggested, for, rather than in the inns of his fantasy, he has slept 'under hedges by day, and in outhouses and hayricks at night, and once [ ... ] in a casual ward'.[6]

Mr Polly's tramping is part of a very specific Edwardian cultural context, as may be seen when the narrator mentions the various books enjoyed by the novel's hero.[7] Amongst these are three works very much part of the Edwardian cultural landscape surrounding ideas of taking to the road: Richard le Galliene's *The Quest for the Golden Girl* (1896); Bart Kennedy's *A Sailor Tramp* (1902); and Hilaire Belloc's *The Path to Rome* (1902). These are all tales of tramping of one sort or another, and they are included even though they complicate the book's chronology: Belloc's book, for instance, was published in 1902, which would suggest that Polly flees his marriage at the absolute earliest in 1917, but there is nothing in the novel (which first appeared in 1910) to suggest that it is set in the future, which, given that Wells was far from loath to figure as a futurologist, indicates that the book's presence is something of an error, and similar problems arise with the publication dates of the other two works. I would suggest, however, that these are 'errors' committed by Wells not through inattention, but because he thought the books' presence in his novel more important than any eventual problems of chronology they might cause for excessively pedantic and eagle-eyed readers.

Mr Polly takes to the road, and in doing so is part of a clear Edwardian cultural tradition. To return to my original paradox, however, why may we say that by exchanging his stultifying lower-middle-class existence in Fishbourne for a freer life, first on the roads and then as general handyman and Jack-of-all-trades at the Potwell, Mr Polly is moving not downwards in class terms but upwards? It is because the tramping tradition into which Wells so cunningly inscribes him, a tradition that, as Lisa Tickner says, would have been 'very evident to [the] original Edwardian audience',[8] was a pastime of the upper middle classes. Mr Polly's descent into the working-class world (or below it, when he sleeps in casual wards and outhouses) was, if made by choice, a journey rarely if ever made, in sociocultural terms, by people of his class position. This can be better seen, perhaps, if we look at his two periods of walking with an eye to their class differences. Mr Polly's tramping is a solitary style of pedestrian endeavour. His apprenticeship days, however, had also seen him walking, going on jaunts as one of the 'three P's'; this was sociable group walking. Miles Jebb, author of perhaps the best book on walking cultures in Britain, the much overlooked *Walkers* (1986), a book always alert to the intertwinings of class and walking, has charted the difference between the upper-middle-class 'tramps' whom we are discussing here and the lower-middle-class 'ramblers' of whom the 'three P's' were examples.[9] By moving from group 'rambling' to individual 'tramping', Mr Polly moves up in the world as he moves through it, a paradox that would not have been lost on any contemporary reader alive to the age's social and recreational mores.

Walking, whether of the individual tramping or group rambling kind, was a key part of British Edwardian culture,[10] but one of the most important figures to examine when we speak of 'tramping' is superficially quite alien to the whole tradition as discussed hitherto; he is nonetheless also one of the most unusual and interesting. Harry Alverson Franck was one of the United States' most famous travel writers and lecturers from 1910 up to the Second World War; he has since faded out of public and critical consciousness, tending to be remembered, when at all, as a source of observations on 1920s China or pre-First World War South and Central America.[11] I should like to make the case, however, that Harry A. Franck was one of the most interesting of incognito social investigators, and that any examination of the subject that does not include him is in incomplete.

Franck's surface biography, so to speak, is simple. He was born in Munger, Michigan, in 1881, and studied modern languages at the University of Michigan. After graduation he taught French in Detroit, and then set out in 1904 on the journey that would make him famous. He circumnavigated the globe, from Milwaukee to Milwaukee, with $104 and a camera. Much of the way he walked; he also stowed away on a liner from Egypt to Ceylon and worked his passage on other boats; he found employment as – amongst other things – a cattleman, circus clown and ticket inspector. He returned to the United States and teaching, but in 1910 published an account of his journeys entitled *A Vagabond Journey around the World*: this was a huge popular and critical success, and he followed it in 1911 with *Four Months Afoot in Spain*, an account of one of how he spent one of his summer vacations whilst a teacher walking through Spain. The success of these books led him to abandon teaching, and he conceived the idea of exploring South America. His chief aim was to walk the Inca roads along the Andes, but he first walked through most of Central America before stopping to work as a policeman in the Canal Zone in Panama. Two books were the fruit of these experiences: *Zone Policeman 88* (1913) and *Tramping through Mexico, Guatemala, and Honduras*

(1916). He then set off, walking the great majority of the way, to Buenos Aires, and slowly returned through Brazil. His account of the first part of his journey was published in 1917 under the title *Vagabonding Down the Andes*, by which point he had joined the army and was a second lieutenant in France, where he served until 1918. In Paris he met his future wife, Rachel Latta, whom he married there in 1918. The 1920s saw the Francks, who would eventually be joined by five children, doing much travelling, especially in China; it also saw the publication of the rest of his South American adventures as well as a series of new books detailing his travels. In 1929 the family moved to England, and later to the South of France, before settling in Pennsylvania, and still the publications kept on coming. The travelling showed few signs of slowing down, but Harry A. Franck was no longer quite as famous a figure he had been when the Second World War arrived,[12] when he enlisted after lying about his age and became what he claimed was the oldest major in the army. He left the war a lieutenant colonel, but published no further books, limiting himself to lecturing, especially on cruise ships, something of a forgotten figure. He died in 1962 of a stroke, having suffered for some time from Parkinson's disease.

This is his *surface* biography, culled from his published works and biographical notes: that of a reasonably successful middlebrow travel writer who had one initial huge success, and then wrote a host of other works that have since accompanied the first through the doors of what Franco Moretti has called the slaughterhouse of literature.[13] His interest in terms of incognito social investigation is limited to his works before his marriage, in which one of his stated aims behind travelling mostly on foot and with so little money was to see how 'the people' really lived in the various countries he visited, and one brief episode of classically Greenwoodian investigation in workhouses in 1930. As we shall see, however, careful examination of the voluminous archive of unpublished material contained at the University of Michigan reveals a much more complex figure, one to whom incognito social investigation was central. Furthermore, although attempts to analyse the psychology of the dead must necessarily tend to become unverifiable speculation on matters unknowable, Harry A. Franck offers so interesting and well documented a case that it would be foolish to overlook it, especially in terms of the possible insights it offers into incognito social investigation more widely.

The existence of the Harry A. Franck archive also makes him unique amongst incognito social investigators. The only other author studied here for whom a comparable mass of documentation has survived is of course

Orwell. However, as we have seen, with the exception of the matter regarding the events narrated in 'Clink', there is a dearth of material relating to his incognito social investigation experiences. With Franck, on the other hand, although he is a figure of immeasurably lesser cultural and historical importance than Orwell, we have not only an array of biographical information, as we do with Orwell, but also of documentation regarding his experiences as an incognito social investigator.

Franck's first book is also in many ways his most important. *A Vagabond Journey around the World: A Narrative of Personal Experience* recounts his journey around the world between June 1904 and October 1905. Its nature as social investigation is signalled paratextually on the title page, with an epigraph attributed to Rousseau: 'Pour connaître les véritables moeurs d'un pays il faut descendre dans d'autres états; car celles des riches sont presque partout les mêmes.'[14] The 'foreword of explanation' then states that his original idea was to carry no money, no weapon, no baggage and no supplies; he relented on this to the extent that he decided to carry a camera with him, as well as $104 to cover any photography costs that he might incur (at journey's end he discovered that he had in fact spent $113 on photography).[15] He sets out his motives for his journey in the foreword:

> As a vocation I had chosen the teaching of modern languages; foreign travel promised to add to my professional preparation. Were I permitted an avocation it would be the study of social conditions; what surer way of gaining vital knowledge of modern society than to live and work among the world's workman in every clime?[16]

He then explicitly states that what he is doing is social investigation: 'The chief object of investigation being the masses, I made no attempt during the journey to rise above the estate of the common man.'[17]

In the account proper of his journey he sets out in much (often wearisome) detail the experiences he had whilst a 'workman in every clime', but it is soon clear, however, that his claim that he made no attempt to 'rise above the estate of the common man' should be taken with an important caveat: he may make no attempt to rise *above* the estate of the common man, but this is not counterbalanced by any attempt to *stay* at the level of the 'common man'; he is more than happy to descend to the level of the homeless tramp, even though this estate may of course be as distant from that of a workman as any more economically fortunate one. The series of socio-economic roles through which Franck passes consists of various working-man's jobs interspersed with a range of different types of unemployment. Although unemployment may seem monolithic insofar as it is a simple absence of work, the situations in which Franck experiences it are many, and his social role may change where his economic one does not. The same phenomenon whereby superficially similar economic roles do not necessarily imply similar social roles may also be seen in Franck's periods of employment – taking on low-paid work of various sorts around the world may superficially resemble, per Franck's introductory comments, the component parts of an enquiry into one world, that of the 'common man' at work, but, just like his more truly incognito investigations into unemployment, it is rather a series of discrete social investigations. This multiplicity of experiences goes towards what makes Franck so *sui generis* a social investigator. An overview of Franck's main jobs may be useful.[18] His first was looking after cattle on the crossing between Canada and the United Kingdom; between Marseilles and Port Said he was a sailor on a liner; he did odd jobs in a consul's house in Cairo; passed briefly for a mechanical engineer in Asyut; was offered the post of French and English secretary to the Greek Orthodox Patriarch of Khartoum (but was refused entry to the Sudan);[19] he stowed away on a liner heading from Port Said to Colombo before revealing himself and being made to work his passage; in Ceylon he was a circus workman and replacement clown; India saw him an undercover inspector on trams in Madras and a tennis ball boy in Delhi; he was a sailor on a windjammer between Yokohama and Victoria; and a series of labouring jobs once back in the United States took him from Seattle to Havre, Montana, where he once again looked after cattle, in what was his final job before his return to Milwaukee.

The range is superficially eclectic. A common theme unites them, however, and it is something that gives the lie to the quasi-scientific motivation that he gives himself in the introduction to his published account. He claims that he wished to live and work amongst the world's workmen, yet the jobs that he finds, for all their surface differences, are very much jobs that, unsurprisingly enough, were likely to be picked up by an itinerant labourer such as he was. These are not jobs amongst different types of worker around the world; they are different jobs amongst the same type of worker the world over. The exception would have been if he had been successful in entering Sudan – although his 'half suspicion' that 'my employment was little more than charity in disguise' does suggest that this would in fact have been in line with his others,[20] insofar as the recipient of such potential charity would necessarily be such a penniless itinerant as Franck was. His jobs are all based upon his rootlessness. Indeed, in the case of Madras, his lack of rootedness in the community is what gets him the job: he was to be an anonymous plain-clothes inspector on the trams whose role was to guarantee that there was no collusion between the uniformed inspectors and the conductors who sold tickets: 'The broker warned me not to build hopes of an extended engagement, rather to anticipate an early dismissal; for the uniformed employés were famed for lynx-eyed vigilance, and my usefulness to the company, obviously, could not endure beyond the few days that might elapse before I was "spotted".'[21] Franck's stated aim of 'gaining vital knowledge of modern society' runs up against the problem that Orwell pointed out regarding Henry Miller, who was 'writing about the man in the street, and it is incidentally rather a pity that it should be a street full of brothels'.[22] The world of work that he experiences is never truly that of the societies in which he finds himself.

This is true a fortiori when he finds himself outside Europe in countries under (British) colonial rule. Here the question of race comes into play and further complicates the situation. The best example of this can be seen in the episode where Franck and other members of 'beachcomber' society perform manual work to put up circus tents in Colombo. He and the others soon become famous as 'white coolies' amongst the native population, who flock to watch them. After the first day's work, two representatives of the Lipton Tea Company come to remonstrate with the beachcombers: by performing manual labour, they risk 'losing caste' and thereby placing all 'reverence for white men' at risk. The solution found is to put the beachcombers into makeshift uniform, for, as one of the Lipton men says (Franck represents his accent, hence the oddities in spelling), 'When a man weahs a uniform, the natives think he is doing something they cawn't do, ye knoaw, and he keeps his cawste.'[23] Franck is in fact totally removed from the surrounding societies: he is not native, yet nor does his 'whiteness' suffice to make him part of the colonial class. His position is absolutely that of a wanderer even when he is staying still and working; the vaunted possibility of insight through work reveals itself to be false.

Even Franck's episodes openly 'tramping', openly living a hand-to-mouth wandering existence, show themselves under examination almost always to be examples of a retreat from the surrounding societies into social groups that are not on the fringes of society in the normal acceptance of that phrase, but rather self-contained societies that may on occasion come into contact with the societies surrounding them (normally when money is needed) but otherwise operate by their own rules; the best example in Franck's writings of one of these parasitic microsocieties, as we may call them, comes in Cairo. Here he falls into company with a community of German tramps who survive chiefly through writing begging letters (usually in English) and mendacious appeals to foreign philanthropists resident in the Egyptian city. Franck's experiences here have nothing to do with Egypt or the 'common man', whose estate here he has very obviously ignored: he is a temporary member of a society quite as foreign in its impecunious way as any collection of rich socialites would be. Furthermore, even this microsociety Franck is experiencing at a remove. He shocks 'die Kamaraden' by wanting to work and by (often, although not always) refusing charity;[24] this solecism is compounded by the fact that he a *real* American, and, as such, more likely to receive help from the philanthropic American missionaries by whom the Germans were usually refused assistance, however much they tried to pass themselves off as their potential benefactors' countrymen. Franck's friend and cicerone to the life of the wandering German, Otto Pia, introduces him to the assembled company as follows:

'Ei! Gute Kamaraden!' he said, 'I have something to show you! Guk' mal! Here is a comrade who is an American – do you hear – a real American, not a patched-up one; and this real American – in Cairo – wants to *work!*'
    '*Work?*' roared the chorus, '*Work* in Cairo – and a real American – Lieber Gott – Ist's den ein Esel?'[25]

Franck is always an outsider, even when amongst those who are themselves outsiders par excellence.

What emerges as Franck's inability ever to become part of a society – he cannot even remain a beachcomber over long – puts him in many ways beyond questions of emicity and eticity. He is always too much an outsider even to *observe* fully; any observation of social mores must be based upon such superficial knowledge that to claim, as he does in his introduction to *Vagabond Journey* that this is his aim must at the very least be disingenuous. He was not unused to this position as an outsider: talking about his childhood in Flint, Michigan, in his unpublished autobiography he at one point says with reference to his never quite truly belonging to any given social group amongst fellow children there, 'Certainly I can recall no heartburning at being on the outside looking in.'[26] Franck's importance lies not so much in *Vagabond Journey* in itself, but in his insistence, in the face of all the evidence in the text, that what he is doing is social investigation. His obsessing over this point makes it much more than an excuse (whether one coined before he set off or after he wrote is of little importance), as does the fact that he carried out an undeniably Greenwoodian piece of incognito social investigation almost two decades after the publication of his first work. We shall examine below Franck's obsession, and its relevance; first, however, we should look at Harry A. Franck's second clear foray into the world of the poor.

The end of the 1920s saw the growing Franck family relocate to England. They lived in a London hotel before renting first a house in Harpenden and later one in Ealing. As with the family's earlier travels, this period too found its way into a book. *Foot-Loose in the British Isles* was published in 1932, and may be fairly described as two books in one. One is a book of travels, detailing Franck's trips, often by bicycle, around the UK, Ireland and the Isle of Man; interleaved with this is the other, a description for his American audience of various facets of English society. One of the parts attempting to offer American readers insights into contemporary English society is Chapter 31, 'The Wages of Loafing'. This is an account of the dole and the controversies surrounding it, and Franck introduces his description of it with a shrewd comparison to Prohibition in terms not of its social effects but of its centrality in the public mind: 'What prohibition is to us the "dole" is to Great Britain: the outstanding problem of the day, the principal subject of conversation, the excuse for any national failings that cannot be otherwise explained.'[27] His tone is generally critical and certainly simplistic (although we must remember that he was writing popular material for a foreign audience to whom too detailed an account was unlikely to appeal): the title already suggests his *parti pris* that the Dole pays people to 'loaf' and is a disincentive to seeking work. The chapter concludes with the author inveighing against the British tax system.

After this chapter, which is very much of a piece with the other parts of the book not specifically based on the author's travels, the reader might expect more commentary on British mores and institutions, or perhaps a description of one of Franck's bicycling trips to the farther-flung parts of the British Isles. The three chapters that follow, however, seem to belong to a different book. They certainly belong to a tradition other than that of travel-writing, for they describe classically Greenwoodian incognito social investigation in workhouses.

The Francks were living in Harpenden, north of London, and Franck describes the town as being one where tramps were constantly passing, up to the rhythm of twenty-eight in a half hour.[28] Franck is curious about these tramps, whom he claims the British no longer notice, having long become inured to their presence, and, on such rare occasions as they do notice them, consider them to be 'unemployables' who would refuse work were any offered to them.[29] He decides to dress as one of them and sleep in workhouses. He walks to Watford, where he sleeps in the workhouse in an individual cell, passing himself off as a Canadian ship's steward. This does not suffice him, however, as for various reasons he had 'missed the roadsters' work and food and nightshirts',[30] as he had turned down an offer of food, been let out early and hence not had to do the usual labour required of casuals, and not bathed and therefore not had to wear a workhouse nightshirt. He walks on to Berkhamsted, where this time he undergoes the 'full' workhouse experience: bath, food, nightshirt, wood-sawing . . . Similar experiences are had in Oxford, to which he continues by foot, bus and hitching. The next day sees him returning to Ealing using the same mixture of transportation.

Franck's report contains little of particular novelty or interest. His description is flat; his conclusions limited. The importance of what Franck did during this Greenwoodian incognito social investigation lies not in the detail, but rather in the strangeness of his having carried it out at all. *Foot-Loose* is not a book specifically about social investigation or the poor, or even about social conditions. In his introductory 'explanation', Franck says that his book is nothing more than 'a collection of the commonplaces of life, the insignificant details that really make or mar living, a miscellany of facts and fancies that pretends to "cover" nothing, either geographically, socially, or psychologically'.[31] It is, as I have said, something of an omnium gatherum, but it is precisely the lack of a guiding principle behind its organization that makes the inclusion of three chapters describing a reasonably arduous undertaking even odder: if there is no structural reason within the text to make such an enterprise necessary, then the question is not so much why one should carry out and include such a thing, but rather why one should give it such relative weight in a context that has nothing to do with incognito social investigation. The reasons for this, I believe, are to be sought in Harry A. Franck's deeply curious relationship with travel.

A true vision of this is only possible through examination of unpublished material, but there are adumbrations of it in *Foot-Loose* (just as there are scattered throughout his published oeuvre). As Franck sets off from Ealing, he peppers his account with references to his former status as a tramp: 'when I first tramped the roads of England in 1900',[32] 'I was less timid on setting out on such a mission in my younger days',[33] 'my first "lift" in Europe – in thirty years'.[34] We even have the strange situation where Franck's excuse to a tramp he meets whilst walking out of London, 'You see, I haven't been on the road before, that is, not for years, and I don't know the ropes',[35] is the absolute truth: Franck quite simply *has* been a tramp before (one of his scrapbooks still contains a ticket dated 25 July 1900 from a Manchester lodging-house annotated 'Neater than the average highclass hotel. Good board from 2d-6d in same house. For laboring men only'). The reader of *Foot-Loose* when it first came out may legitimately have been somewhat puzzled: if they were not familiar with *Vagabond Journey* then these references were odd insofar as they would have no reason to expect that the author had already experienced life as a tramp; to assiduous readers of Franck's work, however (and the University of Michigan archives contain several letters stating that their authors had read all of Franck's books and followed news of new publications carefully), these references would still have been extremely curious. The clear, explicit, message is that Franck was tramping in England in 1900: this predates the exploits narrated in *Vagabond Journey*. This is not the only detail that the reader may find odd. Franck is careful to let his readers know that he has already lived at least in part the life of a tramp; added to this puzzling detail is the fact this in no way translates – as one might legitimately expect – into any sympathy, whether emic or etic, with tramps. After leaving Ealing, Franck walks and hitches to Edgware; in doing so he 'gets below the "sir" line' with his lift and is able to mingle unnoticed with men in a Labour Exchange.[36] However, he goes on to say, 'so far I had not established contact with the enemy...I mean, got in touch with the people I had started out to study'.[37] This pre-emptive disavowal, as it were, of empathy, sympathy and emicity reads even more strangely given the author's insistence on his own previous experiences as a tramp, but these internal quasi-inconstancies may be read as hints towards the true story of Harry A. Franck's multitudinous forays into tramping.

Before we begin to look at some of the problematic and intriguing ambiguities that are to be found in Franck's attitude towards travel and (incognito) social investigation as shown in his unpublished material, we should first look at another aspect of his 1930s workhouse visits. These Greenwoodian experiences described in *Foot-Loose in the British Isles* are also important within the wider study of incognito social investigation for another reason. This is quite simply the fact that the notes he took for it have survived, a unique occurrence.[38] They are contained in one of the tiny diaries that Franck used as notebooks for much of his life. They run from 22 to 25 September 1930, and, given their uniqueness, it is worthwhile offering a transcription:

Monday 22

Ealing Watford

Tried (in vain) to mend R's [illegible - possibly 'puncture'], then in old clothes wandered away in rain, via Wembley to Welsh Harp + on to Watford, where I put up in workhouse + have private cell.

Tuesday 23

Watford Berkhamstead

Wander along in pleasant day for 11 miles, meeting a few bums, reach "Berk" 4 p.m, sit on bench, wander out of town + hide valuables then join bums at "Spike," get bath + night shirt + head to "tea", a [possibly '+'] fair sleep + [possibly a ∪-shaped symbol of unknown meaning] clothes "stoved".

much snoring in night but no other adventures

Wednesday 24

Berkhamstead Oxford

Waked dawn, clothes in bundles, bread + "cocoa," + saw wood; get "ticket" + at 10 to Aylesbury, lunch + mail valuables at Tring bus + walk + catch ride to [the t is uncrossed] "spike" in Oxford, late "supper".

Thursday 25

Oxford Ealing

Another bright lovely day, after noisy scratchy night. "Breakfast," then I scrub hospital walk + reception room, get bread + cheese + wander on via foot, bus + caught ride thru 'igh [it appears that Franck for some reason wished to indicate a form of the name with a dropped aitch] Wycombe, + Beaconsfield to Golders Green + home, to slow bath.

What might we say about this remarkable survival? First, banally, that it matches perfectly what Franck writes about his experiences: this is yet further evidence that his reports are not falsified. More important, however, is the documentary evidence these notes give us about investigative note-taking that is unfortunately impossible for the incognito social investigation texts of more celebrated authors. Other than the basic information of places stayed and means of transport, Franck also signals what he finds particularly noteworthy through his two quite distinct uses of quotation marks. There are those that mark items of linguistic interest – 'Berk',[39] 'Spike', 'stoved' – on the one hand; on the other, there are the scare quotes denoting Franck's disagreement with certain terms' aptness: 'cocoa' and 'Breakfast'.

Let us now move away from Franck's incognito social investigation as recounted in his published works and begin to dig more deeply into his troubled relationship with travel, whether in space or in class. One of the key texts for the understanding of this is the draft of his unpublished autobiography. The very first episode narrated recounts how Franck, aged six or seven, managed briefly to 'jump' a train before falling off; he himself describes this as his 'first stolen train ride' and 'first adventure in hoboing' and connects it to his future career: 'it was the sort of thrill that has come ever since from physical hardship meted out to myself in the name of adventure'.[40] The recognition of his emotions here as the first example of what would become his life's leitmotif, as it were, is of course a form of hindsight, but given Franck's escapades (the term is apt in suggesting escape as an adventure and vice versa) throughout his university days, before any idea of publishing his experiences or travelling professionally had ever come to him, his observation seems justified.

For some three years at the end of the nineteenth century and the beginning of the twentieth he spent his summer vacations as an itinerant worker, a hobo, travelling as far afield as Paris by way of Canada and a cattle boat to England as well as travelling by train (both legally and illegally) all over the central and western parts of the USA whilst working as a casual labourer. Here we run up against a question that in some cases, such as Franck's, may have to remain unanswered and, ultimately, unanswerable. What distinguishes a 'real' casual labourer and tramp from a 'false' one? During the second vacation in which he rode the rails and did casual labour, Franck shipped out of Chicago on an agency ticket.[41] In his autobiography his account of going to the agency is full of ambiguity, an ambiguity that seems unconscious. He goes to the agencies already dressed as a labourer ('my make-up as a laborer appeared to pass muster', he observes as he remembers his walk down the street on which such businesses were concentrated),[42] and notes that this meant that the fee that he paid was the standard one dollar rather than a more inflated sum: 'my semi-disguise was adequate; a "greenhorn" would have been asked two or three dollars'.[43] Why does he describe his garb in such a way? His clothes were labourer's clothes; the work he was doing was that of a labourer; he was doing what he was doing to earn money and to travel. Nothing in any of this necessarily distinguishes him from anyone else who for mixed reasons of need and character is a hobo. There is, of course, the fact that his is a hoboing known before he sets out to have a temporal limit, but the seasonal nature of certain casual jobs means that this is in no way a particularity reserved for impecunious and curious students. We encounter here a point that Barbara Ehrenreich acutely noted in *Nickel and Dimed*: '[I]t may be that I was exaggerating the extent of the "deception" to myself. There's no way, for example, to pretend to be a waitress or not: the food either gets to the table or not. People knew me as a waitress [ . . . ] not because I acted like one but because that's what I was, at least for the time I was with them.'[44] This is true for all those whose incognito social investigation led them to work with the aim of reporting on it; it is also true, *mutatis mutandis*, for those who tramped – one either travels from A to B or one does not, and one's reasons for travelling make no difference: knowing that one is walking 30 miles or riding a boxcar in fear of railway police out of choice and curiosity does not make the miles any less onerous. As we shall see, this doubt over one's status is a recurring theme in tramping narratives; the presence of something so much a part of this form of incognito social investigation in Franck's unpublished autobiography highlights once more how questions of social passing ran through his life at a far deeper level than mere attempts to add 'slumming' as a form of local colour into his travelogues.

Franck's lack of clarity about his motives and status whilst riding the rails may also be seen in the fact that he used his experiences as material for his 1903 thesis for his Sociology 22 class. This was entitled 'Wandering Unskilled Laborers on the Edge of Trampdom' (it was also the first publication for which he was paid, as he received $15.00 from the *Chicago Tribune* when it appeared there). He only made one reference in this to how the information contained in it had been gathered: 'I shall attempt to point out the essential facts in regard to the class as I have seen it myself, having spent one summer among the unskilled dock-laborers of England, one in the wheat fields of Nebraska and the Dakotas, and a third in railroad gangs and steamboat crews between Chicago and the Pacific Coast.'[45] There is a certain disingenuousness here: the suggestion is that his summers were thus spent *in order* to learn the 'essential facts in regard to the class' and that the thesis was therefore the cause; the truth is rather that he wrote the thesis in order to make use of information gathered whilst a hobo, and it was therefore an effect.

A similar lack of clarity about motives is also to be seen in *A Vagabond Journey*. We have seen that in the introduction, necessarily written after the journey, Franck talked of his sociological aims. The unpublished material, on the other hand, talks of how he had originally planned to travel during the summer before returning to the United States to continue teaching – in other words, a vacation jaunt little different from those that he had undertaken as a student. He decided to continue whilst in France, as he had received no information telling him that his services were still required, although this was because he had left no forwarding addresses whereby the school could reach him (they in fact wished to offer him a promotion).[46] However, at some unknown and unrecorded point during his journeying, he did indeed decide (or realize?) that what he was doing was a form of (at times incognito) social investigation. We know this from one of the surviving notebooks, which relates to the last leg of his journey, after he had arrived in Canada from Japan and when he worked his way back to Milwaukee and his parents. This was kept in French 'to forestall possible curious brakesmen or detectives';[47] and its great value lies not in its pedestrian text, which gives little more information than the published account, but rather in the title that he gave to this part of his journal: 'Le Tour du Monde comme Ouvrier – continué'.[48] It may have been a vagabond's journey when it was published, but it was (or rather became) a worker's journey as he undertook it.

Franck's relationship with travel merits further attention for another reason. In examining it, we find light shed on aspects not only of tramping but also of incognito social investigation more generally. In the mid- to late 1940s, Franck wrote various fragments to go towards his autobiography, pieces that never made it into the final draft of that (never-to-be-published) work. One piece was entitled 'Hobo Days', and includes the following reflections:

> In fact, I never so much as mentioned hoboing either in thesis or article. Those hobo episodes could hardly have been included in that staid and overwritten account of my 1910 [sic; this is presumably a typo for 1901, or, possibly, 1902] trip to the Pacific coast and back as a laborer, much less my Sociology 22 thesis. For by the time it was published [in the *Chicago*

*Tribune*] I was a school teacher and the raw facts of life had to be glossed over. [ ... ]

[ ... ] But looking back, I wish at least that I had put in more descriptions of how we lived in sidetracked boxcars, what those boxcar meal times and nights were like. I remember ... but no, I find those days too jumbled in my memory now to be able to draw a worthwhile picture of my experiences at this distance.[49]

Franck's ellipsis holds back a great weight of nostalgia. As one reads through the Harry A. Franck papers (including the sparse remnants of certain acrimonious correspondence with his wife from the 1930s onwards where what remains makes it obvious that he blamed her for forcing him to settle down),[50] it becomes clear that this sense of loss is not only for his youth, but for his travels; these travels, however, should not be limited to the merely spatial, or horizontal, through country after country. There is also vertical travel through class, and an array of details in his papers suggests the degree to which Franck always had the question of 'tramping', which is to say travel in both vertical, class, terms as well as horizontal, spatial, ones somewhere in the back of his mind throughout his life. The late 1930s saw him noting down ideas for possible future articles, 'on the bums in New York City. Spend some days with them on park benches',[51] 'Jump to all main parts of the country, mingle with workers and hoboes',[52] that imply movement in both directions (and this in a man no longer young, whose handwriting was already showing signs of the disease that would kill him). Around the same time he also wrote a curious piece that was never published, 'The Day's Events and Their Background', written, internal evidence would suggest, at some point between the beginning of the Second World War and Pearl Harbor, although quite what 'the day's events' were remains unclear. He twice connects the breadth of his travels in space with the depth of his travels in class, and taken together these constitute the most explicit recognition this highly un-self-aware man ever reached of how his need for travel was not just a question of movement over the Earth's surface: 'While I have talked with kings and dictators and other big shots in many places, my interest, what you might perhaps call my hobby, has been to hobnob with the people, the masses, wherever I have been'; 'I have lived with, and like, the natives of most of the lands that I have visited, partly because my tastes run to what you might call slumming'.[53]

Travel for Franck, then, was in two planes; it was also a drive that approached obsession. The best evidence for this – other than the simple record of his life – comes in notes that he wrote in the early 1930s. Travelling down the coast of Dalmatia, he notes 'I could play about Corcula [Korčula] contentedly for a week myself – which means anyone less discontented with the present outlook could stay for months.'[54] His pleasure in travelling – and this is confirmed by the most cursory look at his books – lies, as he comes very near to stating explicitly here, not in the places to which he travels, but in the mere fact of travelling. It is in a note from Portugal from the same period describing his thoughts after he arrives in a hotel after sleepless nights and a long and tiring walk to find that there is no hot water there that he gives us his most articulated piece on what exactly it is in travel that drives him to be ever on the move:

> That's what these d..n fools who never let themselves suffer can never understand – the intense pleasure of the return to comfort, good meal, good wife, good bed. I probably have been an idiot in setting myself unnecessary stunts that are hard, difficult, dangerous hardships and suffering not at all necessary. But like the man who drinks whiskey, he may hate it as much as I do, but he wants its after-effects.[55]

Also here, in that last sentence, he approaches a realization that there is something of an addiction, a traveller's equivalent of dipsomania or alcoholism, in his insistence on movement and hard travelling. In a note written in Italy too we see him come close to recognizing that there is something not usual in his need to travel: 'I suppose wanderlust in a man my age is much like lecherous old man [sic].'[56] This avowal that his compulsive travelling may be a problem is all the more telling as the word that he uses to describe it is that which he had used in a letter to his prospective father-in-law after doubts had been expressed about the impending marriage: 'I am not looking for a cure of the Wanderlust, since I do not consider it a disease.'[57] Franck's obsession with travelling *was* an obsession, and it included vertical travel in class as much as horizontal travel in space.

The great value of Franck to the student of incognito social investigation is the great mass of unpublished material to read against his published accounts; this, coupled with his general artlessness, allows us the possibility of informed insight into his motivations where we can only speculate for more gifted writers. Any given author's true motivation is ultimately unknowable, as we can only know at best their stated reasons for social investigation, but Franck's case is also useful insofar as it offers us, I believe, an insight not so much into individual motivation as how that motivation may be construed as working socioculturally.

Franck's view of his Wanderlust in his letter to William J. Latta is a form of negative medicalization: the denial that Wanderlust is a disease still implies that it may legitimately be considered such, even though Franck himself does not hold to that belief. This suggests the debate at the end of the nineteenth century and beginning of the twentieth, so expertly explored by Ian Hacking, over fugues in which sufferers travelled compulsively.[58] It is interesting to note that although much of the iconography surrounding these fugueurs suggests that they were compulsive walkers, they are more accurately described as travellers – see, as the *locus classicus*, Philippe Tissié's account of Albert Dadas's travels, which besides pedestrianism, included trains, boats and rafts.[59] Hacking's work is about what he calls 'transient mental illnesses', but I have no desire to endeavour a psychological analysis of Harry A. Franck, whether in terms of today's views on mental illnesses or in those of the various times in which he wrote.[60] However, what I do wish to do is to look at a concept that Hacking introduces when he talks of the 'vectors' making certain diagnoses possible at certain times. This is cultural polarity: 'the illness should be situated between two elements of contemporary culture, one romantic and virtuous, the other vicious and tending to crime'.[61] The concept is extremely useful here, especially as in this case the two poles are 'romantic tourism and criminal vagrancy, one virtuous, one vicious. Both were deeply important to the middle classes, because one stood for leisure, pleasure, and fantasy escape, while the other stood for fear of the underworld.'[62] Here, though, I would like to move away from Hacking's use of this concept in a medical sense to consider how it may be a valuable mental tool for thinking about incognito social investigation generally, and tramping specifically.

The category of 'incognito social investigator' may be considered a social equivalent in vertical travel terms of the medicalized category of fugueur in horizontal spatial ones. The details of the positive cultural polarity in question changes to some extent over the periods examined here, but its basic relationship with the more monolithic negative one does not, I believe. The positive cultural polarity begins as that of research and (quasi-scientific) curiosity, virtues befitting an increasingly self-confident middle-class spectrum of journalists, sociologists and other types of investigative writer; as the twentieth century goes on, the cultural positivity of empathy with the downtrodden increases, as does, somewhat later, that of the value of fluidity of identity. The negative polarity is that same 'fluidity of identity', but seen as a dangerous ambiguity about class positions: the ability to blur class boundaries seen not as a positive characteristic allowing empathy and investigation, but rather as a form of deceit and an invitation to social chaos. The existence of a category, however unarticulated it may be, into which to fit those of the middle classes willing and able to blur the boundaries domesticated the phenomenon. It was made socially safe through an unconscious categorization, just as 'pathological tourism' was made safe by being categorized medically. It is no accident, in this respect, that England saw both the genesis and the greatest development of incognito social investigation. The importance given in England to social and not simply economic class, and all the multitude of clues to it in speech, dress, taste, diet and more, means that this negative polarity was there of a strength to make it psychosocially impellent that those who added ambiguity to class distinctions in the way that incognito social investigators do be seen as part of a non-threatening (however potentially threatening their conclusions and observations) middle-class category and tradition rather than as individual maverick cases threatening the unstated status quo.

If this is true for incognito social investigation in general, it is true a fortiori for that subsection of it that I here call 'tramping', which also fitted analogously in a non-medical way into the relationship of cultural polarities regarding tourism as described by Hacking. Tramping is above all a space where ambiguity reigns: the exact social position of walkers who had no great intention to pass as being poor was often unclear, and this doubt surrounding social roles makes those who took to the roads for their social investigation particularly fascinating yet troubling figures within the panoply of the incognito social investigators examined here.

The social ambiguity of the walker pre-dates the text forms of which we are considering Greenwood *fons et origo* and continues in parallel with the Greenwoodian tradition and other subtypes. Milton's acquaintance Thomas Ellwood was arrested in Beaconsfield in 1661 as a 'sturdy beggar' after preferring walking to riding.[63] The German author Karl Moritz was treated as unworthy of any respect by those whom he met in 1782 as he walked north from London, a mode of transport quite socially acceptable in Germany but not in England.[64] Romanticism saw Keats and his friend Charles Brown walking in Scotland in 1818; 'besides the usual suspicion that they were spies or excisemen' – the former a socially ambiguous professions par excellence for which walkers have been confused with a degree of frequency only surprising if we do not recognize the activity's inherent social ambiguity – 'they were taken for linen-drapers, jewellers, razor-sellers, and, because Brown wore a pair, spectacle vendors'.[65] The ambiguity of walking was recognized by De Quincy, who profited from the fact that unlike many other forms of social unplaceability this was one that could vanish the moment the simple activity of pedestrianism ceased, leaving no trace behind it: 'the scandal of pedestrianism is in one respect more hopefully situated than that of scrofula or leprosy; it is not in any case written on your face'.[66] Edward Thomas, walking along the Icknield Way in 1910, found himself refused a bed in Chisledon, which he attributed to his unclassifiability: he 'was clearly not a country gent, nor a tradesman, townsman or tramp; nor even a foreigner [ ... ]; nor "the hairy and hygienic man in sandals"'.[67] Peregrine Eliot, who would later become the tenth Earl of St Germans, decided in the early 1980s to walk to London; in Somerset a Romani driving a vardo mistook him for a tramp of the other sort and gave him 50 pence to help him on his way.[68] These examples (all taken from Jebb) could be multiplied, and their import is clear: the bivalence of 'tramping' is not merely a linguistic feature; it is also an ambiguity inherent in the activity.

One of the most interesting examples of the ambiguity of tramping comes from Hilaire Belloc. His 1902 book *The Path to Rome* describes a pilgrimage on foot from Toul in the north-east of France to Rome; his insistence on walking (he does on occasion break his initial vow of making the whole journey on foot, but the book remains overwhelmingly an account of a walk), frequent refusal to deviate from the straightest line that he could take between his point of departure and his destination no matter how rough the going and the fact – common, of course, at the time to anyone undertaking such an exploit – that only upon reaching certain pre-arranged places could he receive his funds all meant that confusion over his social status of the type discussed was in no way rare.

His pilgrimage to Rome was not the only occasion on which Belloc's social standing was unclear to those about him owing to the vicissitudes of the walking life. The summer of 1908 saw G.K. Chesterton on holiday in Rye, where he made the acquaintance of Henry James. As Chesterton relates it, James called upon him formally after the correct period indicated by etiquette, and they talked of the literature of the day. Their causerie was interrupted by suddenly hearing Belloc shouting out 'Gilbert', to Chesterton's confusion and James's consternation:

I had every reason to believe that he was a hundred miles away in France. And so, apparently, he had been; walking with a friend of his in the Foreign

Office, a co-religionist of one of the old Catholic families; and by some miscalculation they had found themselves in the middle of their travels entirely without money. [ ... ]

[ ... ]

[T]hey started to get home practically without money. Their clothes collapsed and they managed to get into some workmen's slops. They had no razors and could not afford a shave. They must have saved their last penny to recross the sea; and then they started walking from Dover to Rye; where they knew their nearest friend for the moment resided. They arrived, roaring for food and drink and derisively accusing each other of having secretly washed, in violation of an implied contract between tramps. In this fashion they burst in upon the balanced tea-cup and tentative sentence of Mr. Henry James.[69]

Chesterton analyses this in terms of what we might call real and false class conventions, insofar as the deliberately conventional James is quietly shocked by what Chesterton considers a genuine example of the historical conventions of the upper and upper-middle classes in Britain: a lack of concern over appearance and (although he does not say so) a willingness to tramp in the Edwardian style. This is in itself an interesting point over the ambiguities inherent in tramping: we may legitimately ask ourselves to what extent it was a *British* phenomenon insofar as such a willingness to descend socially, physically and sartorially from one's usual position was more possible in a society in which such eccentricities were accepted and even on occasion socially encouraged in a way uncommon in other class systems. More important, perhaps, is the fact that this episode shows that Belloc's self-presentation in *The Path to Rome* should not be read as being a persona adopted for that occasion, whether by which we mean the occasion of his walk or the occasion of his writing it up. Chesterton's evidence shows that Belloc's persona outside his work, when merely on a holiday, matches that described in his book.

Let us now return to *The Path to Rome* and note a few examples of the confusion over his status in the social hierarchy with which Belloc met during that journey. In Flavigny-sur-Moselle Belloc explains an old deaf man's refusal to tell him where to find a baker's with the presumption that he thought him a beggar,[70] and in Switzerland a peasant has him hold his horse outside an inn, an occupation traditional to the penurious.[71] Not all such confusions were as innocuous as these: in the town of Calestano in the Apennines he is arrested after a woman in an inn refuses him a bed and he is presumed to be some sort of vagrant; he is found not to be penniless (he has 73 liras on his person), but is not released until brought before the mayor in order to have this latter interpret his French. The elderly man to whom he states his case speaks in fact not a word of that language, but picks up on the word *touriste*, almost identical with the Italian, and Belloc is thus set free and able to return to the inn, where he is now feted. Belloc's account of this is interesting:

> The landlady smiled and bowed: she had before refused me a bed! The men at the tables made me a god! Nor did I think them worse for this. Why should I? A man unknown, unkempt, unshaven, in tatters, covered with weeks of travel and mud, and in a suit that originally cost not ten shillings; having slept in leaves and ferns, and forest places, crosses a river at dusk and enters a town furtively, not by the road. [ ... ] Is it not wiser to arrest such a man? Why yes, evidently. [ ... ]
>
> Thus I loved the people of Calestano, especially for this strange adventure they had given me[.][72]

Belloc does more than accept the ambiguity of the road: he enjoys it. He recognizes that he has become an unclassifiable figure: he is not liminal, ambiguously poised between two states, but rather interstitial, an inhabitant of a social and physical space (the road) that connects and confuses categories. His ambiguity is in the eye of the beholder; this, however, includes himself when he self-beholds: it is this acceptance of one's interstitial position whilst tramping that sites it amongst forms of incognito social investigation, as the prospective tramper must bear in mind the possibility of being taken for a tramp before the walk is over.

*The Path to Rome* also offers us an extremely interesting analysis of certain class mechanisms within tramping. That such an analysis – unique, I would say, in accounts of incognito social investigation – should be found in a text of the tramping type is not totally coincidental. It is the most literary type, with practitioners who are more willing to reflect on their motivations and situation. It is not altogether surprising that in an example of the form of incognito social investigation that most deals with ambiguity, including the ambiguity of its very own nature vis-à-vis social investigation, there should be found Belloc's ambiguous analysis of ambiguity.

This comes early in his walk, when he reaches a small town on the Moselle named Archettes. Here he spies almost immediately a signboard announcing the inn 'At the sign of the Trout of the Vosges'. He dines there before setting off again, his fellow-diners sparking a train of thought of great interest that is worth reproducing in its entirety:

> Two things I noticed at once when I sat down to meat. First, that the people seated at that inn table were of the middle-class of society, and secondly, that I, though of their rank, was an impediment to their enjoyment. For to sleep in woods, to march some seventy miles, the latter part in a dazzling sun, and to end by sliding down an earthy steep into the road, stamps a man with all that this kind of people least desire to have thrust upon them. And those who blame the middle-class for their conventions in such matters, and who profess to be above the care for cleanliness and clothes and social ritual which marks the middle-class, are either anarchists by nature, or fools who take what is but an effect of their wealth for a natural virtue.
>
> I say it roundly; if it were not for the punctiliousness of the middle-class in these matters all our civilization would go to pieces. They are the conservators and the maintainers of the standard, the moderators of Europe, the salt of society. For the kind of man who boasts that he does not mind dirty clothes or roughing it, is either a man who cares nothing for all that civilization has built up and who rather hates it, or else (and this is much more common) he is a rich man, or accustomed to live among the rich, and can afford to waste energy and stuff because he feels in a vague way that more clothes can always be bought, that at the end of his vagabondism he can get excellent dinners, and that London and Paris are full of luxurious baths and barber shops. Of all the corrupting effects of wealth there is none worse than this, that it makes the wealthy (and their parasites) think in some way divine, or at least a lovely character of the mind, what is in truth nothing but their power of luxurious living. Heaven keep us all from great riches – I mean from very great riches.
>
> Now the middle-class cannot afford to buy new clothes whenever they feel inclined, neither can they end up a jaunt by a Turkish bath and a great feast with wine. So their care is always to preserve intact what they happen to have, to exceed in nothing, to study cleanliness, order, decency, sobriety, and a steady temper, and they fence all this round and preserve it in the only way it can be preserved, to wit, with conventions, and they are quite right.[73]

Belloc's analysis of how it is the 'respectable' middle classes that preserve 'civilization' is not overly germane to questions of the relationship between social status and 'slumming' (to use a term that I would otherwise avoid, but which I think is apt here), but the main thrust of his argument whereby it is only the rich and/or anarchical that ignore social conventions and are willing to slum it is of great importance and interest.

Belloc's argument may be summed up as saying that only those who do not know the potential difficulties involved in gaining and keeping money are so cavalier about presuming that one can always regain one's social position by simple expenditure, however much one may have decided to slum it beforehand. This strikes me as an excellent summation of much of incognito social investigation, although a rider needs to be added. Passing oneself off as a member of a less well-regarded class is overwhelmingly a pastime – whatever may be the reasons for its adoption – practised by those who presume that their return to the class they recognize as that which is normally theirs is a return that can be achieved almost effortlessly. I differ from Belloc in not believing that money alone is the factor that decides whether one acts in a way that suggests this presumption. Certainty in the belief that one rightfully belongs to the middle or upper classes regardless of one's financial ability to buy once again those classes' trappings is as much a factor as one's economic status, *pace* Belloc's implied disbelief in this (it should not be forgotten that in *The Path to Rome*, as almost everywhere else, Belloc, although never falsifying his views, is often exaggeratedly polemicizing for effect).

Belloc's analysis may also, however, be read as problematic irony over his own role. The possibility of such a reading is suggested by something curious in the very nature of *The Path to Rome*. The book describes a physical pilgrimage from Toul to Rome; it would also not be surprising were we to find contained within it a spiritual pilgrimage too. No growth in self-knowledge, spiritual fervour or any other canonically acceptable improvement would appear to be described, however. It is not a 'spiritual' book in that sense. Nonetheless, I should like to argue that it in fact *does* contain an inner journey as much as an outer one. This, though, is shown rather than described. *The Path to Rome* contains various imagined dialogues between 'Auctor' (Belloc) and 'Lector' (a modern philistine of the type hated by Belloc); it also contains innumerable digressions on a whole host of subjects related and unrelated to the journey in hand. All of this together goes to make it a work that dramatizes *not* its author's self-discovery or spiritual self-realization (as one might expect from an autobiographical pilgrimage narrative) but rather something that paradoxically is more obvious yet harder to see: his *journey* of self-discovery. In other words, the non-physical journey that Belloc undertakes is presented in the same way as the physical one: Rome goes undescribed, for it is the road that matters; any psychological or spiritual changes achieved by Belloc go undescribed, as it is the arguments he had with himself and the thoughts that he entertained whilst on the road that matter. He shows his readers both an internal path and an external, but the goal of the pilgrimage *is the pilgrimage itself.* This focus on methodology, as it were, justifies a reading of Belloc's analysis that sees it as an ironic problematizing of the question of tramping and class.

The irony, of course, is that Belloc, for all his ruminations against those who do not follow the middle-class code that he claims guarantees civilization's survival, would himself appear to be an example of a 'man who boasts that he does not mind dirty clothes or roughing it', and therefore either an anarchist opposed to civilization or a rich man ignorant of the value of the things. Neither category strikes one at first sight as something to which Belloc would care to claim to belong. We know from Chesterton and the episode in Rye quoted above when he and Henry James were interrupted by Belloc returned from tramping in France, however, that 'Belloc [was] legitimately proud of having on occasion lived, and being able to live, the life of the poor.'[74] This refers to the summer of 1908; it is fair to presume that amongst the occasions to which Belloc made reference were some experienced during his pilgrimage walk to Rome. We also know that Belloc was famous as a solitary walker in days when to walk alone nearly always meant tramping and all that that implied. We may thus fairly ask why Belloc introduces this possibility of having accusations of hypocrisy or double standards levelled against him. One answer may be that he is implying that he belongs to a third category that he leaves unstated but implicit: those neither middle class (and preserving the conventions) nor rich (and deliberately flouting them), but poor and therefore without any choice. He has no choice but to appear poor, although of the same social rank as those who look upon him askance; he is, albeit temporarily, outside the class binary that he sketches. This interpretation cannot but suggest yet further self-aware knowingness on Belloc's part about what we might call the methodological ambiguity that has demonstrated itself as inherent in tramping: how much is Belloc 'pretending' to be poor here? Indeed, what value does a concept such as 'pretence' have within a context such as tramping?

Below the ambiguity of class is another layer, however. Belloc talks in detail of the rich, but not of the other category, the anarchists. This may suggest a certain sleight of hand whereby the reader is not meant to dwell overmuch on the possibility that Belloc belongs to this class, unlike the obvious ambiguities raised by his discussion of wealth and class. However, throughout the book 'civilization' has a certain bivalence depending on whether it is to be taken as the positive older Catholic tradition so praised by Belloc or the newer post-Reformation phenomenon that he so often disparages. There is therefore a buried hint here that the author is an anarchist by nature 'who cares nothing for all that civilization has built up and who rather hates it' *for a given value of 'civilization'*.

Above and beyond these problematizing issues, however, is another level, which I think is the most important layer of ambiguity in Belloc's analysis. He is forcing his readers into the position of the middle-class guests in the inn. Just as they find themselves confronted with the ambiguities generated by his unclassifiability based upon visual cues, so the readers find themselves confronted with the ambiguities generated by his unclassifiability based upon the analysis he makes of his situation.

That these various ambiguity-creating levels, which are clearly grounded in an understanding of the fact that he is writing in a form to which ambiguity is central, are not meant to be resolved but are instead there as ultimately unresolvable points comes in the one-sentence paragraph with which Belloc ends his musings and returns to his main narrative: 'I find it very hard to keep up to the demands of these my colleagues, but I recognize that they are on the just side in the quarrel; let none of them go about pretending that I have not defended them in this book.'[75] Belloc drives the ambiguities home. He talks of 'my colleagues' but he also talks of 'none of *them*': his position is made absolutely unclear. A further piece of confusion is thrown in by the phrase 'go about pretending': what is its relationship to the whole question of his going about and possibly pretending to be poor, or middle class, or walking through necessity, or walking through choice? The ambiguities multiply; Belloc leaves them unresolved and unresolvable, for he knows that what he is doing is the acme of ambiguity, and wishes to leave the reader in a fog of confusion where boundaries blur, in the interstitial space that is the tramp's road.

The tramping phenomenon subsided after the First World War. Partially this was for the very practical reason that increased motor traffic made road-walking increasingly difficult. This is an obvious point, but the only incognito social investigator who seems to have noticed it is Robin Page in the 1970s.[76] Page himself tramped from Hastings to London, but was very much an exception: the only two post-1918 trampers of note in England are Orwell and Franck, but the former stayed within the sprawl of London and so avoided the problems posed by the increase of traffic and the latter also used public transport (he also clearly had a lack of care regarding physical danger that makes him rather unrepresentative).

Outside England, however, the interwar years in less mechanized countries did see at least one other important figure. This was a writer not usually considered as a social investigator, yet whose *sui generis* journey was, we are semi-explicitly told, first envisaged – in a characteristic mixture of 1930s zeitgeist, anachronistic Edwardian taste for tramping and semi-mediaevalist romanticism – as a way to descend amongst the poor. The writer is Patrick Leigh Fermor, and the journey his 1933 walk across Europe. In his introduction to his reminiscences, couched in the form of a letter to Xan Fielding, he wrote in 1977 that his aim was:

> To change scenery; abandon London and England and set out across Europe like a tramp – or, as I characteristically phrased it to myself, like a pilgrim or a palmer, an errant scholar, a broken knight or the hero of *The Cloister and the Hearth*! All of a sudden, this was not merely the obvious, but the only thing to do. I would travel on foot, sleep in hayricks in summer, shelter in barns when it was raining or snowing and only consort with peasants and tramps.[77]

The existence of technologically less-developed regions meant a partial stay of execution for the tramping tradition as it faded into the modern travel-writing tradition, but it was not only a transport system that created a dichotomy between walking for pleasure and driving for necessity, leaving modern homelessness as above all a physically static phenomenon, which meant that tramping as a form of incognito social investigation died away. Related to this process whereby walking became a leisure activity is that whereby it became a specialized one, especially in terms of what one carried. Walkers of the types discussed here (whether tramps out of necessity or trampers out of curiosity) before the 1930s carried at most a small satchel when pockets would not suffice; this had already given way to forms of rucksack by the time Patrick Leigh Fermor set out. Miles Jebb, who has the best description of this change,[78] reaches a conclusion that says rather more than he realizes: 'The heavy-duty backpack, as we now see it, is a symbol of self-sufficiency, and its bearer is proclaiming a message just as explicit as when clothes told of class distinctions.'[79] As we have seen with Belloc (who set off with 'in a small bag or pocket slung over my shoulder, a large piece of bread, half a pound of smoked ham, a sketchbook, two Nationalist papers, and a quart of the wine of Brulé'),[80] one of the key points about tramping was the ambiguity engendered by observers' inability to distinguish someone walking for pleasure or curiosity from someone walking through necessity. As the distinction became visually more obvious with the advent of particular luggage (and later clothing), this ambiguity vanished into the past. These changes in how one walked caused the possibility of accidental incognito social investigation (as in Belloc) or incognito social investigation as merely one aspect of a much wider project (as in Leigh Fermor) that had hitherto existed to be lost.[81] As tramping was the form of incognito social investigation that most had to do with questions of ambiguity and identity, a whole range of insights and issues vanished with it.

We have looked at the golden age of tramping, but James Greenwood himself also provides us with a precociously early example. In this case, however, Greenwood cannot be granted the palm as originator of the (sub-)form; tramping is clearly also part of the history of other cultural traditions going back long before the 1880s. *On Tramp* was published in 1883; it details how Greenwood tramped from London to Bedford, staying in various types of cheap lodging and describing the people met upon the road. We do not meet here the ambiguity over the tramper's real or perceived role that we find in other tramping accounts, as Greenwood's interest is so focused upon meeting tramps that he avoids polite society wherein such doubts may arise.

Nonetheless, *On Tramp* does contain ambiguity. This, however, is of a different sort; it comes out in the unconscious struggle in Greenwood's text between emicity and eticity, and creates a book where ambiguity grows out of the fact that the book the author tried to write (and thought he was writing) is not necessarily the book that one reads.

It should not be thought that *On Tramp* does not also contain the form of ambiguity that we have seen is proper to the tramping tradition. There is this too, as can be seen in an episode that occurs between Hitchin in Hertfordshire and Shefford in Bedfordshire. Two men, both tramps of one sort or another, invite him to share a chicken that they claim to have bought and are cooking over the embers of a fire that they have lit in a wood off the road; they are generous because Greenwood has bread to share with them. Greenwood finds himself in an ambiguous position morally (should he eat the chicken and thus become complicit in what he presumes to be their theft thereof?), but of more interest is the ambiguity of his position vis-à-vis the tramps as observers. The tramps are eating their chicken (Greenwood refuses his portion) with their knives, and Greenwood begins to worry for his safety; his unease is increased when one of his new companions observes that the journalist has not been on the road very long, deducing this from the quality of his flannel shirt. The two real tramps set to discussing whether they would rather have the shirt or its value, and one starts feeling the fabric. Greenwood understands that he is to be robbed, and claims that he can hear a dog approaching; this frightens his companions away. Whether or not Greenwood was right in thinking that his two new acquaintances had theft on their mind is of little import here. Of interest is how, in a quite different cultural context from that of the Edwardian tramp (in both senses of the term), we still meet with the ambiguity of the road. Greenwood is not observed by members of the middle classes uncertain how to judge him, but rather by tramps; these, however, believe him to be neither what he is pretending to be (a real tramp) nor what he really is (a journalist and incognito social investigator) but rather fit him into another category: that of the tramp who is not a 'regler' on the road. They see him, as it were, as a tramp, but a dilettante tramp – a category that is in itself ambiguous, neither real nor false in either direction, so to speak.

This characteristically 'road'-based form of ambiguity, however, is not where the real interest of *On Tramp* lies. This is rather in the complex question of its intended audience and the gap between Greenwood's intentions and his achievement.

*On Tramp* sets itself out as an account of Greenwood's tramp from London to Bedford. It *is* an account of this, and we have no reason to believe that anything of what it states is false. However, the way the book organizes and presents its account, whilst (as far as can be known) at no point mendacious, is misleading. The first is its relationship with immediacy. In begins, if not exactly *in medias res*, with context-free meditation on tramps leading to the decision, never truly explained, other than a desire to discover whence 'arises this incurable propensity for "tramping"' and what 'the particular delights of tramp life' may be,[82] to go on a tramping expedition as an incognito social investigator. Published in 1883, it contains no explicit references to when the events that it recounts took place. It does state the day that Greenwood set off – Monday 18 June – and gives a few other dates that allow the reader to calculate that it took the author five days to reach Bedford: 18 June was indeed a Monday in 1883. The reader, then, would be quite justified in reading Greenwood's book and presuming it to be an account written very soon after the events related, making it akin to 'A Night in a Workhouse'. Such an impression would have been reinforced by various pieces of paratext. On the title page, Greenwood has 'THE AMATEUR CASUAL' emblazoned below his name;

this is a call to remember that the author became famous for a piece of journalism that was a success not only because it was clamorous and ground-breaking, but also because it was *methodologically* seminal, as it was the immediate publication of articles based on notes taken in disguise. This recollection of what we might call Greenwood's trustworthiness and immediacy is reinforced by the presence of 'A Night in a Workhouse' alongside other books of his in the back matter advertising other books by the publisher, Diprose and Bateman.

This trust in Greenwood would have been ill founded. *On Tramp* also contains reference to the death of 'Mad Lucas',[83] the tramp-friendly hermit of Wymondley,[84] as having taken place 'some thirty odd months ago' (Greenwood)[85] or 'three years ago last April' (an itinerant umbrella mender whom Greenwood meets).[86] According to Greenwood, James Lucas died on 17 April 1874,[87] which places us in June 1877 – the 18th of which was also a Monday. The book's events therefore took place six years before its publication; it is not the immediate account that it implicitly purports to be, but rather a later recollection.

It might be argued that the lack of clarity over the year in which the action takes place points merely to a delay between composition and publishing, and the fact that this is passed over in silence is nothing more meaningful than the common commercial desire not to be seen to be offering a product that is not as new as possible. This view is contradicted by another point in *On Tramp* where the clarity of the account is not what one would expect had it been written immediately after the event. As one reads *On Tramp*, the approximate route taken by Greenwood seems reasonably clear (with overnight stops in bold): London – Barnet – Potters Bar – Bell Bar – **Stevenage** – Wymondley – St Ippolyts – **Hitchin** – **Hatfield** – Welwyn – **Stevenage** – **Hitchin** – **Shefford** – Bedford.[88] There is no reason why a casual reader should do anything more than note the stages of this journey – if indeed even that is done; the more likely outcome, of course, is mere acceptance of the fact that Greenwood visited these places, with an understandable lack of interest in the exact details thereof. We shall look at exactly why these would appear to be the stages of Greenwood's journey below; first, though, we should look at why we may make such presumptions about the level of attention that should be ascribed to the public for *On Tramp*.

That casual readers were the public at whom *On Tramp* was aimed can be seen from the fact that it was published by Diprose and Bateman as part of their series 'Diprose's Railway Literature'. This is announced at the top of the front cover; it is also repeated in a half-page notice on the first page of the back matter, which is chiefly a list of other books in the series (including several by Greenwood). The series is advertised as comprising 'readable and attractive books for travellers'; it includes a potpourri of light reading, much of which is rather of the type that later generations would classify as stocking fillers.

Prospective buyers of *On Tramp*, seeing it for sale somewhere (one imagines a railway bookstall in one of the great London termini), would, one presumes, in spite of a famous dictum, have judged it by its cover. This shows a tramp standing pensively outside the door of a lodging-house of some sort whilst two men loaf by a milestone in the background. The background is rural, although what can be seen of the lodging-house suggests a slightly more urban context: it is a red-brick building with some of the panes in the window appearing to have had stones thrown through them, and a stick figure has been scrawled on the wall. This mixture of urban and rural is deliberately non-committal: the perspective purchaser cannot know whether Greenwood is 'on tramp' through the country or the town; in those pre-blurb days, this must have meant an increase in the possible public. The most interesting detail of the cover is text rather than illustration, however (or, more accurately, it is text as illustration). Above the stick figure, an announcement is fixed to the wall reading as follows:

Lodjings

For

TRAvilers

$4^d$

Per Night

The chaotic mixture of letter forms and the haphazard approach to orthography already suggests something about Greenwood's text that will be discussed below: in its obvious suggestion of (comic?) ignorance, it is pushing an image of the poor that is in line with Greenwood's quite clear prejudices as put on show in *On Tramp*. More significant is the sign's relationship with the book's prospective audience. As has already been noted, *On Tramp* was published as part of the series 'Diprose's Railway Literature', and the back matter has a large announcement proclaiming that the books in the series are 'readable and attractive books for travellers'. 'For travellers'/'For TRAvilers': Greenwood's book was marketed as a contrast between these two groups. Here the modern train-taking leisured reader with money for luxuries such as books; there the poor outdated pedestrian: the latter can read of the former for his or her delectation as the train speeds along, Greenwood's critical gaze mirroring that of the more fortunate traveller as he or she looks out of a carriage onto a changing scene that may well include unfortunate and footsore 'TRAVilers'.

Railway travellers of the 1880s looking for light reading and chancing to pick up a book on tramps by the famous James Greenwood that carried suggestions of confirming in them their moral superiority to 'the tramp tribe', we may then conclude, were unlikely to have whiled away their time calculating the exact details of the author's itinerary. Had they done so, as has been said, the obvious result resembles something very much like the journey given above; but close reading and examination of a map of Hertfordshire explodes any possibility that this was the precise journey undertaken by Greenwood. It can be seen that the posited 'obvious' reading gives a total of six nights spent on tramp; we know, however, that Greenwood set off on 18 June and that the 21st found him between Hitchin and Shefford, in which latter place he slept (the date comes from a note included 'for conscience' sake' that promises remuneration for the owner of any hen stolen 'on or about the 21st of June' from 'a person residing somewhere between Hitchin and Shefford'),[89] before walking on to Bedford and the end of his adventures. This makes the total of six nights quite impossible: Greenwood started out on the 18th and finished on the 22nd, not sleeping in his tramp persona on the last day, for a total of four nights out. The correct total and itinerary can be achieved by removing the doubled towns from the above itinerary and modifying things slightly, so that we now have: London – Barnet – Potters Bar – Bell Bar – **Hatfield** – Welwyn – **Stevenage** – **Hitchin** – Wymondley – St Ippolyts – **Shefford** – Bedford.

If we accept Greenwood's statements, this alone could in fact have been his route. It was said above that Greenwood is not actively mendacious, only misleading, and let us look at exactly how this comes about. The misdirection over his itinerary comes above all in the second chapter. The first ends with Greenwood, who has described his walk up to a mile before Bell Bar (a hamlet between Potters Bar and Hatfield), saying that 'if I wished to make sure of a lodging that night, I had best push on'.[90] The following chapter begins 'I had no idea, when I halted for the night at Stevenage, that I was within a mile of the spot held in affectionate remembrance by habitual tramps,'[91] and goes on to relate the story of Mad Lucas. To the casual reader the inference is obvious: Greenwood spent his first night in Stevenage. This would have been a tramp of somewhere between 20 and 30 miles, depending on where exactly he started in London, something of which the reader is not informed: a long walk, certainly, but one far from impossible or even unlikely in the days before motorized road transport complicated pedestrian use of the highway. After Greenwood treats his reader to a long digression on the life and eccentricities of James Lucas and his visit in his tramp's persona to the late hermit's deserted house, he continues with an account of how he spent a highly uncomfortable night in a cheap pub dormitory in Hitchin. The paragraph describing this ends, and that following it begins as follows:

> With the sun yet young in the heavens, I repeated the words yet once more, as I joyfully stepped across the threshold, – 'Never again! A clover field, the lee of a haystack,– anything rather!'
> With the accumulated dust of several hot miles thick on my shoes, I looked in at the 'White Swan', the last wayside house of entertainment for man and beast before the town of Hatfield is reached[.][92]

Once again, the inference to be drawn is obvious: from Hitchin, Greenwood went to Hatfield by way of a pub called the White Swan. One might at most wonder why he backtracked like this, as doing thus instead of stopping at Hatfield meant an unnecessarily long tramp on the first day. Such an interpretation is reinforced by the layout of the paragraphs: they are set as normal text, without the smallest hint of an asterism or any other type of section break.

This interpretation breaks down when we realize that reading Greenwood's account thus leads us to contradictory versions of how many days he spent tramping; this becomes clearer when we realize that the White Swan in question is certainly a pub on the road to Hatfield, but it is not between there and Hitchin, as one might expect given the inferences that we have suggested that a causal reader may draw. Rather, it is in Bell Bar,[93] which we last saw as the place to which Greenwood was heading before remarking that he needed to push on to find his night's accommodation, accommodation that the casual reader would have inferred to have been in Stevenage. In other words, notwithstanding the total lack of any marking, textual or typographical, to indicate it, the whole section from the opening of Chapter 2 to '"Never again! A clover field, the lee of a haystack,– anything rather!"' as quoted above is an interpolation of matter relating to the third day of Greenwood's tramp into his account of the first day. This is why, in the presumed 'casual reader's interpretation' posited above there is the strange repetition of certain overnight stays leading to an impossible number of days spent on the road.[94]

Why is this lack of clarity important? It is important because it demonstrates the degree to which *On Tramp* is *not* an immediate account: so confusing an interpolation – whether its causes be author's carelessness or editor's intent (or, for that matter, vice versa) – is surely unthinkable in something written and published almost coterminously with the events described, as 'A Night in a Workhouse' was. As has been said, it is very much casual reading, 'railway literature'; this, which can be seen in the text's clear presumption of a lack of attention on its readers' part, influences the contents and the book's curious stance vis-à-vis its emicity and eticity. Greenwood sets out his *parti pris* very clearly as he begins his book. Tramps are 'idle drones', 'fat and comfortable in their laziness'.[95] His unexplained curiosity regarding them is openly not unprejudiced; his account, we may more than legitimately suspect, will not be merely etic, but biasedly so. However, although this prejudice may on occasion translate into obviously negatively biased introductions, conclusions and commentary regarding the various slices of tramp life that he meets on the road, Greenwood's eagerness to *present* such slices of life, an eagerness, I would argue, conditioned by his writing a book aimed at a 'casual' audience, means that he often presents those he meets in such a way as to increase their self-presentation and minimize the impact of his editorializing.

*On Tramp* is full of portraits of individuals on the road; Greenwood's eagerness to present coupled with an unshakable confidence in his ability to convince with his commentary – to convince, too, an audience not only reading casually but also likely to be predisposed to think the worse of tramps – means that these allow his various interlocutors to speak for themselves in a way that in many respects goes against an aim that he has implicitly said to be biased. The best example of this comes in Greenwood's second encounter of note on the day that he falls in with the two tramps whom he presumes to be chicken thieves. After his escape from them, Greenwood meets another, less worrying, tramp, whom he says he would not have described had it not been for the fact that 'he was the most perfect specimen [of the "common cadger kind"], both as regards "get up" and impudence it had been my lot to meet with'.[96]

Greenwood endeavours to interview the tramp about his attitude to work, but it was in fact the interviewee who first apostrophized the interviewer, asking him for ''arf a pipe of terbacker'.[97] Greenwood, who does not comment either to his interlocutor or reader regarding the rather curious fact that the tramp repeatedly addresses him as 'genelman', attempts to upbraid his new companion:

> 'I should feel ashamed, if I were you, to beg of a man as poor as yourself'.
>     It was worth several pipes of tobacco to watch the varying expressions of the man's countenance as I administered to him this mild rebuke. Presently, with a short laugh, and with a bit of a scowl, he remarked –
>     ''Ow's your brother Job?'
>     I replied that it was unknown to me that I had a brother of that name. 'It's Job Blunt *I* mean,' said the tramp; 'if you ain't one of the Blunt family, may I be butchered'.[98]

In their edition of Greenwood's text, Freeman and Nelson gloss 'Blunt' as flash slang for money, which is certainly a possibility (interesting, too, that Partridge notes that it is obsolete except for when used with the article, when it is still current amongst tramps). This would suggest that the tramp has to some extent seen through Greenwood's disguise and sees him as at least relatively wealthy, just as had the two whom he had met earlier. However, this does not explain the use of 'Job'. This was also flash slang for a guinea, which would continue the theme indicated by the reading of 'blunt' as money, but such a reading seems rather hard to support insofar as no further reference appears to be made to Greenwood's supposed wealth. Partridge also gives 'job' as a variant spelling of the verb 'to jobe', however, which was Cambridgeshire slang for 'to reprimand', and Cambridgeshire is certainly near enough to the border between Hertfordshire and Bedfordshire for it to require no leap of faith to imagine a tramp from that county being met by Greenwood on his travels. This area of meaning, where 'Job' may either be some form of 'jobe' or a simple reference to the Biblical Job's connection to complaints, suggests an interpretation of the tramp's words whereby Greenwood is himself being rebuked for the lack of manners he shows in 'jobing' one who is in fact a total stranger and speaking overly *blunt*ly to him. In this reading, Greenwood's 'interview' with the tramp becomes something of a comedy of errors, with mutual misunderstanding over questions of identity further complicated by the fact that what we are given is of course Greenwood's account of events.

Greenwood offers the tramp a pipe of tobacco on the understanding that he tell him when it was that he last worked for a meal; the tramp tells him that it was the very morning of that day, which meets with incredulity, but is explained as having been stone-breaking in a workhouse. The tramp introduces his explanation with an insistence that he is telling the truth: 'You're a open-spoken kind of cove, and I'll be open-spoken to you.'[99] The inclusion of this suggests Greenwood probably interpreted it as his interlocutor insisting that he was being honest. Given the likely meaning of 'Job Blunt', however, I would suggest that the tramp is not so much protesting his honesty as setting out his right to speak as bluntly as Greenwood clearly does. This reading is reinforced by his comment a little later, 'Who you are and wot you I don't know, and us two being alone, ser-'elp me I don't care, and so I'll tell you plain [ . . . ,] but I'm challenged to be plain spoke, and I'll stand to it.'[100] He then goes on to explain how his life is hard precisely because (as Greenwood's account clearly indicates) he is healthy and lazy. To accept work, he says, may mean depriving of their situation someone trained to the job and indeed brought up to work; tramping, anyway, *is* work, he claims in a prefiguring of Orwell's observations regarding begging in *Down and Out in Paris and London*, as it means being out in all weathers for no reward but frequent ill treatment; being strong and healthy means only that in workhouses he is given heavier labour to do and before the bench longer sentences to serve.

Greenwood reports the tramp's words; he also reports how he left the tramp lying by the side of the road with his face covered by his hat. The message is clear: this is the perfect example of the healthy and strong yet lazy and feckless cadger; Greenwood may have been an ambiguous figure in the tramp's eyes, but this only led to the interviewee being more open than he would have been with a more classifiable interviewer. I think that Greenwood not only misread the situation, but misread it in such a way as to publish an account of his failure as a journalist under the impression it recounted a success. He believes the tramp is condemning himself because he misunderstands the tramp's insistence on his right to speak bluntly as an insistence instead on his honesty. All of the tramp's replies are polemic and intelligent; they are made into relatively ridiculous self-serving self-justification by Greenwood's interjected questions and commentary. Greenwood does not notice the tramp's opposition to him as his interviewee's bluntness (unlike the interviewer's!) lies not in simple rudeness and a breach of the usual rules of social engagement but in a refusal to allow his interlocutor to push him conversationally into the 'expected' answers. This is a remarkable episode: the nominal interviewer, a journalist and writer, is ill mannered and unclassifiable, and accepts statements based more upon their tone than their content, which he in fact shows himself unable to grasp; the nominal interviewee, a tramp who openly states that he will not work, is polite, yet manages to make Greenwood look a fool. Greenwood is so unaware of this that he publishes against his own best interests. The paradox, of course, is that by failing to be the interviewer and journalist that he was aiming to be and thought that he was succeeding in being, Greenwood in fact achieved something that may fairly be considered the theoretical ultimate goal of journalism and incognito social investigation: he allows his subject total freedom of expression, unregulated by the middle-class textual control normally inherent in the fact that the social investigator has necessarily to record his or her experiences and conversations after the event and thus, *nolens volens*, make of the account a Procrustean bed where the poor have their words and being fitted to their observer's ideology.

## NOTES

1. For discussion of the concept of 'interstitiality', see Chapter 7.
2. Wells, H.G. 2005 [1910]. *The History of Mr Polly*. London: Penguin, p. 123.
3. Ibid., p. 122.
4. Ibid., p. 160.
5. Ibid.
6. Ibid., p. 162.
7. The best introductions to the Edwardian tramping phenomenon are Tickner, Lisa. 2000. *Modern Life & Modern Subjects: British Art in the Early Twentieth Century*. New Haven and London: Yale University Press, pp. 54–65 and Southworth, Helen. 2009. 'Douglas Goldring's *The Tramp: An Open Air Magazine* (1910–11) and Modernist Geographies'. *Literature & History* 18:1, pp. 35–53.
8. Tickner, *Modern Life & Modern Subjects*, p. 54. Tickner is in fact talking about Augustus John's 'obsession with gypsies and "tramping"', but the observation holds just as true regarding *The History of Mr Polly*.
9. Jebb, Miles. 1986. *Walkers*. London: Constable, pp. 130–68, especially p. 153.
10. A good example of this can be seen if one notes the relative prevalence in the essays of one of the great public literary figures of the Edwardian age, G.K. Chesterton, of scene-setting that shows the authorial voice on a country walk (for example, Chesterton, G.K., 1910. 'The Telegraph Poles'. In his

*Alarms and Discussions*. London: Methuen & Co., pp. 21–7, p. 21); this despite what we know of Chesterton's deep distaste for going on recreational walks (see Ker, Ian. 2011. *G.K. Chesterton: A Biography*. Oxford: Oxford University Press, p. 201).

11. See for instance Clifford, Nicholas. 2007. 'With Harry Franck in China'. In Kerr, Douglas and Julia Kuehn (eds.), *A Century of Travels in China: Critical Essays on Travel Writing from the 1840s to the 1940s*. Hong Kong: Hong Kong University Press, pp. 133–45. A recent exception to the lack of critical interest in Franck's writing itself as opposed to interest in the things that he describes is Driever, Steven L. 2011. 'Geographic Narratives in the South American Travelogues of Harry A. Franck: 1917–1943'. *Journal of Latin American Geography* 10:1, pp. 53–69.

12. Driever makes the excellent point that the 1930s saw Franck's books moving away from travel literature 'more suited to the armchair by the fireplace' to books for tourists to take with them, and this was accompanied by a falling-off in sales. Driever, 'Geographic Narratives', p. 62.

13. Moretti, Franco. 2000. 'The Slaughterhouse of Literature'. *Modern Language Quarterly* 61:1, pp. 207–27.

14. 'to understand the true customs of a country you have to descend into other classes, as those of the rich are the same almost everywhere': my translation. This is in fact a slight misquotation: the original begins 'il faut descendre dans d'autres états pour connaître les véritables mœurs d'un pays'. Rousseau, Jean-Jacques. 1967 [1761]. *Julie; ou, La Nouvelle Héloïse*. Paris: GF Flammarion, p. 166.

15. Franck, Harry A. 1910. *A Vagabond Journey around the World: A Narrative of Personal Experience*. New York: The Century Co., p. xiv.

16. Ibid., pp. xiii-xiv.

17. Ibid., p. xiv.

18. I take here Franck's version of his travels as given in *Vagabond Journey* to be a reliable account of his rather incredible experiences. This faith is based upon the fact that all of the scrapbooks housed in the Special Collections Library of the University of Michigan confirm what he writes. Ann Arbor, University of Michigan Library (Special Collections Library), Franck, Box 30.

19. Khartoum does not in fact have a Patriarch; one presumes the exact Orthodox title was lost in translation at some point.

20. Franck, *Vagabond Journey*, p. 232.

21. Ibid., p. 310.

22. Orwell, George. 2000 [1940]. 'Inside the Whale'. In *A Patriot After All: 1940–1941* [*The Complete Works of George Orwell*, ed. Peter Davison, vol. 12]. London: Secker & Warburg, pp. 86–115, p. 88.

23. Franck, *Vagabond Journey*, p. 282.

24. All non-English terms are spelt as Franck spells them.
25. Ibid., p. 197.
26. Ann Arbor, University of Michigan Library (Special Collections Library), Franck, Box 5, *Tales of a Vagabond/Making of a Vagabond.*
27. Franck, Harry A. 1932. *Foot-Loose in the British Isles: Being a Desultory and Not Too Serious Account of Sixteen Months of Living and Peregrinating Hither and Yon throughout Great Britain.* New York and London: The Century Co., p. 316.
28. Ibid., p. 331.
29. Ibid., p. 333.
30. Ibid., p. 341.
31. Ibid., p. viii.
32. Ibid., p. 332.
33. Ibid., p. 334.
34. Ibid.
35. Ibid., p. 335.
36. Ibid., p. 334.
37. Ibid., p. 334.
38. Ann Arbor, University of Michigan Library (Special Collections Library), Franck, Box 8, folder 1930–1932, 1934–1936.
39. In the published version (see Franck, *Foot-Loose*, pp. 358–359) he spells the contracted form 'Bark', presumably to indicate a pronunciation with /ɑː/ rather than /ɜː/.
40. Ann Arbor, University of Michigan Library (Special Collections Library), Franck, Box 5, *Tales of a Vagabond/Making of a Vagabond.*
41. A system existed whereby for a small fee employment agencies would pay labourers' tickets to their place of work (very often in railroad construction or maintenance somewhere).
42. Ann Arbor, University of Michigan Library (Special Collections Library), Franck, Box 5, *Tales of a Vagabond/Making of a Vagabond.*
43. Ibid.
44. Ehrenreich, Barbara. 2011 [2001]. *Nickel and Dimed: On (Not) Getting By in America.* New York: Picador, p. 9.
45. Ann Arbor, University of Michigan Library (Special Collections Library), Franck, Box 5, 'Wandering Unskilled Laborers on the Edge of Trampdom'.
46. Ann Arbor, University of Michigan Library (Special Collections Library), Franck, Box 5, *Tales of a Vagabond/Making of a Vagabond.*
47. Ann Arbor, University of Michigan Library (Special Collections Library), Franck, Box 8, 1905.
48. 'The Tour of the World as a Worker – continued'. My translation. Ibid.
49. Ann Arbor, University of Michigan Library (Special Collections Library), Franck, Box 5, *Tales of a Vagabond/Making of a Vagabond* fragments.

50. Ann Arbor, University of Michigan Library (Special Collections Library), Franck, Box 1.
51. Ann Arbor, University of Michigan Library (Special Collections Library), Franck, Box 6, Suggestions for Books, Articles, and Novels.
52. Ibid.
53. Ann Arbor, University of Michigan Library (Special Collections Library), Franck, Box 6, 'The Day's Events and their Background'.
54. Ann Arbor, University of Michigan Library (Special Collections Library), Franck, Box 5, Proposed European Book.
55. Ibid.
56. Ibid.
57. Harry A. Franck to William J. Latta, 8 January 1919. Ann Arbor, University of Michigan Library (Special Collections Library), Franck, Box 1, 1919.
58. Hacking, Ian. 1998. *Mad Travelers: Reflections on the Reality of Transient Mental Illnesses.* Charlottesville and London: University Press of Virginia.
59. Hacking gives a translation of this document, ibid., pp. 135–48.
60. Although a term that Tissié used to refer to Dadas's problem, 'pathological tourism' would be the perfect shorthand for Franck's life. Quoted in ibid., p. 27.
61. Ibid., p. 1.
62. Ibid., p. 81.
63. Jebb, *Walkers*, p. 22.
64. Ibid., pp. 22–23.
65. Ibid., p. 63.
66. Quoted in ibid., p. 61.
67. Ibid., p. 119.
68. Ibid., p. 150.
69. Chesterton, G.K. 1988 [1936]. *The Autobiography.* [*The Collected Works of G.K. Chesterton,* vol. XVI]. San Francisco: Ignatius Press, p. 210.
70. Belloc, Hilaire. 1985 [1902]. *The Path to Rome.* Harmondsworth: Penguin Books, p. 31.
71. Ibid., p. 108.
72. Ibid., p. 181.
73. Ibid., pp. 45–46.
74. Chesterton, *Autobiography*, p. 210.
75. Belloc, *The Path to Rome*, p. 46.
76. Page, Robin. 1973. *Down among the Dossers.* London: Davis-Poynter, pp. 145–6.
77. Leigh Fermor, Patrick. 2004 [1977]. *A Time of Gifts: On Foot to Constantinople, from the Hook of Holland to the Middle Danube.* London: John Murray, pp. 12–3.
78. Jebb, *Walkers*, pp. 169–170.

79. Ibid., p. 171.
80. Belloc, *The Path to Rome*, p. 19.
81. An important exception to the near-total lack of tramping narratives after the Second World War is a remarkable book (Holzach, Michael. 1985 [1982]. *Deutschland umsonst: Zu Fuß und ohne Geld durch ein Wohlstandsland; Mit einer Deutschlandskarte und dem eingezeichneten Wanderweg*. Frankfurt am Main and Berlin: Ullstein Sachbuch) by a West German journalist who in 1982 published his account of how in 1980 he spent six months walking from Hamburg to Lake Constance and back again, picking up casual work but setting off with no money at all. Although a fascinating work, it is of limited relevance to the field of study here because Holzach tells nearly all those whom he meets exactly what he is doing: it is not incognito social investigation even in the ambiguous way that such accidental examples as Belloc's are. A British equivalent is Carroll, Charlie. 2013. *No Fixed Abode: A Journey through Homelessness from London to Cornwall*. Chichester: Summersdale.
82. Greenwood, James. 2008 [1883]. *On Tramp*. In Freeman, Mark and Gillian Nelson (eds.). *Vicarious Vagrants: Incognito Social Explorers and the Homeless in England, 1860–1910*. Lambertville: The True Bill Press, pp. 141–80, p. 142.
83. Regarding Lucas, see Whitmore, Richard. 1983. *Mad Lucas: The Strange Story of Victorian England's Most Famous Hermit*. Hitchin: North Hertfordshire District Council.
84. Greenwood spells this without the e.
85. Greenwood, *On Tramp*, p. 151.
86. Ibid., p. 148.
87. Whitmore gives 19 April as the date of Lucas's death (*Mad Lucas*, p. 65); this discrepancy can be explained by the fact that the 17th, the date that Greenwood gives, quoting the *Hertfordshire Express* (*On Tramp*, p. 151), was the day on which the unconscious and dying Lucas was removed from the house in which he had immured himself (Whitmore, *Mad Lucas*, pp. 1–3).
88. St Ippolyts is given simply as 'Ippolits'.
89. Greenwood, *On Tramp*, p. 169.
90. Ibid., p. 147.
91. Ibid.
92. Ibid., p. 157.
93. http://pubshistory.com/HertsPubs/Hatfield/WhiteSwan.shtml, accessed 28 January 2014.
94. For completeness' sake, Greenwood's itinerary and the dates thereof must have been as follows (the places of departure and arrival in brackets):

18 June 1877 (London)–Hatfield
19 June 1877 Hatfield–Stevenage

20 June 1877 Stevenage–Hitchin
21 June 1877 Hitchin–Shefford
22 June 1877 Shefford–(Bedford)

95. Ibid., p. 141.
96. Ibid., p. 172.
97. Ibid.
98. Ibid., pp. 172–3.
99. Ibid., p. 173.
100. Ibid., p. 174.

# CHAPTER 5

# The Daily Grind: T. Sparrow, Olive Christian Malvery and the World of Work

*Down and Out in Paris and London* marked the general end of investigation into the homeless as a productive type; legal and technological changes at the same time put an end to tramping. The dominant form would become exploration of work carried out by those of lower social classes. It is why this may have been and how it relates to the form's becoming associated with women writers to which we must now turn.

We have already talked about incognito social investigation texts in terms of their status as a text type in truth concerned more with its own methodology than what it describes; we need now to look at where, as a text type, it fits within social frameworks. I would argue that incognito social investigation texts are a strongly middlebrow form; this, however, necessarily brings us to the troubled question of how exactly we wish to define 'middlebrow'. It will be defined here by way of a *via negativa*, so to speak: the middlebrow does not set itself up as ('mere') entertainment as the lowbrow does; nor does it challenge as the highbrow does. I do not mean by this that the 'lowbrow' *is* always only entertainment, but that it presents itself as such and is perceived as such; nor do I wish to limit the 'highbrow' to any particular type of challenge – its challenge to its readers may be formal, intellectual, political, social . . . Nor should 'challenging' be read as synonymous with 'difficult': there is, for instance, nothing particularly 'difficult' about suggesting, as Stephen Reynolds does in *A Poor Man's House*, discussed in Chapter 7, that the life of the poor, *considered emically*, is better than the life of the middle and upper classes, but this

© The Author(s) 2017
L. Seaber, *Incognito Social Investigation in British Literature*,
Palgrave Studies in Life Writing, DOI 10.1007/978-3-319-50962-4_5

does challenge those non-working-class readers whom he might legitimately have expected to be his audience. The key point, in this example, is that Reynolds's analysis is emic: an etic representation of the superiority of non-middle-/upper-class life would remain, in the sense used here, middlebrow, as by remaining within its likely reader's system of values it offers no challenge.

Incognito social investigation texts, despite their various implicit and explicit protestations to the contrary, are overwhelmingly etic; only a small fraction succeed in doing what most promise, and not only give an observation-based portrait, but also do so in the terms of those observed rather than those observing. This already makes the wider genre middlebrow in general, but there are further reasons for supposing the subset of texts concerning the world of work to be especially middlebrow within this context. The Greenwoodian tradition, with its focus on the 'residuum', on deep poverty, squalor and hardship, although still middlebrow, was a distinctly less respectable form – ideologically middlebrow, as it were, but less middle class in practical terms: it always courted accusations of voyeurism, spectacularism and a potentially dangerous fascination with the unwholesome side of things. Settling in communities, always the rarest form anyway, tends to suggest that somewhere behind the author's actions is an idea or ideology questioning the status quo, and is thus another form of approach to the highbrow. Tramping always seems to tread an uneasy path between lowbrow and highbrow: it can, as in much of Franck's work, be so devoid of intellectual content as to move towards 'pure' entertainment; it can, as with Belloc's journey, be the pretext for a series of reflections challenging the status quo. The world of working-class work avoids the Scylla and Charybdis of the highbrow and lowbrow more easily than the other forms of incognito social investigation can manage. When it offers views on social problems it tends to offer practical solutions. This is unsurprising: each workplace, each job, each trade, will have its own localized problems; such problems – whether of overcrowding, sweating, poor management, low pay or any of a host of others – are much more likely to suggest practical, local solutions than are broader, societal problems such as homelessness. Such localism suggests reform rather than revolution as a solution, and reform in this sense is resolutely top-down and thus etic. Those texts regarding work that do suggest a more structural change are not however necessarily therefore emic. Texts such as those by Polly Toynbee do suggest changes that are not merely local, but they are nonetheless changes suggested by a middle-class journalist for a middle-class readership, and therefore of the same fundamentally hegemonic nature as those suggested by eminently etic Victorians such as Stallard.

'Work', of course, is not a monolithic concept. The term is not used here in an economic sense: we are not considering work here in terms of what it earns the worker or what it produces, but rather in terms of how certain actions are classified socially. 'Work', in the sense used here, is that which the society in which it takes place classifies as something done either for economic reasons or in order to achieve a certain aim, which is to say not for motives that are religious, leisure-based or solely idiosyncratically personal. Of course, in the latter case, the reasons for wishing to achieve a given aim may be, let us say, religious, but the need to work is not. To explain this distinction, we may take the case of someone such as Samuel Barnett: his work at Toynbee Hall in the general sense obviously came about through religious motivation; however, his work considered on a day-to-day basis can only have been dictated by the immediate necessities of achieving certain goals. In the use of 'work' here, therefore, Canon Barnett's 'work' in the sense of his mission is not to be considered 'work' in the sense of social perception; the daily 'work' that he did because of that mission is. The same would be true of a poet or artist: creation is not 'work'; that which one does in order to create is. In the former case, that of economic reasons, this is not to say that the reasons behind the actions classified as 'work' *are* necessarily economic, nor that the motives may not belong in fact to some other category: what is important here is social perception rather than economic reality. By way of example, anyone who could live off accumulated capital yet still continues to work is clearly not working out of personal economic necessity; nonetheless, the social perception is that what they are daily doing is 'work'. In other words, 'work' is socially recognized and recognizable: it is actions rather than structure. In practical terms for questions of incognito social investigation, 'work', which is to say the actions comprising it, is that which is observable and, most pertinently here, *that which is imitable.*

I have insisted on this definition of 'work' with relation to incognito social investigation for practical reasons. The focus on work as a social category rather than as an economic one, this reduction of it to observable actions removed from economic context, is a deliberate simplification, but it is a deliberate simplification reflecting that practised by the journalists and writers who took various forms of work as the object of their investigations. If one wishes to investigate and recount the life of a housemaid, factory operative or street seller, then one cannot deal with unseen underlying causes in regard to one's disguising oneself: one can only follow, more or less mechanically and more or less faithfully, the visible actions of those whom one includes in that category. An incognito social investigator cannot have been led to the forms of work in question by the same forces that have led to it those whom he or she (as we shall see, usually she in social investigation concerning work) is investigating; he or she can only repeat the surface characteristics, not the structural ones. This does not mean, of course, that in their analyses of the situations that they have investigated, certain incognito social investigators do not also look beyond the merely superficial and observable. Nonetheless, however insightful and subtle the analyses of what 'work' may be and the role that it has within society, they will nearly always be based upon an initial choice of disguise limited to the observable surface.

A useful side effect of understanding 'work' in this sense is that it allows us to include in our examination here accounts of street begging. Begging, in the physical sense of asking passers-by for money is observable work. This point was famously made by Orwell in *Down and Out in Paris and London*:

> Yet if one looks closely one sees that there is no essential difference between a beggar's livelihood and that of numerous respectable people. Beggars do not work, it is said; but, then, what is *work*? A navvy works by swinging a pick. An accountant works by adding up figures. A beggar works by standing out of doors in all weathers and getting varicose veins, chronic bronchitis, etc.[1]

Orwell does add an explicit economic level to his interpretation of begging as work, insofar as he discusses the reasons for which beggars are 'despised' and the fact that what they do is work is not recognized. Nonetheless, by basing himself on the physical actions of the beggar – he begins his analysis with the observation that the little money that London beggars make is 'a poor return for standing eighty-four hours a week on the kerb, with the cars grazing your backside',[2] which is a perfect summation of the observable physicality of much of a London street beggar's work – he is recognizing the concept of 'work' as a set of actions that can be examined outside their economic context.

The value of allowing begging to be considered as work lies in the degree to which pretending to be a street beggar for a day was considered a common pastime of journalists in the late nineteenth century. There are various examples of it, although none, I would argue, of particular importance or merit within the wider body of incognito social exploration texts.[3] Their importance lies rather in their inspiring probably the best-known fictional presentation of incognito social investigation, Neville St Clair/ Hugh Boone in Arthur Conan Doyle's 'The Man with the Twisted Lip'.[4] The tale of how the journalist Neville St Clair discovers on his day's expedition for copy as the disfigured beggar that he can make more money from public sympathy than he can by writing, and of Sherlock Holmes's investigation of his disappearance, may take its inspiration from journalistic accounts of incognito social investigation as a street beggar, but as Audrey Jaffe has argued, its true interest lies in matters other than incognito social investigation. Doyle's story is of great importance to studies of incognito social investigation not because of any insights it might in itself offer on that subject – it offers very few – but because of the simple fact that it offers what is almost certainly the best-known fictional representation of it, *and that representation is false.* Street begging has never been either the most widespread or most influential form of incognito social investigation; incognito social investigators writing on work do not give up their journalism or writing to take up for real what they once feigned.[5] To contemporary readers Neville St Clair would have been a reasonably familiar figure, and his lack of typicality would not have been of particular importance; in later years, when street-working journalists were no longer a known, if not necessarily common, feature of newspapers or magazines, the whole complicated question of incognito social investigation is reduced in its best-known fictional representation to a question of how much 'dishonest' beggars may make. Insofar as incognito social investigation is known outside *Down and Out in Paris and London,* it is the image of Hugh Boone the dishonest beggar and Neville St Clair the dishonest journalist that remains. Street begging is in itself, I would repeat, not an especially important form of incognito social investigation; it is worthy of attention simply because its presence in Doyle's story acts to skew such public perception of it as has remained now that its heyday is long past.

The most widespread form of incognito social investigation centred on a form of work that is not the mistakenly canonical street-begging, but rather something less obvious: organ-grinding. Barrel organs were a common feature of the London streetscape in the late nineteenth and early twentieth centuries.[6] A list of the articles treating journalists' experiences as temporary organ-grinders shows the popularity of the form and the period in which it flourished: Eva Bright, 'How the Other Half Lives: The Organ-Grinder' (1894);[7] T. Sparrow, 'London Street Toilers' (1894);[8] Frances Bourne, 'A Lady's Experiences as an Organ-Grinder' (1900);[9] Olive Christian Malvery, 'Music in the Byways' (1905).[10] Four texts in a decade may not appear many; if we consider, however, the extreme specificity of the (sub-)subtype, then the very fact of there being more than one makes it worthy of note.[11]

False organ-grinders have been studied in detail by Laura Vorachek. Hers is an excellent study, although she underestimates the degree to which ethnicity and class are two categories that bleed into one another and cannot be as easily distinguished as she would like when considering how people reacted to journalists' disguises (was it the 'ethnicity' of 'ethnic' costumes that allowed women 'to ramble anonymously in urban environments',[12] or was it the differences in class belonging that they communicated?), and should be referred to for its close-argued detailed analysis of these texts and their illustrations. Her conclusion, however, that 'social investigation involving cross-cultural dress illuminates gender issues more than the plight of the urban poor, its ostensible purpose',[13] is rather problematic: incognito social investigation is treated as a non-problematic background against which questions of gender are played out. It is stated as a bald fact that (incognito) social investigation has as 'its ostensible purpose' the illumination of 'the plight of the urban poor'. This accepts the text form's self-presentation, not recognizing either how it is a reflexive form concerned with its own methodology or how it follows journalistic fashions. Early examples of incognito social investigation were as much about *investigation* as they were about the *social*; later ones were for an audience familiar with the shifts in the degree to which the genre was fashionable. With this in mind, it is worthwhile returning to Vorachek's statement, as it contains a vital truth almost in spite of itself, a truth that becomes visible only when the whole corpus of incognito social investigation texts is borne in mind. Texts involving passing for organ-grinders *do* go more towards illuminating gender issues than they do towards illuminating the plight of the urban poor. However, the importance of this lies not in the texts themselves, but rather at an intertextual level (although perhaps 'contextual' would be a better term): incognito social investigation texts dealing with 'work', of which the organ-grinding texts and related matter explored by Vorachek are a sub-type, are an extremely gendered subform within the wider corpus. Organ-grinding texts *are* important in gender terms, but above all when read against other types of social investigation texts.

The first text, Eva Bright's 'How the Other Half Lives: The Organ-Grinder', is of interest not merely because of its chronological primacy. It was part of a long-running series, 'How the Other Half Lives', of which the *English Illustrated Magazine* published twenty-two instalments between 1894 and 1897. In itself, taken as incognito social investigation, Bright's article does not contain any particularly outstanding interest; its interest on other levels has already been illuminatingly analysed by Vorachek. However, although (as we shall see) Bright was in many respects a failure as a social investigator, her piece does nonetheless contain various points of interest. It was inspired by an article in the *Telegraph*, described in the opening of Bright's article as offering 'visions of Alnaschar-like splendour in the profession of organ-grinding';[14] the *Telegraph* piece may thus be taken as the original inspiration for all the organ-grinder pieces, with the pre-existing *English Illustrated Magazine* series, of which it was the third piece, following two incognito social investigation pieces by Elizabeth L. Banks, providing the impetus for the incognito element. Bright's description of her attempt to be an organ-grinder demonstrates that, qua incognito social investigator, she had not learnt much from the almost thirty years of examples that separated her from Greenwood. She disguises herself with care, but has no knowledge of where to hire a barrel-organ other than a vague story from an acquaintance that he had been disturbed whilst living in Hammersmith by an organ hirer's; this leads her to a fruitless visit to the house of one 'Signor Garcia'. Leaving Garcia's abode, she encounters a policeman, who directs her to Notting Hill; here she is informed that she has been sent to an organ builder's, where they are currently working on an instrument for the President of the Royal Academy. She is finally sent from here to the nearby organ hirer whom she has been seeking; now, one would think, the true focus of her journalism can begin. It is already worth noting that the first two-and-a-half pages of her five go by this way; half of her article is *not* concerned with 'how the other half lives', but with her misadventures in trying to discover it in order to describe it. This may appear to be another example of the wider genre's focus on its own methodology, but the openness with which the social investigator puts herself at the centre of her enquiry belies this. The opening half of her article is about herself; it ends too not with a recapitulation of what she has witnessed and described, but rather her relationship to it: 'As I drove homewards the events of the day seemed to resolve themselves into a kind of "Walpurgisnacht" dream, were it not that my blistered hands, aching wrists, and almost shoeless feet, assured me of their stern reality.'[15]

Bright does not even succeed in her ostensible aim of disguising herself: acting upon the information of Herr Gern, the organ builder of Notting Hill, she goes, in her disguise, to Mary Place; here she is met by 'a deputation waiting to receive me – it had leaked out that I was a journalist, and the men were anxious to air their grievances'.[16] The 'classic' incognito social investigator's ostensible position is to act as a conduit whereby the 'voiceless poor' can be overheard, so to speak, and have their voices relayed to those who are not poor; being incognito is taken to be a *sine qua non* for allowing accurate reporting. Bright presents herself as wishing to speak for organ-grinders, a privilege that disguise will allow her. Instead, she finds that it is her *lack* of disguise that allows it: she becomes both an implicit representative of the journalistic world to which she and the author of the *Telegraph* article belong in an inversion of the normal social investigator relationship, and thus doing is made – will she, nill she – into a vehicle for the organ-grinders, the poor, to convey their views. Her failure is her success.

Bright's article's interest lies not in its content proper, which is to say, not in its description of what it sets out to describe, but rather in the very fact of *what* it describes. It provides further proof that very often the real interest of incognito social investigation texts lies not in what they describe but in the presumptions underlying their very existence and methodology. This is doubly true in the case of Bright's article, owing to its placement within the 'How the Other Half Lives' series. The first three articles – on crossing sweepers, flower girls and organ-grinders – were incognito social investigation (although, as we have seen in Bright's case, 'incognito' here should be taken somewhat *cum grano salis*); of the nineteen that followed, only one more, the sixth (also by Elizabeth L. Banks, author of the first two articles), that on dressmakers' apprentices, was an example of incognito social investigation. The others are a heterogeneous mixture: interviews, descriptive urban pieces and some by the Essex writer S.L. Bensusan that are more rural sketches than descriptions of how any supposed 'other half' may live. There is in fact *no* common thread uniting the pieces other than their taking as their nominal subjects those performing work that spans the working-class scale – from crossing sweepers who are far below the poverty line to prison warders and engine drivers, who are edging towards the lower middle classes. Incognito social investigation of the sort based upon work is clearly 'domesticated' (for want of a better term); it has lost the scandalous charge it had in Greenwood or that it would have again in Ehrenreich. Here it is not even held in enough consideration to merit recognition as a methodology apart. The *English Illustrated Magazine* series included four accounts of incognito social investigation, yet it was not even in any way bruited that it contained such things. We can see here how the Greenwoodian methodology had already been internalized into journalism, so to speak: it is nothing more than another way of looking at, and writing about, those who, the author and publisher feel it fair to presume, are not represented amongst a publication's readership but are rather 'the other half', who have nothing in common except what they are *not*: they are not of the middle class that is presumed to read such accounts; they may safely be used as a source of copy with no attention needing to be paid to choosing one investigative methodology over another. Novelistic rural romanticizing à la Bensusan is as meaningful and useful a way of describing the 'other half' as the potentially more scientific methods of a Banks or Bright. No differentiation is required: *all* of the 'other half' are fit material for *any* approach. Incognito social investigation is no longer interesting or innovative; it may provide a little entertainment to its readers, but not necessarily more than any other form of writing about the poor.

That there was, in some sectors at least, an implicitly dismissive journalistic view of incognito social investigation as a methodology in the 1890s may be seen in the second article published by the *English Illustrated Magazine* detailing an incognito exploration of the life of the organ-grinder, Frances Bourne's 'A Lady's Experiences as an Organ-Grinder' from October 1900. It was not part of the 'How the Other Half Lives' series, which had reached its conclusion with Bensusan's piece on 'the gipsy' three years earlier. It is remarkable that a piece so similar to Bright's – the similarity is particularly marked early in the articles, where the focus is on the author's staining her skin brown and dressing as an 'Italian' before having to find somewhere that hires out barrel organs rather than the manufactories thereof to which she first erroneously goes – should be published only six years later in the same magazine. Here, however, the process of domestication affecting incognito social investigation at the time had reached its logical conclusion. Although Bright's article was superficial and the series of which it was part gave no weight to incognito social investigation as a methodology, the 'How the Other Half Lives' articles did at least have the ostensible aim of educating readers about other sections of society. That this aim was rarely more than a sprinkling of 'seriousness' to dignify a hodgepodge of pieces otherwise unconnected is irrelevant: what is important is the simple fact that it was thought necessary to include at least a façade of investigation. Bright's piece begins with reference to public conversation raised by newspaper coverage of organ-grinders and she explicitly states that her aim in disguising herself was to *learn*: 'The article set me thinking, finally I resolved to test the matter personally.'[17] Whatever the real result of Bright's desultory 'investigations', she glosses what she did as a learning experience, and thus by implication something that will impart knowledge to her readers. Such justification, disingenuous though it may be, is wholly absent from Bourne's piece, which begins:

> It occurred to me one day that to go round the streets of London with a barrel-organ, in an Italian costume, with stained face, clumsy boots, red handkerchief, and earrings, would form an experience at once exciting, adventurous, novel, and attractive; and having once given room in my mind to the idea, it grew and grew until it attained such alarming proportions that, unlike most things, I was fain to encourage it in order to get rid of it.[18]

Her incognito social investigation experience is presented solely as a lark; its genesis lies not in any curiosity regarding organ-grinders and how they live but merely in the entertainment that the escapade may bring her. When she uses a small shop as a changing-room, the owner is represented as asking whether Bourne is a detective, and the author reassures her that she was no detective, but 'only an ordinary madcap, with a new idea'.[19] This is pure entertainment, but without even the fig-leaf of instruction: 'A Lady's Experiences as an Organ-Grinder' is focused on the 'lady' who writes rather than on any organ-grinder whom she impersonates or meets. Her one 'insight' is that people in rich areas of the West End are more likely to give generously to an organ-grinder, even though they do not greatly enjoy the music, than people in the City, who do enjoy the music. That the rich give more generously than the poor *may* be an insight worthy of analysis, but presented without analysis it is but a poor gleaning. Bourne's piece is one of the nadirs of incognito social investigation in all its forms; it has degenerated from Greenwood's original scandal through various waves of popularity to being merely one of an array of equally meaningful (and thus equally meaningless) methodologies in the hands of the various 'How the Other Half Lives' authors, where it nonetheless had at least retained some odour of instruction, before becoming nothing more than the 'madcap' escapade of 'a lady' who can even claim originality – 'a new idea' – for something that had been recounted *in the same magazine* some six years earlier.

That the process of degeneration of 'work'-based forms of incognito social investigation in the 1890s ran in parallel with a continued use of the methodology for more serious ends can be seen from another piece examining organ-grinders appearing the same year as Bright's piece. This was 'London Street Toilers' by T. Sparrow, published in the *Newbery House Magazine*, which shows how even so limited a field as 1890s incognito social investigation journalism focusing on organ-grinders can contain enormous differences. The *Newbery House Magazine: A Monthly Review for Churchmen and Churchwomen* was an Anglican publication appearing between 1889 and 1894, becoming the *Minister* in 1895 before ceasing publication in 1896. It was a rather high-minded periodical, and Sparrow's pieces, one suspects, came as something as light relief after a rather steady diet of pieces on religious music and theology. Notwithstanding its rather general title, Sparrow's piece focuses on organ-grinders and is divided into her experiences of 'Street Life' and 'Slum Life'. No greater contrast to the pieces by Bright and Bourne could be imagined. Whereas the two *English Illustrated Magazine* authors begin with long descriptions of their travails with make-up and costume and their problems in finding a barrel organ with which to accompany their jaunts, Sparrow's description of how she organized herself in her investigation hardly exists. She decides to undertake the experiment, and then:

> A week later, and I was domiciled with an organ-grinder and his wife, having made a bargain with them, that I should be treated as one of the family, eating what they ate, and drinking what they drank. The man was to take me on his round with the organ the first day: for the remainder of the week I was to manipulate the machine unaided.[20]

Her motivations too differ. Hers is neither an escapade à la Bourne nor a suspiciously lackadaisical hunt for facts à la Bright, but an investigation. It is emblematic that whereas Bright's piece was inspired by another newspaper article, the inspiration for Sparrow's grew out of an investigation (the word is hers)[21] that she had already begun. The first impulse, she tells us, came from seeing five men 'on the right side of thirty, neither blind nor deaf nor dumb' grinding their organs on the same street on the same morning.[22] The manner in which this motivation is expressed may suggest that what one is about to read is a denunciation of these able-bodied men who have no better occupation. Such a reading is subtly undercut by Sparrow's use of the form 'grinded' rather than 'ground' to refer to the five organ-grinders' activity; this may be read as simply being non-standard (a reading further suggesting a coming denunciation), but it may also be read as a semi-technical term, and Sparrow's use of it a way to suggest that what is coming will give a certain professional dignity to those described. This latter reading will be borne out by the remainder of the article.

Indeed, not only does Sparrow start from a clearly investigative stand-point, but she also begins with new data upon which to build her investigation, although how this was discovered she does not relate:

> I had often read how organ-grinders were mostly Italian, how they dwelt in the vicinity of Hatton Garden, and hired their organs by the week from a large emporium; but my first discovery was the fact that, at least, Westminster organ-grinders lived in Westminster, did not bind themselves to be Italians – though many dressed as such, and mostly owned their organs, or hired them from one another.[23]

*Before* she begins her incognito social investigation, Sparrow has already discovered more than Bright or Bourne after they have completed theirs. She starts from a point already beyond the semi-exoticizing 'Italian' stereotype; the organ-grinders whom she investigates are 'real', with all the complexity that this implies. They are themselves as capable of pretending to be Italian as any dilettante social investigator is.

Sparrow's genuine status as an investigator is evinced in her willingness to learn and the enthusiasm that leads her to begin her presentation of her investigation proper with a question and answer that challenges her readers' presuppositions: 'Did you know that organ-grinders cultivated a distinct code of manners? They do, and to learn it takes time and intelligence.'[24] Hereafter follows one of the most non-judgemental of *all* incognito social investigation accounts. Sparrow describes the organ-grinder's work with neither condescension nor criticism; more remarkably, her presentation of those amongst whom she lives not only recognizes that they are not 'lazy' (presenting her awareness of the physical difficulties involved in forthright terms very rare in incognito social investigation texts in general, especially in the 1890s: 'To call an organ-grinder's life an idle life or a lazy one *is to show you know nothing at all about it*'),[25] but also recognizes the technical mastery involved in organ-grinders' work. This recognition of the *expertise* needed to carry out what was (as is clear from the other pieces discussing organ-grinders) otherwise regarded as a trade requiring at most brute stamina is remarkable.

Sparrow's refusal to judge can also be seen in her description of the 'Rests', penny-an-hour lodgings for resting, washing or sleeping. These, she says, are frequented by the 'lowest of street-traders, beggars with false arms or wooden legs, imposters as to blindness, lameness, dumbness, &c.'.[26] Should the police come visiting, a system of passwords allows the majority of the clients to leave hurriedly, and 'a few *bonâ fide* cress-sellers, cornet players, or apple-women are left, who are never known to "rat" on their companions'.[27] The description is precisely that, a description: no moral judgement is passed on either those who flee or those who remain. Sparrow's conclusion regarding these 'Rests' is interesting, insofar as it balances an emic advantage against an equally emic disadvantage: 'On a wet day to be able to dry one's drenched clothes if far from home is a decided gain, but to have to consort with such a low class of criminals rather militates against the advantage.'[28] Given Sparrow's previous refusal to condemn the 'low class of criminals' to be found in 'Rests' and the fact that she limits herself to describing them neutrally, I see no reason to presume that her recognition of the disadvantages involved in frequenting the same lodgings as them to be anything other than the recognition, steeped in emicity, of the fact that those whom she might legitimately expect her readers to take to be all part of the same urban underclass are amongst themselves differentiated and subject to recognized social gradations.

Sparrow's article shines with a refusal to judge hugely rare in accounts of incognito social investigation. More powerful than the individual examples of what Sparrow records or passes over is the whole tone of her piece. It breathes *not* tolerance (in Pasolini's sense of the term as what occurs when those holding power decide that certain groups not holding power are to be allowed to behave as they will, without there being any question, however, of the power relationship changing),[29] but rather acceptance. Sparrow criticizes what she sees as criticizable, but does so from her reaction to what she sees rather than from anything broader.

A good example of the difference, as I understand it here, between acceptance and tolerance can be seen in Sparrow's description of the diet in the household whose life she was sharing:

> About food the less said the better. Their knowledge of cooking is so crude that they do as much as possible without it. We had gin in our tea for breakfast with dry bread. We had ale for dinner with a bloater, or a bit of pork, or a stew with more onions than anything else. Cheese and fat bacon formed a supper which made all our confreres envious, while dripping or margarine were considered a tasty relish that helped to wash down mouldy bread or potatoes gone dry. But the chief thing was drink.
>
> A man would forego his supper and never think about his tea, but he must be starving indeed if he did without his pipe and a glass of something by his side. Children were given many a taste, or helped themselves as they ran to and fro with the jug. If a woman felt 'down' she took a glass: if she felt 'up' she treated a friend. Joy was commemorated by a liquoring up, sorrow was endured on the same lines. The sober partook at home, the unsober away from home, but it was only too evident that both classes suffered from such a constant drain on their digestion, temper, and pockets.
>
> But their capacity for pleasure compensates in some degree for what seems such a sordid existence.[30]

There is certainly criticism here – knowledge of cooking is 'crude'; constant drinking damages health, happiness and wealth – but they are superficial. Sparrow describes, noting what to her are the negative aspects, but neither condemns nor tolerates. In other words, she says neither that the subjects of her observation *should* or *should not* do what they do: she simply says what it is that they do and her reactions to it. Sparrow's casual acceptance of gin for breakfast at the physical level mirrors her acceptance of breakfast gin-drinking at the social level: she may or may not *like* it, but she accepts it, neither criticizing nor tolerating it.[31] The absence of the former is clear; the absence of the latter can be seen in her negative comments on excessive drinking or knowledge of cooking: she has no intention of pretending to like things that she does not; she is not willing to hold the organ-grinders to standards that differ from hers. She will not make allowances: she accepts but does not tolerate. Rather than recalling any of the other Victorian incognito social investigators, whose accounts all show greater levels of editorializing (of what type is irrelevant; it is always a form of refusal to let the poor speak for themselves), Sparrow's work here is reminiscent of the much earlier work by the far from incognito Mayhew: there too we see description leavened by personal comment, but without the sensation of there being a voice behind the text, as it were, continuously judging the poor against middle-class standards. Sparrow's standards as evoked here *are personal*; she criticizes certain things, but she criticizes them because *she* does not agree with them, and neither criticizes nor agrees with them with explicit reference to a system rather than her personal reaction.

The same, one suspects, would be true vis-à-vis her response to behaviour at the other end of the social scale. She ends her account with a description of her visit to an organ-grinders' 'hop'; her description of it is as accepting as one has come to expect by this point. She describes too one of the differences between this social event and other more exalted ones, and ends with a recommendation:

> There was no host, and chaperones were conspicuous by their absence; people came in as they liked in ones, twos, or threes. Introductions were unnecessary: you could speak to any one if you liked, or you could let them alone. The great idea was – ease, and in this many a West-end entertainment could learn a lesson with profit.[32]

That this is the only point at which she draws an explicit comparison with social events frequented by a different class suggests that for Sparrow this was one of the most important differences that she witnessed. Her lack of any explanation for her views here suggest once again that what we have is a *personal* opinion rather than one that is part of a wider criticism (of West End society on this occasion) that has behind it a stated ideology to which one can refer.

This is not to deny that Sparrow's views, her social standards, her ideas of what is good or bad, were formed by social and class ideologies, nor that the standards against which she judges the poor whom she is studying were those of her class. The distinction between *personal* and *social* criticism (whether condemnation, tolerance or praise) as understood here lies not in certain authors' ability to reach their conclusion *ex nihilo* with no influence from society's ideologies, but rather in differences in presentation of ideologies, without reference to the aetiology thereof. There is no sense in 'London Street Toilers' that an appeal (implicit or explicit) is being made in any way to an ideology shared by Sparrow and her readership. The fact that such an ideology exists is of less importance here than the fact that its existence goes unpresumed. She does not allow herself to do her readers' work for them: if they wish to draw wider lessons based upon their pre-existing middle-class ideologies regarding other social classes, they may do so, but Sparrow will not offer them anything other than accounts of what she has observed and her reactions thereto. Sparrow is a rare example amongst incognito social investigators of someone able to act as a means of transmission of information about the poor to the middle classes without colouring the information transmitted with appeals to shared prejudice or ideology, yet who is still willing to offer more than a purely anonymous, neutral and depersonalized version of what she sees. In 'London Street Toilers' Sparrow successfully walks the tightrope between being an investigator whose intrusive editorializing voice falsifies what is seen by imposing a level of interpretation that creates complicity with the readership against those investigated and being an investigator whose attempts to be absent from the text mean that this becomes a flat account where the *partis pris* do not even have the courage of their convictions, as it were. Sparrow has the courage to show her prejudices openly; she has the intelligence not to treat them as anything more than *her* prejudices.

That the remarkable facility for achieving a rare balance between trying to hide one's ideology or prejudices and allowing them to dominate one's reporting to become what we might call an unspoken conspiracy between readers and writers demonstrated by Sparrow in her piece on organ-grinders was not limited to that sub-subform of incognito social investigation may be seen from her second 1894 piece in the *Newbery House Magazine*: 'London Street Toilers: Cress Sellers'. This shares much of the character that makes Sparrow's piece on organ-grinders so important within the spectrum of incognito social investigation; however, as we shall see, in it we can also see a movement towards a coming into line with the majority of texts of this sort that would be accentuated as the decade went on.

The focus in this second piece, obviously enough, is cress sellers rather than organ-grinders, but the opening passages, where it is explained that the street selling of watercress is considered amongst the poor as one of the lowest rungs on the social ladder already recall the earlier work in starting *in medias res* as far the investigation is concerned. Very interestingly, the brief description of how Sparrow organized her time as a cress seller (the brevity of the description mirrors the equivalent description regarding organ-grinders, as does the method used, which was simply to ask someone to accept her as a temporary lodger and pay for the privilege) includes what one may presume to be the commentary of the old woman with whom she lodged on the whole business: 'there was little opposition to the "leddy's freak"'.[33] As we have seen in the comparison of Sparrow with Bright and Bourne, Sparrow presents what she does in terms far removed from a 'freak' or anything else equally 'madcap'. Once again, we see Sparrow's ability to refrain from comment: she does not defend herself to her readers against this suggestion, trusting in their ability to discern what she would wish to communicate as truth.

Sparrow's piece on cress sellers differs from that on organ-grinders in that the former is more personalized. We learn much more about the family with whom she lodges, and the bulk of the account is taken up with their individual travails rather than the general ones experienced by cress sellers as a class. This leads the later piece to run the risk of presenting a facile pathos: the daughter of the woman with whom Sparrow lodges is dying after a difficult childbirth when they leave to sell cress, and her mother accepts that she will die in their absence. There is a definite touch of melodramatic pathos in the scene in which the aged mother, Hannah, takes leave of her daughter, Grace, who has been abandoned by her husband, for the presumed last time. This is the scene, with Sparrow's sole comment thereon:

[Hannah] took a tress of the woman's hair and kissed it lovingly, and her old face changed.

'Curse him,' she muttered several times, and her bent frame shook with strangled sobs.

The suppressed grief of old age is a terrible sight, and I turned to the children.[34]

The scene – the hair-kissing, the imprecations against the absent son-in-law – is clichéd. This is not to say that it is not true: clichés become such for a reason. What is of note here is not the scene per se, but Sparrow's response to it. Equally clichéd, in textual terms, would have been an authorial response at a higher key, whether criticizing working-class male fecklessness or further patheticizing the two women into semi-symbolic figures. Yet Sparrow does not take this path. We see that she does not absent herself from the text: we have her comment on the scene. This comment, however, is intensely personal: it is not presented as such, but the fact that in so emotionally charged a situation – charged, too, with what we might call cultural triggers – the only point that she considers important enough to comment upon is something (the 'suppressed grief of old age') that one might legitimately suppose to be minor (in a context of death and abandonment) suggests that the comment is there because she, and she alone, thinks it is what is most striking. Sparrow reports a clichéd scene, but her response to it refuses cliché.

Sparrow's faith in her readers' hermeneutic abilities includes a refusal to invoke them and their judgements. There is only one direct invocation to her readers' experiences in these two texts, and this, in 'Cress Sellers', is anomalous. Sparrow sells cress on the streets accompanied by Artie, the dying woman's middle child, a toddler. She meets Hannah again by chance, and gives her the five pence that she has made to buy food for her eldest grandchild, the five-year-old Sally, who has stayed at home to nurse her mother on her deathbed. She and Artie stay out a little longer, and as they decide to turn homewards she apostrophizes her readers: 'I don't suppose one of my readers can realise what it is to be hungry, lame with fatigue, and cold to pain, and yet not have a penny to pay for a 'bus home.'[35] Sparrow does *not* appeal to anything shared by her, a middle-class journalist and her middle-class readership. Rather, she invokes the difference between her and those who read her; she always refuses her readers a facile identification with the author, just as she does not allow herself a facile identification with the poor whom she studies.

Sparrow is simultaneously absent from, and present in, her text. She is absent as an editorializing voice; she is present as an individual personality. This rarest of positions allows the poor to speak without patronizing them with what can only be a feigned objective neutrality. Sparrow squares this circle, as it were, and in doing so places her two 1894 *Newbery House Magazine* articles amongst the very best of incognito social investigation texts. I should like to examine one final example, as it represents perhaps the pinnacle of Sparrow's achievement at resolving the problem of eticity and emicity.

When Sparrow finds herself lost in the fog with Artie, by now too tired to walk and drowsily crying for milk, she becomes frightened, as she can afford neither transport nor food. She sees people passing who could alleviate her distress, and reaches a decision:

> My compassion for the ailing child drove me to a desperate step. If I could not sell I could beg; who would refuse a copper to one in such plight as I?
> So I told a stout gentleman, in a fur coat, I had lost my way, and would he give me a copper. But he waved me majestically away with a silver-headed umbrella. Then I tried a portly man with grey whiskers, who stopped and

asked me if the child was ill, but when I said I feared so, he hurried off at a great rate, calling over his shoulder, 'go to the hospital; this is the way infection is spread.'

[ ... ]

[ ... ] I saw a working-man coming along with a bonny boy of four, trotting by his side. His face I fancied, and said impulsively –

'For the sake of your own child, do give me a penny to get mine some milk.'

He stopped at once, and put a coin into my hand.

'Take sixpence,' he said kindly, 'and get something for yourself too.'[36]

Barring that sole adjective, 'desperate', no commentary is offered on what is in fact a momentous decision. Sparrow *begs*: only theft and prostitution lie below this in the 'respectable' middle class scale of values; no other incognito social investigator so lightly descends to this level. Indeed, Sparrow's social descent is not even to 'begging' *tout court*. It may start with semi-honest versions of her situation – she *is* 'lost', although where she has to return is not her home; the child *is* not well, although through hunger rather than illness – but her begging is successful when she resorts to what is very near to a direct lie: 'For the sake of your own child, do give me a penny to get *mine* some milk.' Artie is not her child; at most, she could cavil over the exact meaning of 'mine' – it is 'true' in this case if taken to refer to temporary possession rather than its usual sense when referred to a child by a woman – but such a quibble is but a poor defence. Whatever her motives, Sparrow here is unambiguously a dishonest beggar; and it is worth noting that not only does she not refuse the sixpence to 'get something for yourself too' but also spends what is left over when she has fed Artie on an omnibus ride home for them both, thereby unambiguously profiting personally from what can be accurately referred to as mendacious begging. Of course, 'mendacious begging' does not usually connote what Sparrow does here, which may quite rightly be read as emergency philanthropy. Sparrow also does not step out of character, which would, one imagines, have procured more rapid help for little Artie; her dedication to her investigation outweighs her philanthropy. Sparrow's begging, in one light or another, reflects badly on her within the text; within the wider world of incognito social investigation texts, her willingness to make hard choices and present herself negatively is rare and praiseworthy; rare and more praiseworthy still is the fact that she has the courage to do so without signalling it to her readers, a courage resting upon a desire to leave them to reach their own conclusions.

The passages from Sparrow that we have hitherto analysed all show why she merits so high a place in the annals of incognito social investigation. The conclusion of 'Cress Sellers', however, adumbrates the unfortunate fact that such social investigation, whether incognito or otherwise, as she undertook after 1894 shows decreasing unicity and comes into line with the great mass of other reports.

The years following 1894 saw an array of articles, chiefly published in *Quiver* and usually titled or subtitled 'The Penniless Poor' or 'As One of the Penniless Poor' (the 'as' being potentially misleading regarding the fact whether Sparrow was incognito or not). These, with two important exceptions, are descriptive, impersonal and etic, a far cry from the two remarkable personalized emic pieces discussed at length above. In one, from 1896, 'The Penniless Poor: A Doss-House near the Docks', she first confides her wish to see inside the dosshouse to a policeman, an act in many ways emblematic of middle-class respectability and trust in the law. Told by this worthy that such a thing is impossible, she speaks to a female cleaner at the dosshouse, who tells her that she needs to speak to the manager, Mr Smith. The cleaner shows herself less than willing to trouble him over Sparrow's stated desire to look around, and the journalist responds with an unmistakable display of middle-class privilege and arrogance: '"Send for him, please", I said, with an air of authority. "I have to see him on important business."'[37] Faced with such a tone (not to mention the interruption to her work cleaning the rugs), it is little wonder that the cleaner 'scowled, but obeyed'.[38]

The earlier T. Sparrow is gone; all the emicity that this piece shows in its reasoning about the problems working men have in procuring decent clothes does not change the fact that the promise shown in the *Newberry House Magazine* articles has not been realized. Sparrow no longer accepts those whom she is studying: the most telling phrase in her litany of condemnation of the habits of the poor comes perhaps in the 1897 piece 'The Cry of the Canal Children', where, having discussed the freedoms available to 'Master Tommy', the typical (and stereotypical) canal child, she continues:

> But Master Tommy and his kind do not know what is good for them.
>     I can conceive of no life so utterly demoralising as life on board a barge, with a crew both godless and cruel.[39]

More openly and unashamedly etic statements would be hard to find.

At this point, a possible conclusion would be that Sparrow's two pieces for the *Newberry House Magazine* were exceptions, produced perhaps for a somewhat different readership (although the exact difference in shades of Anglicanism leading to such marked differences of emicity and eticity would be hard to pinpoint), rather than positing a gradual change in her opinions (even though eticity and judgementality certainly increase over time in her work). However, two pieces, one for *Quiver* in the 'Penniless Poor' series (thus suggesting that to attribute her change to a deliberate choice made when not writing for that journal is misleading) and one from the *Strand Magazine* (thus indicating that her emicity was not solely a poise adopted for the *Newberry House Magazine*), argue against this interpretation.

The first of these, published in *Quiver* in 1895, is entitled 'As One of the Penniless Poor'; it is the first in that occasional series, its subtitle 'I. – Palm-Workers'. It defines the class that Sparrow would go on to study in her series in *Quiver* ('those who [ ... ] cannot make enough to more than keep body and soul together – and *never will*'),[40] and states what one would presume to be her methodology for the rest of the series (that 'I.' in the subtitle alerting the reader to its continuation): 'This is the class that interests me, and to enlist people's sympathy in [sic] their behalf, I resolved to go and live among them, and practically test what they had to endure.'[41] The tantalizing promise of a whole series of incognito social investigation would not, alas, be realized, for Sparrow's following examinations of the penniless poor are solely descriptions from outside. The methodology of 'Palm-Workers' itself does not allow easy classification as incognito social investigation, although it is certainly presented in such a way as to suggest that identification:

> Casting about for a means to fulfil my plan, I came across an old woman who told me she was a palm-worker, so was her daughter; but that work was so slack she feared she would not be able to keep the two rooms which housed the family consisting of six persons.
>
> I had never heard of palm-working, but I asked if she would take me as an indoor apprentice, and I would help with the rent. No doubt she thought I was 'strange', but times were too bad for her to be critical; and on my paying three shillings in advance, it was agreed I should arrive the next evening at her domicile with my belongings.[42]

Sparrow would soon discover that palm-working was making canvas items, the name deriving from the use of a palm-thimble used in sewing very hard materials to protect the hand whilst driving a needle through. Other than this, however, the passage raises more questions than it answers. How did Sparrow 'come across' the old woman? What exactly was her host's view of Sparrow's 'strangeness'? The final question in fact rather includes the previous two: to what extent is this *incognito* social investigation?

The first question admits of a partial answer. At the end of the article, Sparrow speaks of having 'got a charitable lady' to befriend her erstwhile landlady and her family; this, and other hints dropped in the course of the *Quiver* articles, suggests that Sparrow was by this point moving in philanthropic circles (or, more accurately, was open about her doing so); one may legitimately presume from this that Sparrow met her old woman at an event organized by a philanthropic individual or group.

This gets us no further in resolving the wider question of Sparrow's incognito status. She may have been introduced to the palm-worker as a journalist; she may have merely been known as one of the ill-defined philanthropic class; she may already have been incognito at their first meeting. If we accept Sparrow's account of events, then the most honest and straightforward, that she was known to be a journalist, is the least likely: if the palm-worker was aware of the reasons behind Sparrow's desire to apprentice herself to her, then there was no reason to think her 'strange'. If Sparrow was already 'fully' incognito, then the 'strangeness' that she presumed the palm-worker would attribute to her may simply have lain in her being someone unknown asking for apprenticeship in a relatively unskilled trade. If the palm-worker knew, however, that Sparrow, was in some way slumming it, even though she was unaware that her putative apprentice and lodger was doing so for copy rather than any other motive, then the question of the exact nature of what it means to be an incognito social explorer becomes more interesting.

Sparrow certainly shared her hosts' lives: she slept on the floor in a room shared with another woman and her two children; she lived on their meagre diet; she set to learning the dangerous trade, and noted rather sadly that her fear in damaging her hand led her to have a distinctly reduced earning capacity compared to 'Gran'. We can never truly know her exact status vis-à-vis 'Gran' and the family that welcomed her; however, we may presume that to any casual observer calling in on them she would have been indistinguishable from her hosts. This is one of the central points distinguishing the form of incognito social investigation based upon work from that created and exemplified by Greenwood: whereas investigators in the latter tradition must show their mask to all whom they meet, those in the former may don and doff the mask according to circumstance. Investigation in the Greenwoodian tradition has as its role the gathering of information about the poor: the only way this can realistically be achieved in this context is by never allowing the mask to slip: the poor have to feel that they can speak, as it were, without fear of being overheard on the one hand; on the other, one must present the same mask to those who are not poor in order to see how one is then treated. With investigation into work, however, where the focus may be narrower, this is not necessarily the case. If, like the organ-grinders considered above, one wishes to explore the public's attitudes towards those who work in the streets, then an incognito state need not be maintained with all those who do that job. Conversely, if, like Polly Toynbee in the 1970s, one is working in a factory in an attempt to understand the views of the workers, management may on occasion be informed of one's pre-sence;[43] indeed, one may even, like Celia Fremlin, have been invited there *by* management.[44] Only for those who, like Barbara Ehrenreich, wish to explore the whole question of how one becomes employed as much as what one does when one is does a complete incognito status become a necessity.[45]

'Palm-Workers' is of interest because of the questions it raises concern-ing incognito status; it is also the only one of the long 'Penniless Poor' series that shows a level of emicity in any way comparable with the remarkable level shown in the *Newberry House Magazine* pieces. This is partially seen in an absence of criticism that contrasts with the barbs that would appear in later pieces; more interestingly, however, it can be seen in how Sparrow's pseudo-apprenticeship ends. She is lodging and working with 'Gran', her daughter Hannah and Hannah's children; after an unspe-cified number of days, another daughter (presumably), 'Liza, returns one wet night with a sick five-year-old boy:

> What tragedy her coming covered I never knew. Her return was accepted with passivity; she shared their board and lodging, and was grudged nothing.
>
> She and her child slept in my room, and Hannah did vouchsafe to say to me, the first morning after her arrival –
>
> "'Liza's out of work, so she'll stay with us for a bit. She thinks her boy is sickening for fever, and wants a bit of nursing'.
>
> 'Ought he not to go to the hospital?' I exclaimed.

'What's the good,' she said laconically, 'till we know what's the matter? Maybe he's only light-headed from starvation'.

Still, under the circumstances, I thought my room was preferable to my company, and having got a charitable lady to befriend them, I gratefully took my departure.[46]

There is deep ambiguity in 'preferable' and 'gratefully': is Sparrow leaving to safeguard her health against possible contagion or in order to help the family at the possible expense of her copy? The two interpretations have to coexist, resisting any attempt to collapse them into a single certain reading. The emicity is not here. It lies rather in Sparrow's lack of editorializing: whereas in later 'Penniless Poor' articles such a scene would almost certainly involve some form of moralizing – perhaps criticizing the fecklessness of the poor, perhaps bemoaning their ignorance in matters medical; perhaps, if moralizing of a different but no less invasive sort, criticizing the societal structures that lead to such a situation – here Sparrow passes over matters in silence. The one interjection she records is narrative, not editorial; she pays the family what is perhaps the greatest compliment the middle-class social investigator can pay: she lets their story tell itself.

No more, however, would such trust be shown in *Quiver*; hereafter she became increasingly critical as an invasive presence, condemning or tolerating, but never accepting. The only exception is another 1895 piece, one which appeared in the *Strand Magazine* in July under the title 'In the Heart of Hop-Land'. This, in a prefiguration of Orwell's far more famous trip, describes how Sparrow accompanied Beery Bill, a Houndsditch hawker, and his family hopping. It is in many ways one of the most curious narratives examined in this work.

Once again the reader is faced with a lack of any explanation regarding Sparrow's status. She is apostrophized as 'miss' by Beery Bill and his family, which suggests that to them at least she is not incognito; however, she (without comment) begs for food and shelter along with the others, which must mean that she was incognito to the wider world, and her acceptance by the wider group of hop pickers suggests that she remained incognito outside Bill's family circle. Interestingly, Sparrow does offer an explanation of her presence in Beery Bill's house when he and his wife Amelia first decide to go hopping, which supposedly casual presence leading to her decision to join them. The one-sentence paragraph is rather unusually set between parentheses: '(Perhaps here is the place to introduce myself, as an individual in quest of personal experience, and able to vouch for the truth of what follows)'.[47] The non-specificity of this conceals more than it reveals. More interesting is to read this self-presentation against something that Beery Bill is given as having said a little earlier regarding an increase in popularity in hopping and a commensurate decline in the quality of the people going: '"Farmers used to know their 'ands and take them reg'lar year by year. Now anybody goes – even toffs!" The scorn in the last word was indescribable.'[48] 'Toffs' are a sign of slipping standards; these standards may also be moral, as Bill's other warnings about how 'mixed' the hopping company is show. Bill's saying this in Sparrow's hearing suggests that she is herself no toff. Read in conjunction with the self-presentation a few short paragraphs later, Sparrow's ambiguity increases: she is (we must presume) neither toff nor one of Beery Bill and Amelia's class; but what she tells us of her status is only in fact a description of her motivation. She is a curious figure in both senses of that adjective: her only distinguishing feature, it would appear, is her curiosity, and this leaves her oddly mysterious and undefined.

The other great oddity of the text is the presence in it of bizarre incidents, the author's reaction to the melodrama of which strengthens her emicity as well as increasing her indeterminate status within the article. One wonders whether these incidents may represent a degree of fictiona-lization within the text; however, given their absence from all of the other pieces similar in content, if not tone, written by Sparrow, I see no reason not to accept the article's documentary nature at face value. One of the girls with whom Sparrow is hopping dies of consumption; her body is laid out by night in front of the house of the farmer with whom the hoppers are disputing their pay with a note attached to her, a piece of doggerel attributing her death to hunger. The result of this macabre *mise-en-scène* is an increase of a penny a bushel, with the final line of the article noting Beery Bill's admission, many weeks later, that he had got the idea from the Surrey Theatre. Sparrow displays a complete lack of shock at this tactic, noting only that they were 'all too low to resist this gruesome plan'.[49] Indeed, not only does she not object (the inclusive 'we' is also worth noting), she concludes the episode – which importantly is only part of the larger, more important, story of the struggle over pay – by saying: 'We accepted the terms and turned in. The lesson had done good on both sides.'[50] Sparrow includes herself amongst those profiting from this use of the girl's corpse; furthermore, she rather incredibly does so without any comment on her own reactions, a reticence that reinforces her position as the one incognito social investigator with the emic confidence to allow matters to speak for themselves. The sole comment, that final line about both sides having had good done to them by this grisly subterfuge, reads, in its understated tone and complete lack of any explanation of just what this might mean, as nothing more than a weak sop thrown to conventional morality. What lesson has there been? Sparrow in fact describes nothing that can be seen as such, and her conclusion rings hollow, emic in its throwaway pragmatism. This is also the only explicit case of an incognito social investigator joining in with any sort of industrial action; Sparrow clearly has no qualms about contributing to change in the situation in which she finds herself. She has confidence enough in the reality of what she describes not to worry about whether she may be influencing events; yet again, her confidence extends to her refusal to make too much of what she observes and is involved in.

Yet more indicative of Sparrow's acceptance of events comes in what follows an earlier death. One of the women in the party travelling down to Kent has a child who dies in the night whilst everyone, Sparrow included, is asleep in a disused barn. The group leaves the little corpse there, and Beery Bill and another man fire the barn, presumably with some (rather ill-conceived) aim of concealing what had happened. Once again, Sparrow's lack of reaction is noteworthy, highlighting her ability to accept, as Beery Bill's ruse to help draw attention away from what has happened leads to one of the most bizarre episodes in any account of incognito social investigation. Before Sparrow realizes that the barn has been fired, she is rejoined by Bill as he returns from his act of arson:

> When we were well under way in the sunless dawn he joined us again.
> 'That's an orkard piece of business,' he said to me, jerking his thumb to where the dead child lay, shroudless and uncoffined. 'I must ask you to cut with me and do the rest o' the journey by train. If they track us, it will save the others not to be found among 'em'.
> So I changed attire with his wife; he shaved, or scraped off rather, his grisly beard, and thus disguised we trudged in an opposite direction to our travelling caravan. [51]

The meaning of this passage is not completely clear. Beery Bill is one of the two men who set fire to the barn, so it is more likely that he be tracked (although quite how anyone should know that he is the object of their search is unclear); why, however, should anyone particularly wish to track

Sparrow? Is the disguise to make Sparrow look less respectable, Bill's wife more respectable, both or neither? Are Sparrow and Bill decoys? The precise sense of their actions cannot now be seized; what remains is the clear message that Sparrow was happy to take part in a ruse designed to mislead the authorities. She had yet to know, she says, that the barn had been fired, but concealing the sad death of the child – her sole concession to conventional morality and sentiment is the two adjectives applied to him here – is in itself an act far from allowable by usual standards. That Sparrow is so willing to flout convention and legality is in itself unusual in incognito social investigators (especially in the subcategory of explorations of the world of work); what is even rarer, and more praiseworthy, is that this is clearly not in any way an attempt to *épater les bourgeois*: hers is the confidence of silence; emic acceptance of people and events that manifests itself in trust in herself, those whom she observes and those to whom she narrates. Very few other incognito social investigators could boast such achievement, and T. Sparrow deserves to be reckoned amongst the very top flight of writers in the form.

The tragedy was that she could not keep up such superlative work. We can never truly know why this may have been, and analysing the psyches of the long dead is a fruitless and ultimately pointless task. However, some glimpse into the personal background is afforded by her file in the Royal Literary Fund (RLF) archives; from this we may tentatively posit why Sparrow wrote some of the very best incognito social investigation pieces yet was not able to avoid becoming another patronizing journalist prioritizing her requirements and beliefs over those of the people whom she was investigating.[52] T. Sparrow – the initial stands for Tissie, a family nickname – was born Anna Mary Sparrow in Lancashire in 1859. She wrote under T. rather than A. Sparrow, as there were already two other journalists, she says, writing under that name when she started. She was a professional journalist and writer, but her budding career ran into problems when, at some point a little before 1897, she had to care for her paralysed brother. This problem was added to the fact that she had already by then started to suffer from deafness. Her brother died in 1897, by which time Sparrow had spent all her earnings and savings on caring for him. There then began what she calls her 'black period', between 1897 and 1907, when she 'did hack journalism on any penny or ½ journal that would take me' in order to help provide for her brother's five children. She retired in 1909, living on a £50 annual pension from another brother, Professor of Law at Liverpool. It was his imminent retirement and the cessation of the pension that impelled her to write to the RLF. She was unsuccessful, turned down owing to insufficient literary merit; a card in her file from Sir Sidney Lee, registrar to the Fund, accepts that this must be the case but regrets it.

Sparrow was a professional journalist and writer, but she was more than that. Her letters to the RLF clearly cast her as a professional social investigator too, although to what degree incognito as opposed to semi-incognito remains unclear. It should be noted that when she speaks of her writing here it is to her pre-1897 signed, non-hack, work that she is referring. This may be seen from the letter in which she speaks of her *literary* work as belonging to her earlier days: her later work, she clearly believes, in no way qualifies her for recourse to the Fund. Sparrow's introductory letter to the Fund explains the method through which she tried to help the cause most dear to her, and lists the positive social results against the negative personal ones

> [My work] was all devoted to the same purpose:- The removal of slum-dwellings & improvement of conditions under which the poor work. The handsome Tenements at Millbank Westminster called Turner Buildings – Ruskin Buildings etc are the result of my vigorous onslaught on the Slum landlords of the District where to prove my facts I lived for long periods & worked with Organ-Grinders – Flower-Girls, Palm Workers etc. So strenuous were my efforts that my health broke down. I became deaf & my eyesight seriously impaired.

We must of course take such statements in such a context with a pinch of salt: Sparrow, after all, is writing what amounts to a begging letter. However, this view of the first part of her career is also backed up by those from whom she had requested references; again, although the caveat must still stand, there is no reason, especially when we see the consistency between this and what we read in her journalism, not to accept this account of things.

The decrease of quality in Sparrow's signed work from 1897 onwards we may attribute to her personal situation; we may also wonder whether the real poverty and terror of poverty engendered by her unfortunate circumstances led her to have less sympathy with the working poor of whom she was now one. She continued her job – or her vocation, perhaps – publicizing the problems of those who could never earn enough to live in any way comfortably, yet who would do the same for her when, as she says in a *cri de cœur* in one RLF letter, 'I worked till I dropped on my knees – I worked *after*'? No-one could offer Sparrow what she wished to offer the poor (how clearly here we see that 'the poor' are socially constructed and not economically!); a subconscious bitterness and lack of patience – acceptance becoming tolerance – should not surprise us.

This leaves us, however, with the problem of Sparrow's pre-1897 writings, where, as we have seen, there is a mixture of remarkably accepting and emic pieces such as those from the *Newbery House Magazine* with much more mundanely tolerant and etic pieces. If her grim personal circumstances cannot be blamed here, to what may we ascribe the cause? I would suggest that it is to be found in something that makes Sparrow unique amongst journalists who practised incognito social investigation. Her profession was not journalism *tout court*, it was incognito social investigation journalism. No other writer known to me so doggedly pursued so niche a calling. That, even in an age when incognito social investigation in its various forms was almost a cliché, Sparrow's dedication to her self-imposed task was seen as something unusual can be seen in her explanation for her failure to achieve greater fame:

> I lived the life of the poor, not for days but for weeks together & wrote my experiences in the Daily papers, *Magazines* & *Monthly Reviews*. There was always a feminine clique against me as they said I did it for vulgar notoriety.

If Sparrow is right that such charges were levelled against her, then she cannot be referring to her incognito social investigation work in itself, as such an activity, even when undertaken by a woman, was by then far from innovative enough to render one notorious (although its lack of originality may have opened one up to charges of vulgarity). Rather, Sparrow could be accused of courting notoriety because of the *single-mindedness* of her work and her seeming wish to corner the market in this journalistic text form. This repetition and professionalization of experience, I would suggest, led to Sparrow becoming inured to what she saw – not, however, in terms of poverty and suffering itself, to which she remained sensitive, but to any possible novelty represented by the ideologies and lifestyles of the poor. Her senses dulled not to material things but to more subtle questions. She gradually and partially lost her methodological freshness, the bloom wore off what had become a mechanical repetition; her integrity did not allow her material sensitivity to be affected, but honest surprise and acceptance gave way to more cynical mature tolerance – and in the process one of the most interesting, original and culturally courageous of incognito social investigators sank into a journalist perhaps more obsessive than many others but no more interesting than them.[53]

A little later, another journalist could make a possible claim to a similar level of specialization in incognito social investigation: Olive Christian Malvery. Judith Walkowitz, who has written at length about Malvery, describes her as 'an established cultural icon in Edwardian London'.[54] She arrived in London from the Punjab at the beginning of the twentieth century to train as a singer at the Royal College, and became first a renowned reciter and elocutionist and then journalist and lecturer.[55] Her series 'The Heart of Things', published in *Pearson's Magazine* from October 1904 onwards, detailed her experiences in a range of incognito social investigation roles; their variety and the professionalism that she brought to her task may be seen in the description that she gives of a room that she rented, central to the various slum areas that she wished to visit:

> In this room was stored a large amount of carbolic, Keating's powder, and other disinfectants, and a varied assortment of old clothes to suit the different characters I intended to impersonate. To anyone studying the various grades of life in the working and submerged classes, it will of course be apparent that one disguise would not effectually carry any person through the various phases. For instance, a factory girl is different in a hundred small ways, in the fashion of her clothes, in her manner of walking and talking, from the girl employed in a small shop. Then again, a tramp is wholly different from a woman who obtains small jobs and seeks refuge in the various shelters. The coster girl has not much in common with the labourer's daughter, and a street singer is entirely different from an organ-grinder.[56]

All of the roles mentioned are in some way played by Malvery and described in her book, and this evidence may appear to suggest that Malvery has as much right as Sparrow to be considered a specialist incognito social investigator; I would argue, however, that it would be wrong to posit such an equivalence. The articles making up 'The Heart of Things' series were republished, with a little revision, in book form in 1906; the book was entitled *The Soul Market*, but the subtitle appended thereto was '*with which is included "The Heart of Things"*'. Malvery here no longer appears so specialized a figure: we have her impressions of America as gleaned from a lecture tour; the story of her first encounter with London and London society; part of the second series that she wrote for *Pearson's*, which was on the 'alien' (for which read 'Jewish') question. We have here a range of subjects quite unlike that shown by Sparrow. There is, none-theless, a unifying theme running through Malvery's work: it is all auto-biographical. 'The Heart of Things' is as much about one who, in Walkowitz's words, 'forecasts her own destiny to be an exceptional woman, a great traveler herself, one who would penetrate the "surface-glamour of hospitality" in the metropolis' to see things as they truly are as it is about life amongst the poor women of London.[57] Indeed, the photographs that accompanied Malvery's account are overwhelmingly of *her* in various guises: Malvery's descriptions are, ultimately, more about the describer than the described. Whereas Sparrow can be curiously (and praiseworthily) absent from her texts, Malvery is always present, always the centre of narrative attention.

Even if Malvery were less obviously a 'star' journalist and her work less about her autobiography, the various incognito social investigation pieces contained in *The Soul Market* would still indicate a less specialized approach than Sparrow's. This may be best seen in Chapter 5, headed 'The British "Jungle" – What I Saw of the Preserved Food Trade'. The nod to Upton Sinclair's *succès de scandale* is clear (Sinclair too went undercover to research his novel), but Malvery's stated aims were less revolutionary:

> When I first conceived the idea of enlisting myself in the great army of daily workers in the factories, I did not intend taking part in any reforms other than those which concerned the workers. Indeed, I had no idea of the revelations which work in such places would bring to me. It was long before the agitation in regard to clean food had begun, and I had paid no attention to the matter of food preparation; my chiefest interest lay in the workers of factories and the stories that I am here going to relate are merely the outcome of personal experience while trying to gain a knowledge of factory girls and their lives.[58]

Her stated interest is factory girls and their 'stories' (the use of the word here, unqualified as it is by any negative adjective, carries perhaps a slight suggestion that human interest rather than denunciation is the focus); hers did not set out to be a muckraking account of factories, but rather a look at those who work in them. However, notwithstanding Malvery's state-ment of intent, and her putative role as an incognito *social* investigator, this section of *The Soul Market* is in fact not about workers but workplaces:

its focus is *not* 'factory girls and their lives', but the squalor and sharp practices of jam factories, bakeries and meat preservers. One 'story', and one story alone, is given involving people rather than practices, and this is a secondhand account of a young costermonger who fooled a butcher into giving him a piece of meat for less than its true value. This is undercover investigation and this is investigative journalism, but is not incognito social investigation. Nothing is learnt about people (or rather, if anything has been learnt it is not being communicated to the reader). Malvery's vaunted interest in the conditions of the poor is here a concern for what her readers eat; her disguise may have allowed her to interact with people whom otherwise she would not have been able to meet, but no knowledge regarding them gained therethrough is produced.

That Malvery's interest is as much in work as in the people who do it can be seen in the very variety of the roles that she plays. In a single chapter of *The Soul Market*, 'The Story of the Shop', she manages to fit investigation of four different jobs: coffee-shop waitress, draper's assistant, barmaid and countergirl in a fish-and-chip shop. This is not the only case of her performing comparative studies, so to speak, of different types of employment, but it is the best example of how such compression of material leads to superficiality. Describing and analysing people is a more complex task than describing jobs, and Malvery tacitly accepts this in her focus on quantity over quality. What she is therefore offering her readers is not so much insight, even feigned insight, into the lives of the working poor as a pageant of types of working woman, considered not even as character types but as types of job.

This lack of deep interest in the people who are her supposed subject matter is not contradicted by Malvery's donating her royalties and performance fees towards the building of two London shelters for homeless women, which she then donated to the Salvation Army and Church Army.[59] When she *does* interact with the poor, her attitude (however far from openly) is very much *de haut en bas*: she wishes to improve more than help, and the control implied by her building shelters and choosing to which organizations to give them is of a piece with this. Her refusal of emicity and (here the contrast with Sparrow can perhaps be best seen) her inability to compromise her principles when faced with those of women not from her class or ideological background are best demonstrated in her relationship with drink.[60]

The evidence presented in *The Soul Market* shows Malvery very prone to accept drink as one of the chief problems of the poor: one of the chief causes of destitution, she claims (offering no proof), is men spending '95 per cent. of their earnings in the public-house', the pub being an 'evil'.[61] The first adumbration of this *parti pris*, and how strong Malvery's views on it were, comes in one of the first episodes of incognito social investigation that she recounts, when she posed as a street singer: '[we] adjourned to a coffee-shop. The woman would have preferred a "pub", but I objected, so we discussed our plans over some extremely muddy coffee.'[62] Malvery is willing to risk estranging someone who may help her into the world that she wishes to explore over this point of principle; unlike Sparrow, she shows no willingness to compromise. She will not even add gin to her coffee to warm herself up when starting work at half past four in the morning in the fish-and-chip shop, a use of alcohol that verges on the medicinal![63] Her antipathy to drink and pubs, we have seen, is such that she is willing to put her enterprise at risk because of it; it also not only colours her view of those whom she is investigating (which we may consider indicates a failure on her part, but by which we should not be surprised: of all a priori ideological judgements regarding the poor, that one of the chief sources of their problems is drink is one of the most common, then as now), but also more interestingly means that she is blinkered *with regards to her own methodology*.

This occurs when Malvery wishes to investigate the life of coster-mongers. She talks of the 'weeks of working and planning before I could translate myself into a *bonâ-fide* coster girl',[64] before going on to outline a few salient points about her practical methodology:

> It is in no wise easy to 'slip' into a new life. Among the 'people', as we term the labouring and poorer classes, an outsider is very quickly recognised. I found, however, that my foreign appearance [Malvery was Anglo-Indian] really helped me, for as I dealt mostly with women and girls, they made their own stories about me. By maintaining a discreet silence, I managed to get through. Being small and young-looking too, helped me. I get tired very quickly and show it, and poor Mr. C., who was nearly always with me, got the rough side of several 'gentle' tongues for ill-treating me. It helped wonderfully to have a man so big and burly, and such a splendid Cockney actor, to assume command of me. Together we were able to do what one alone could never have accomplished.[65]

She recounts her first experience of costering, and how it was a success; her methodology clearly worked. She wishes to have a change of scene, and meets Liz, a costerwoman that she knows from the market in Covent

Garden. She and Mr C. tell her that Malvery has come into some money and wishes to become a proper costerwoman so that Mr C. no longer has to work; Liz takes her to hire a barrow and to rent a room from a Mrs Rummings. All of this is duly achieved. After she has paid a week's advance rent, Malvery continues her story, but the scene and tone shift, a change marked by a new paragraph (especially visible as that preceding was of but a brief single sentence) beginning with the bald statement: 'And now followed a sad experience' (the slight solecism of starting a sentence with 'and' also strengthens the degree to which this should be read as emphasizing the importance of what follows).[66] What is this 'sad experience' that Malvery thus marks out for special attention? The women go to the pub to celebrate the fact that a deal has been struck. The day is a Monday, which Malvery says is the traditional day for working-class women to drink in London. Nothing is described of what she sees in the pub that is so sad or so shocking; given her prejudices, we may presume that had she genuinely witnessed anything to justify her powerfully negative judgement she would have found a way to convey it to her audience, notwithstanding the care she took (as Walkowitz observes) 'to offer very little in the way of naturalistic detail regarding the dark side of London life' in order not to offend the editorial conventions of *Pearson's Magazine* and the sensibilities of its readers.[67] Nonetheless, her disgust in what she sees is such that she now stops narrating her experience and begins editorializing, adding the following piece of what one might hope is hyperbole (but fear is not): 'I grew convinced that the framers of our laws could do no better than immediately make a law forbidding all women to be served with drink in public-houses.'[68] Her method, so carefully laid out at the beginning of the chapter, has succeeded: she is accepted by costerwomen as one of their own, not only in the sphere of work but also socially. No better illustration of her acting ability could be offered, one might think, yet the achievement inherent in being invited for a drink is hidden to her; she sees only the feared pub and working-class women briefly besporting themselves there, not her success in being there to witness it and describe it to her middle-class public – and thus no description is forthcoming, merely condemnation.

Malvery's stance on drink and the pub leads her into further contradiction. When she undertakes her whistle-stop tour of 'shop' work, immediately before describing her time as a barmaid she recounts her experiences as a live-in floorwalker at a large draper's shop. She finds much to commiserate regarding the life of the floorwalker – or 'counter-slaves' as she calls them – and the 'hardships of their lives.[69] The quality of the food supplied is 'shocking', and not enough time is given to eat it comfortably; nor is there enough of this poor provender to meet the needs of the workers.[70] Notwithstanding the provisions of the Shop Hours Regulation Act of 1886, shop assistants at the draper's where she was employed were not allowed to sit, as the third time they were caught doing so meant that they were discharged under the pretext that they were 'ill'.[71] To this list of workers' woes are added those occasioned by the draconian rules that those sleeping in have to live under – fines were levied for daring to decorate one's room, arriving late for breakfast; anyone leaving a light on after the doors were locked in the evenings (eleven o'clock with the exception of Saturdays, which were midnight) was discharged;[72] although Malvery's recognition that such rules were far from fair on the workers is somewhat tempered by her judging such arbitrary threats to people's continued employment solely as 'frivolous, and merely vexatious'.[73]

The shop assistant's lot is far from a happy one, and Malvery brings her description of it to a close with the affecting image of a 'poor shop-girl' dealing with a difficult customer, and managing to smile and humour her whilst '[s]uffering pain, and weary almost to the point of sinking'.[74] The reader may fairly wonder how such work compares to others, but any idea that the next job examined, that of the barmaid, is any way better is soon removed by Malvery's opening description of the hardships of that life. She details the prejudices that she says most people from all classes hold against barmaids, defending them against those who do not realize that they have to protect their virtue whilst strenuously resisting temptation and surviving insults, bad language and the company of the drunk.[75] She then launches into a denunciation of such a form of employment:

Indeed it is a hard life: no Roman slave lived a harder. From early morning until late at night one has a constant round of severe work. When not serving, one is cleaning. The girl is often subjected to the bad temper of a harassed mistress, or the familiarities of a drunken master. Scarcely taking any outdoor exercise – being too tired to go out during the two or three 'rest-hours' which the custom of the trade allows these girls in the afternoon – the barmaid soon loses all her good looks, and is ruthlessly discharged. It is of little wonder that many of these girls succumb to the temptation of drink, when it is always at their elbow. [ ... ]

The atmosphere of a public-house must weaken, in the course of time, the most exemplary, and undermine both health and moral calibre. It is an unnatural life for any young girl to live. Youth is destroyed. And to be pretty and young are qualifications demanded of a barmaid. It has often excited my compassion to see the early age at which some of the girls I know, engaged in this pernicious business, are discharged as worn-out.[76]

No similar diatribe is offered, in terms of length or tone, for any of the other jobs Malvery explores in the chapter dedicated to them, and we must presume that barmaiding is uniquely negative amongst her experiences. Once the reader has accepted Malvery's condemnation of female bar work, however, he or she must then read her description of it, and it is here that a naïve acceptance of her judgement becomes difficult. Whether or not one agrees with that judgement is not the question: reading Malvery's description of her time as a barmaid simply leaves us unable to understand how that judgement is formed and what it has to do with the life that she describes.

We can already see this process beginning in her criticism. A barmaid is '*ruthlessly* discharged' if she loses her looks. If we compare this with what is said about the floorwalker's job, the negative charge implied by the adverb is hard to justify. Shop assistants may be discharged from the draper's shop for leaving lights on or for sitting, neither of which has any relevance to how qualified they are for doing their job: sacking for such reasons is clearly not something that Malvery favours, but the rules themselves are 'frivolous, and merely vexatious' and certainly not 'ruthless'. It may be wrong that youth and good looks are a barmaid's qualifications (although Malvery does not argue this), but her qualifications they were, and as such surely discharging somebody when he or she no longer has the qualifications required cannot justly be described as 'ruthless' if firing someone for reasons quite unrelated to the job is merely 'vexatious'.

Malvery's double standard regarding the comparison between the pub and the draper's shop continues. Although the hours that she describes are long (from half past seven in the morning to a little after half past midnight with a three-hour break) and the work clearly hard, she offers but one piece of evidence towards how terrible the life was: 'One of the worst sights I think I noticed' – the hedging suggests other horrors unrecounted, but so ardent a campaigner against the evils of pubs would surely have included them for her readers' instruction – 'was a young woman who gave a little baby, only a few months old, sips from her can'.[77] Against this is an array of not only positive points, but points that almost seem designed to show work behind a bar in a more favourable light than work in a draper's: 'Much better breakfasts were provided than those given to me at the draper's where I had worked';[78] 'I was allowed forty minutes for dinner',[79] as opposed to twenty-five at the draper's, five of which were often spent reaching the dining hall;[80] 'There was a seat in the bar, and no objection was made if I or my companions sat down when there were no customers to serve';[81] 'At three I went to "rest". I invariably spent this time walking or riding on a tram' ('invariably' – this on the page following the complaint that barmaids are too tired to get outdoors during their time off!).[82]

All of Malvery's own evidence goes against the conclusions she appears to draw. It is clear, of course, that her judgements were formed before her experience and underwent no change because of them. Of more interest vis-à-vis Malvery's capacity of being dazzled by her own prejudices to her own abilities is the very fact that the gap between what she describes and how she judges it is so obvious. She has such an ingenuous certainty in her own rightness that she clearly cannot see the disparities that she creates. Never would it appear to her what jumps out of her text here: that she has lived the barmaid's and the shop assistant's lives deeply enough and done their job (and thus her job) well enough to reach, and potentially communicate, a genuine insight – 'unrespectable' work can offer better conditions than 'respectable'. Malvery's methodological tragedy is that she investigated better than she knew. Her blindness to her own actions and beliefs, coupled with a refusal to compromise and an unbending eticity, means that her descriptions can never rise above themselves, never be much more than a source of data rather than a place to go for insight.

## NOTES

1. Orwell, George. 1997 [1933]. *Down and Out in Paris and London* [*The Complete Works of George Orwell*, ed. Peter Davison, vol. 1]. London: Secker & Warburg, pp. 174–75.
2. Ibid., p. 174.
3. It is in fact distinctly rarer than its image in fiction and the public imagination might suggest. I am aware of two examples: 'Begging in the Streets of London. – I'. *The Echo* 9 January 1884, p. 1 and 'Begging in the Streets of London. – II' *The Echo* 10 January 1884, p. 1, and 'A Day as a Professional Beggar'. *Tit-Bits*, 17 January 1891, p. 232.
4. Regarding the story's relationship with the journalism of the day, see Calami, Peter. 1999. 'Art Imitates Life: Participant-Observer Journalism and The Man with the Twisted Lip'. Unpublished lecture notes, Toronto Public Library, call no. 823.91 D598 B575 V. 22, NO. 8, and Jaffe, Audrey.

1990. 'Detecting the Beggar: Arthur Conan Doyle, Henry Mayhew, and "The Man with the Twisted Lip"'. *Representations* 31, pp. 96–117. For a more general overview of Sherlock Holmes's relationship with social investigation, see Seaber, Luke. FORTHCOMING. '"Many Acquaintances, and Those in the Most Different Classes of Society": Sherlock Holmes as Social Investigator' in Tom Ue (ed.) *Mapping Arthur Conan Doyle's Modernities: 1887–1929*. Manchester: Manchester University Press.

5. The partial exception to this last point is Stephen Reynolds, but he is a highly anomalous figure.

6. See Vorachek, Laura. 2012. 'Playing Italian: Cross-Cultural Dress and Investigative Journalism at the Fin de Siècle'. *Victorian Periodicals Review* 45:4, pp. 406–35, pp. 408–10.

7. Bright, Eva. 1894. 'How the Other Half Lives: The Organ-Grinder'. *English Illustrated Magazine* 11, pp. 1007–12.

8. Sparrow, T. 1894. 'London Street Toilers'. *Newbery House Magazine* 2, pp. 248–55. Hereafter cited as 'Organ-Grinders' to avoid confusion with her other piece for the *Newbery House Magazine*, 'London Street Toilers: Cress Sellers'.

9. Bourne, Frances. 1900. 'A Lady's Experiences as an Organ-Grinder'. *English Illustrated Magazine* 24, pp. 18–24.

10. Malvery, Olive Christian. 1905. 'The Heart of Things. IV. – Music in the Byways'. *Pearson's Magazine* 19, pp. 149–57. This is contained in Malvery, Olive Christian. 1907 [1906]. *The Soul Market, with Which Is Included 'The Heart of Things'*. London: Hutchinson & Co., which is the edition that will be cited here.

11. As to *why* the ten years in question witnessed this phenomenon, see Vorachek, 'Playing Italian'.

12. Vorachek, 'Playing Italian', p. 408.

13. Ibid., p. 407.

14. Bright, 'How the Other Half Lives', p. 1007. 'Alnaschar' refers to a story from the *Thousand and One Nights*; one wonders if this is criticism of the *Telegraph*'s stance, as Alnaschar's wealth was purely illusory...

15. Ibid., p. 1012.

16. Ibid., p. 1009.

17. Ibid., p. 1007.

18. Bourne, 'A Lady's Experiences', p. 18.

19. Ibid., p. 22.

20. Sparrow, 'Organ-Grinders', p. 248.

21. 'Further investigation warming me to my work'. Ibid.

22. Ibid.

23. Ibid.

24. Ibid.

25. Ibid., p. 251. Italics mine.
26. Ibid.
27. Ibid.
28. Ibid.
29. See Pasolini, Pier Paolo. 1976. *Lettere luterane*. Turin: Giulio Einaudi, p. 23.
30. Sparrow, 'Organ-Grinders', pp. 253–54.
31. See too her comment on one of the things that she learnt in her week as an organ-grinder, '[I] had increased my vocabulary of abuse' (p. 252): she has learnt more ways to swear, and this is presented as a simple fact rather than as a moral judgement on the iniquities of the poor or a reflection on their freedom of speech as opposed to a middle-class reticence.
32. Ibid., p. 254.
33. Sparrow, T. 1894. 'London Street Toilers: Cress Sellers'. *Newbery House Magazine* 9, pp. 489–494, p. 489.
34. Ibid., p. 492.
35. Ibid., p. 493.
36. Ibid.
37. Sparrow, T. 1896. 'The Penniless Poor: A Doss-House near the Docks'. *Quiver* 31, pp. 68–71, p. 69.
38. Ibid.
39. Sparrow, T. 1897. 'The Cry of the Canal Children'. *Quiver* 32, pp. 366–9, p. 366.
40. Sparrow, T. 1895. 'As One of the Penniless Poor: I. – Palm-Workers'. *Quiver* 30, pp. 225–8, p. 225.
41. Ibid.
42. Ibid., pp. 225–6.
43. See Toynbee, Polly. 1971. *A Working Life*. London: Hodder and Stoughton, p. 157.
44. See 'Mass-Observation' [Celia Fremlin]. 1987 [1943]. *War Factory*. London: The Cresset Library.
45. See Ehrenreich, Barbara. 2011 [2001]. *Nickel and Dimed: On (Not) Getting By in America*. New York: Picador.
46. Ibid., p. 228.
47. Sparrow, T. 1895. 'In the Heart of Hop-Land'. *Strand Magazine* 10, pp. 450–6, p. 451.
48. Ibid., p. 450.
49. Ibid., pp. 455–6.
50. Ibid., p. 456.
51. Ibid., p. 453.
52. All quotations and information following come from London, British Library, Loan 96 RLF 1 2916. I owe knowledge of the fact that Sparrow

had applied to the Royal Literary Fund to Cross, Nigel. 1980. *A Select Catalogue of Applicants to the Royal Literary Fund 1790–1870 with a Historical Introduction*. Unpublished PhD thesis, University College London, no page number.

53. A further level of explanation for the fact that Sparrow did not keep up the superlative level of work evident in the pieces discussed here is to be found in Laura Vorachek's suggestion that Sparrow's consciousness of her middle-class status and the possibility that the 'feminine clique' against her was motivated by a sense that certain journalistic 'tricks' were below her class dignity. Vorachek, Laura. 2016. '"How Little I Cared for Fame": T. Sparrow and Women's Investigative Journalism at the Fin de Siècle'. *Victorian Periodicals Review* 49:2, pp. 333–61, pp. 350–1.

54. Walkowitz, Judith R. 1998/1999. 'The Indian Woman, the Flower Girl, and the Jew: Photojournalism in Edwardian London'. *Victorian Studies* 42:1, pp. 3–46, p. 7.

55. Ibid.

56. Malvery, *Soul Market*, pp. 202–3.

57. Walkowitz, 'The Indian Woman, the Flower Girl, and the Jew', p. 5.

58. Malvery, *Soul Market*, p. 90.

59. Walkowitz, 'The Indian Woman, the Flower Girl, and the Jew', p. 8.

60. Malvery's strong eticity – or, in this case, more simply, her uncomprehending disdain (the term is not too strong) of those amongst whom she temporarily lives – can also be clearly seen when she talks of working-class eating habits. The best example of this comes in her first costering experiment, when she writes 'I always kept some meat lozenges and Plasmon biscuits [a renowned health food of the early twentieth century] in my pocket, and so managed to escape with very small quantities of the food taken by the people with whom I lived' – the use of so loaded a verb as 'escape' is remarkable – before going on to note that she has 'never met a coster girl or a factory girl who could cook decently' and relating her attempts to teach her hosts how to cook and her success in introducing cinnamon into their lives (Malvery, *Soul Market*, pp. 138–9). This speaks for itself.

61. Ibid., p. 197.

62. Ibid., p. 33.

63. Ibid., p. 164.

64. Ibid., p. 134.

65. Ibid. On Malvery's 'foreign appearance', see Walkowitz, 'The Indian Woman, the Flower Girl, and the Jew', passim, especially p. 8.

66. Malvery, *Soul Market*, p. 142.

67. Walkowitz, 'The Indian Woman, the Flower Girl, and the Jew', p. 10.

68. Malvery, *Soul Market*, pp. 142–3.

69. Ibid., p. 158.
70. Ibid., pp. 156–7.
71. Ibid., p. 157.
72. Ibid., p. 155.
73. Ibid.
74. Ibid., p. 158.
75. Ibid., pp. 158–9.
76. Ibid., p. 159.
77. Ibid., p. 161. Fittingly, and rather hilariously, Malvery's remonstrance is met with an indignant instruction to mind her place and not interfere with her betters. She does not seize the opportunity to adduce this as an example of the impenetrability of her disguise ...
78. Ibid., pp. 159–60.
79. Ibid., p. 160.
80. Ibid., p. 156.
81. Ibid., p. 160.
82. Ibid.

# CHAPTER 6

# If Men Do These Kind of Journalistic Feats . . . : Elizabeth L. Banks and Woman's Work

In T. Sparrow and Olive Christian Malvery we see two poles of emicity and eticity, both writers also having a fair claim to recognition as specialists in the field. When Sparrow first started to specialize in the early 1890s, close to a decade before Malvery, she was not the first, however, to invent herself as a serial incognito social investigator amongst working women. Sparrow's *annus mirabilis*, 1894, also saw the publication of one of the most important collections of pieces detailing undercover experience of work: Elizabeth L. Banks's *Campaigns of Curiosity: Journalistic Adventures of an American Girl in London*. Like Malvery after her, Banks was a figure of some celebrity; whereas the Edwardian writer presented herself very much as a figure primarily philanthropic, the Victorian one was a more honestly self-publicizing journalist. Banks was an American, born in Wisconsin in approximately 1870, who worked in various journalistic roles in her home country before moving to England in 1890 to attempt to establish herself as a more serious journalist than she felt it was possible to be in the United States.[1] A chance reply to an essay of Kipling's was published in *The Times*, and she awoke to find herself famous; she then became an increasingly celebrated journalist, 'the American Girl in London'.[2] Mary Suzanne Schriber and Abbey Zink have amply explored her relationship with 'Americanness' and the 'New Woman',[3] but their most interesting analysis for our purposes here is what they have to say about Banks's situation vis-à-vis the history of journalism. The 1880s in America had seen the birth of a more sensational form of journalism, one involving 'stunt work'; normally

© The Author(s) 2017
L. Seaber, *Incognito Social Investigation in British Literature*,
Palgrave Studies in Life Writing, DOI 10.1007/978-3-319-50962-4_6

undertaken by women, this involved journalists performing 'daring' feats for copy: 'daringness' could range from rapid circumnavigation à la Phileas Fogg (Nellie Bly, the most celebrated 'stunt girl' did this between 1889 and 1890) to less strenuous activities such as travelling beneath the East River to see a tunnel being dug (as done by the *World*'s reporter Meg Merrilies).[4] One of the central activities of this form of reporting is incognito social investigation. Some was of a sort that had no element of class passing (Nellie Bly's success in having herself committed to an insane asylum; Annie Laurie's visiting a leper colony), but much was: Meg Merrilies working as a shop-girl in Macy's or begging on Fifth Avenue, for instance.[5] Banks certainly wrote in this tradition, but the less sensationalist journalistic climes of London also of course had their own tradition. Indeed, the difference between Banks and Sparrow or Malvery lie not so much in form or content as presentation of the author, and if we limit ourselves to the sole texts, there is little in Banks's writing that would in itself suggest to the reader more in common with Nellie Bly than James Greenwood. In other words, there is nothing particularly 'American' or 'stunt' about Banks's campaigns of curiosity, but there is about her *Campaigns of Curiosity*. Banks's persona, there in her book's subtitle, owes much to an American, self-promoting, journalistic tradition, which can be compared with Sparrow's lack of self-publicizing. Malvery, the last of these three 'specialists', clearly *does* have a public persona to present to her public, but compared to Banks's it is distinctly less brash. Malvery takes pains to suggest not so much her philanthropy as her *knowledge* of philanthropy; she investigates the poor because she is already in some way expert, and her self-presentation obviously aims at convincing her readers of her suitability as a social investigator. Banks, on the other hand, in the preface to her collection of pieces offers chiefly anecdotes relating to the uproar some of her work has produced. Malvery self-promotes insofar as she tries to show herself fit for the task that she has taken on, but Banks self-promotes in a simpler sense: *she* is interesting and therefore what she has experienced and narrated will be interesting.

Banks's book collects six investigative articles from the preceding year, four of which are examples of incognito social investigation. Two of these were the opening articles in the *English Illustrated Magazine*'s important 'How the Other Half Lives' series. The titles given to these when republished are 'Sweeping a Crossing' and 'A Day with the Flower Girls', and both are instructive examples of Banks's rather unusual judgements on those whom she investigates.[6] Of particular note is something that Banks says regarding them in her preface. She thanks the Editor of the *English Illustrated Magazine* for allowing her to republish them, after which acknowledgement she limits herself to this comment on her two articles: 'They do not take up any very serious social or moral problems, and so need not be further referred to here.'[7] Banks's dismissal of these two pieces is very much in agreement with their overall tone. They are light, and no real pretence is made of serious social commentary, other than a suggestion that the author wishes to ascertain whether it is true, as urban legend would suggest, that street-sweeping can be an unusually profitable business – that 'hundreds of London sweeps are growing opulent at the expense of poor but kind-hearted pedestrians';[8] or that, as she archly claims to believe (in a good example of her style and the relative lack of seriousness it implies), 'smiles and fame and a fortune await the dainty dealer in *boutonnières*, who, attractive herself, and attractively attired, will take her stand for a few weeks at Oxford, Piccadilly, or Ludgate Circus'.[9] The chief focus of her articles is herself and her tone. A good example is the stress she lays on her clothing, especially when, as a tyro crossing-sweeper she wears an old white jacket, and her 'costume was not quite the orthodox thing for a sweep'.[10] It is instructive to note that whereas the republished version in *Campaigns of Curiosity* is accompanied by a photograph of Banks in her street-sweeper's garb, the original magazine publication has a full-page drawing illustrating Banks in the moment, as she narrates it, when it first came to her mind to take an interest in crossing-sweepers. This shows Banks and her clothes quite literally at the centre of her narrative: her long dress takes up most of the centre of the viewer's gaze, its light-coloured trim and her long white scarf providing, along with Banks's face, the chief points of colour that stand out against a mainly dark background where dull working-class figures undifferentiatedly lurk.

Although Banks clearly sets herself out as an entertainer rather than a serious commentator in these pieces, 'Sweeping a Crossing' does show certain interestingly emic points. She recognizes that what sweeps do is work; a sweep is 'not a beggar, but a man of business, however humble his line of operations may be'.[11] The sweep may even be something of an artist, tracing geometrical figures into the dust.[12] Just as crossing-sweepers are legitimate workers, however lowly, they too have their trade secrets. Having failed to make any money outside Baker Street station, Banks moves to the corner of Vigo Street and Regent Street, but does not sweep, preferring merely to stand there in her disguise so as not to risk accusations of stealing somebody else's pitch. Here she falls into conversation with a real crossing-sweeper:

> 'It's hard times,' he continued with an attempt at being sociable. 'I've only took in tuppence today, but I've done some big splashing on the rest of 'em'.
> 'Splashing! What for?' I asked.
> 'Well, ye must be a new un if ye don't know that trick! When I asks a man or a woman for a copper and they doesn't give it, I splashes 'em; that's all'.
> What a pity I had not heard that before I took up my stand near Baker Street Station![13]

Banks, it would appear, is siding with those whom she observes rather than those on whose behalf she is observing. Rather than expressing her indignation about such minatory behaviour and the lack of respect towards one's betters that it indicates, she not only passes over it with no comment on its morality, but also suggests that she too would be more than willing to adopt such distinctly un-middle-class tactics to increase her takings.

There is another interpretation, however, of Banks's seeming emicity here. Her piece on crossing sweepers ends with the following suggestion, made to those sweepers whom she had interviewed after her incognito experiences: 'I have recommended to them that they get some sort of halfpenny-in-the-slot machine and place it in such a position that passersby must see it and feel it incumbent upon them to contribute a halfpenny.'[14] It is difficult to believe that this is anything other than a deliberate attempt at humour.[15] Read in this light, most of Banks's assumed emicity can be seen as humorous.[16] Her 'emic' willingness to 'splash' is simply a joke – a middle-class journalist thinking of doing such a thing! – in the same way that her improbably 'etic' suggestion that crossing-sweepers equip themselves with slot machines is.

A further instance of an apparently more serious moment from Banks that leads to humour comes when she includes a table of accounts from her flower-selling, working out that she showed a profit of 2s. 4d. for her day's work, and calculates that she could aim to make a realistic maximum income of 18s. a week.[17] Her discovery does not leave her any clearer, she claims, with regards to her curiosity over flower-sellers' earning potential: 'Yet I have been told that the majority of the London flower-girls usually take in more than twice, and sometimes three times that amount of money during the week, and I am in a quandary as to how the thing is done.'[18]

This, in itself, is humour: a faux-naïf presentation of herself as baffled by an urban myth's refusal to stand up to investigation. In the original publication in the *Illustrated English Magazine*, Banks's piece on flower-sellers ended here, on this slightly ironic note aimed at the author herself, as well, even more slightly perhaps, at a public also willing to believe such stories of working-class wealth. The version given to *Campaigns of Curiosity*, however, continues for two more paragraphs. The first of these is a one-sentence note that perhaps her quandary regarding the gap between flower-girls' purported income and what she found that she could make may be resolved through knowledge of the various tricks of the trade that the girls use. This brief addition may be read as a note of seriousness, of 'investigativeness'; I would argue, however, that its primary function is in fact to complicate one's reading of what follows:

> Although I have not, perhaps, spent as much time in investigating into the condition of the flower-girls as some may think necessary before passing an opinion, I am bound to say that, from what I have seen and learned of them, I cannot look upon them as a particularly deserving class of individuals. They are unprepossessing in appearance, loud and rude in their manners, and I am inclined to think that the morals of many of them would not bear a close scrutiny. Some charitable ladies who have attempted to work among them say that they are a difficult class to reach, and that sympathy and kindness are usually wasted upon them. Not having tried the work of reformation, I am not able to speak authoritatively on that point; and I should not care to go as a missionary amongst them. They impress me as being of a too combative disposition to make pleasant companions.[19]

After the 'seriousness' of her asides on flower-girls' professional tricks such as further subdividing the bunches that they buy in the market, we may be tempted to read this as serious commentary. Yet the tone, with its excessive hedging ('I am inclined to think', '*particularly* deserving', '*usually* wasted'...), combined with the distinct understatement of the final sentence does not fully convince. There is an undeniable undercurrent of mockery towards those who would presume to judge and engage in 'the work of a missionary'.

Schriber and Zink argue that 'Banks was faced with the challenge of being perceived as "womanly" while being taken seriously as a journalist', and that she 'met this challenge with the tool of humour'.[20] This is an excellent observation; their conclusion, however, that Banks characterizes the personae that she creates as 'incompetent' in order to 'expose the seriousness of her undercover investigations' by setting up tension between her professionalism as a journalist doing a 'man's' job as opposed to her incapacity to perform well the 'woman's' work her disguises imply is less easy to accept.[21] If we look at the two pieces of incognito social investigation examined above in the context of the British tradition, I would argue rather that Banks instead undercuts the seriousness of that tradition. The very thing that she is engaged in is faintly ridiculous; that she can do it so well yet still slyly hint at the foolishness of doing it at all underlines her abilities, her genius, even, for this sort of journalism. Banks's humour is aimed, ever so subtly, at readers and editors: she stands in the middle, the central figure, balanced between her professionalism and her recognition of the lack of importance of some of the things that this very professionalism can lead her to be obliged to do.

An editor asked a sensible journalist to do foolish things to please a (foolish) readership: the unspoken subject of Banks's pieces for the *English Illustrated Magazine* is herself. Perhaps no other incognito social investigator is as secretly cynical as Banks about the worth of the genre; perhaps no-one else so successfully showed an ironic awareness of the fact of writing within a genre.

We have Banks's own account of matters to demonstrate her awareness of the existence of a tradition as well as her self-awareness towards her eventual position in it. In 1894, the year in many ways of her greatest fame, she was the subject of a profile in the *Young Woman* magazine, which said:

> A year ago it seemed as if the height of ambition of a 'smart' London journalist was to pass the night in 'seedy' costume, reclining on a newspaper spread over the flags in Trafalgar Square, so that he might rush into print the next day with a narrative of *les miserables* who had been his fellow-lodgers upon the cold ground. Miss Banks argued, If men do these kind of journalistic feats, why not a woman?[22]

Quite how much is the interviewer, Marion Leslie, adding her own detail of recent journalistic fashions and how much is Banks's own contribution is of course unknowable; nonetheless, the idea of not only writing in a tradition but also of remaking that tradition in an image more suited to the new type of female journalist is clear. It should be noted, however, that by 1893 the tradition was approaching its thirtieth birthday, and the early

1890s were not the central moment in the tradition that is suggested here; it is also a fortiori false that this was the 'newest of new journalism'.[23] Be that as it may, Banks was obviously fully aware of the existence of the Greenwoodian genre, but to it she brought her undisputed talents for self-promotion and subtle irony. She leavened a text form that was self-consciously 'serious' with humour coming from an American journalistic tradition. We may also credit her for granting a new importance to the presence of the investigator's personality in the text: that she was a 'star' journalist is of less weight in this context than the fact that her personality is intrinsic to her texts' interest. This too is a way of making incognito social investigation less 'serious', less 'heavy': once the first wave of the novelty of the concept had passed, and entertainment became increasingly more the goal than information, then who, after all, would not rather read something enlivened by the presence of a self-consciously feisty narrator (present too in lively illustrations and photos) than something where the narrator was at best absent and at worst a relatively dour moralist?

Not only is Banks key in marking the point where incognito social investigation became *fun*, but she was also a hugely important pioneer in another sense, although not with the pieces that we have been examining hitherto, important though they are. Banks's first incognito social investigation piece was published as a series in the *Weekly Sun* in 1893 under the title 'In Cap and Apron'. That this was the founding work of female incognito investigation would alone make it of supreme importance, yet it is more even than that. 'In Cap and Apron', *pace* the idea that Banks was drawn to it by the thought that she too could doss à la Greenwood or his imitators in Trafalgar Square, is emphatically *not* a work in the Greenwoodian tradition. It is the beginning of a new tradition: that of investigating the lives not of the poorest of the poor but a class several steps above them in the hierarchy. The Banksian tradition is incognito social investigation looking at the lives of those in service; for half a century it chronicled the fading away of the world of servants and their employers. Elizabeth L. Banks, then, is as crucial a figure in the history of these related text types as Greenwood; she is the second *fons et origo* in the broader genre's history, and 'In Cap and Apron' as important a work as 'A Night in a Workhouse'. Although in her interview Banks does not explicitly state that she was thinking of the creation of a new form of incognito social investigation other than insofar as it was to be carried out by a woman for the first time, her interviewer's listing of the (specifically Greenwoodian) spheres in which incognito social investigation had contributed to the amelioration of the lot of its object of study, 'the life of the slums, the doss houses, and the casual wards, to say nothing of investigations into the conditions of the homeless sleepers in Trafalgar Square',[24] does suggest a reasonably conscious desire to open up new territories.

As Banks relates it, the inspiration for 'In Cap and Apron' came when she was watching a young woman sewing. She had, she says, for two months been trying to think of a way to ameliorate the situation of this example of the female urban poor, and pity led her to suggest what she thought might be a way to improve her lot. The seamstress's skills are not such to garner her a shop-girl's job, nor is her handwriting good enough for her to do any secretarial work. She can only sew, she says, but the journalist is struck by inspiration: she will employ the poor seamstress as a housemaid, with all found. The reaction with which she is confronted is not that of her Lady Bountiful fantasies:

> The girl had risen from her chair and, to my astonishment, confronted me angrily, her cheeks aflame and her eyes blazing.
>    'Did you come here to insult me?' she demanded, stamping her feet. 'I go out to service! I wear caps and aprons, those badges of slavery! No, thank you. I prefer to keep my liberty and be independent'.[25]

This outburst (although we may suspect a touch of poetic licence in the reporting of the words) sets Banks thinking about the rhetoric of 'independence' and 'liberty' that she hears from a range of underpaid women of various classes, all of whom are united by their horror of the lack of liberty endured by those who go into service: the imposition of cap and apron, those 'badges of slavery'; only having one night off a week; the prohibition of having followers; a general sense that hunger is preferable to the loss of independence that even service with everything found would be.

She thus decides that abstract consideration of the problem alone will not aid her in understanding whether the horror in which so many hold service is justified; nor, however great how powers of sympathy, will her experiences as an employer of housemaids.[26] She must experience the world of those forced to wear cap and apron herself.

She finds that investigating *this* world of work is distinctly more complicated than taking up work in the street or pretending to be indigent: one must wait for a suitable opening to present itself and then convince one's perspective employer to take one on. No suitable position can be found advertised, so Banks decides to take the unusual step of turning the tables, advertising for a job herself as 'Housemaid, Parlourmaid, or House-Parlourmaid'.[27] This brings an array of responses – 159 replies of various sorts. These range from serious enquiries about her experience and abilities to a bizarre proposal of marriage; few, very few, offered her in any way the opportunity that she was seeking. When she did achieve an interview of some sort, it rarely went well: here she was immediately turned away for having a fringe (a style of cut often forbidden to house-servants); there refused for not looking robust enough. A Mrs Green took pity on her and slipped her half a crown and a letter of recommendation to a high-class employment agency, but did not give her a place as Banks's arms were too short, she believed, for her to be able to perform some of the tasks that would have been required of her. A Mrs Weldon subjects Banks to such a questioning that Banks has to hold herself back from answering her in kind, but her restraint does not avail her, as she is still not given the job.

Interestingly, Banks does not accept the first place proposed her. This is as a parlourmaid in a house in Cambridge Terrace, but the house is one where there are twenty lodgers living: 'I would have accepted it but for the fear that at the end of the week's trial she was to give me I would be too much reduced in flesh and spirit to linger long on the earth.'[28] The degree of work involved in carrying twenty people's meals upstairs on trays is enough to convince the journalist that this would be too extreme a step in her quest for knowledge. What is of importance to the wider question of incognito social investigation of this sort here is the issue of choice. Whereas someone acting (in both senses of the word) in the Greenwoodian tradition has very little choice about the role that they must play, someone following the Banksian tradition, such as Banks herself, must choose where exactly in the working-class hierarchy they wish to (endeavour to) place themselves. There is no need here to seek to descend as low as possible in the social hierarchy; no dubious pleasure or consolation in 'going to the dogs' of the sort that Orwell claimed to have found in Paris.[29] One of the most fascinating questions raised by the tradition started by Banks is that regarding where the incognito social investigator (and the reading public) draws the line separating those observed from those observing (and vicariously observing). Banks has no difficulty in refusing a job that she thinks would be too physically difficult, and has no qualms about the opportunities for investigation, discovery and reportage missed; nor is there anything to suggest that she thought her readers may see such a refusal in any way as a dereliction of her self-imposed duty to provide them with information otherwise unavailable. Yet there must, logically, be a line drawn somewhere. If the subgenre is to exist, if it is to have any sense, then there must exist a level of employment, reported refusal of which would constitute a breach of the tacit agreement between writer and reader. If Banks had held out for a job as an upper servant, it would surely have been legitimate for her readers to complain that her experiment was meaningless; but from what point exactly in the servant hierarchy was such a principle valid? It would be interesting to conduct a diachronic study of incognito social investigation tracing which jobs have been considered valid sites of Banksian social investigation at which moments.

Banks surmounts her various problems, and at last succeeds in finding a position as a housemaid near Portman Square in the household of a Mrs Allison (a pseudonym, as are all of the employees' names that Banks records). A letter informs her that her new employer believes that she will 'be able to smooth over many of the rough places' for the neophyte Banks, and provide for her 'a comfortable home'.[30] Any possible optimism created by this reveals itself to have been unfounded. The household is portrayed as badly run, Mrs Allison as bad-tempered and expecting the maximum work for the minimum price, even when such an outlook is economically counterproductive, and the whole experience is tiring, dispiriting and a good introduction to the negative side of service. Banks correspondingly decides to leave; in order to avoid having to pay Mrs Allison a month's pay in lieu of notice, she determines that it is better to be dismissed without notice, receive a month's pay but forfeit that servant's talisman, a character. She succeeds in this by complaining that the breakfast allocated to the servants, bread and coffee, is not enough, and that she must have meat (an insistence that was one of the points that revealed to the *Weekly Sun*'s readers that Banks was American rather than British).[31] Her fellow servants are shocked by her recklessness in acting thus and forgoing a character; while Mrs Allison is shocked by Banks's refusal to stay on, as custom and an employee's caution would dictate, until she is 'suited' with another housemaid.

Banks's next position is as a parlourmaid for a Mrs Brownlow in Kensington. Here the contrast, as Banks tells it, is like day after night. Mrs Brownlow (one wonders whether the pseudonym here owes something to Oliver's saviour in Dickens's novel, especially as Banks compares herself to Oliver Twist when she is discharged without a character by

Mrs Allison because she 'had the audacity to "ask for more"')[32] is a marvellously considerate mistress, and the house is well run. Indeed, it is better run with the help of 'Lizzie Barrows', as Banks calls herself throughout her time as a servant. Banks's efficiency, on the other hand, does not endear her to the housemaid, Alice, who is eventually discharged. Banks organizes a replacement through the *Weekly Sun*, and leaves Mrs Brownlow's service, although not before she has survived serving at a reception where one of the guests is a publisher who knows her, to whom she has to slip a note imploring his silence.

A particular point of interest about 'In Cap and Gown' lies in the fact that we have unusually detailed reflections from its author on its writing. Banks's 1902 autobiography contains precious insights into the writing methods (rather than the investigative methodology) of one of the most important and influential of all incognito social investigators:

> I also did what might possibly be termed a little 'posing' during the course of my narrative, by letting it appear that I was not well up in the art of housework [ … ] I acted thuswise for the purpose of trying to break up the monotony of the daily life of myself and my fellow servants, thus furnishing somewhat more interesting 'copy' than I otherwise could have done. All work and no play is bound to make one a dull journalist.[33]

This might at first sight seem an admission to a certain degree of fictionalization in the work that made Banks's name. If we read it thus, then we should recognize that it is something of a courageous level of openness to display: this is in a book coming out only nine years after a media sensation, and any seeming attempt on the author's part to diminish in any way its supposed veracity must surely be taken as a level of honesty that at the very least risked damaging her career.

I would argue, however, that what Banks is admitting to is not fictionalization as it would usually be recognized. It is constructive to use *Down and Out in Paris in London* as a comparison here, as it is another work in which we have the author's admission – admittedly for private rather than public knowledge – of where his work departs from the 'truth', in Orwell's notes on the copy that he gave Brenda Salkeld.[34] The most important fictionalization in Orwell's book is the point that he annotates laconically: 'This incident is invented to explain trip, but all the experiences described hereafter are authentic.'[35] 'This incident' is the wholly fictitious failure of the equally fictitious 'B.' to provide Orwell with the job looking after a 'congenital imbecile' that he had promised him. The patient and his family, we are told, will return in a month, until then, Orwell has to survive on the 19s. 6d. that is all he has with him. We have already examined why Orwell practised this deception; it suffices here to note that this is true fictionalization. It creates a narrative that changes the way we read *Down and Out in Paris and London*; it suggests Orwell is genuinely down and out rather than an incognito social investigator; it aggrandizes the narrator, suggesting his knowledge is not only hard come by, but also unsought. Banks's admission, on the other hand, is something more subtle (and, I would suggest, at the deepest level an example of her ironic self-awareness).

We might say that she belittles herself instead of aggrandizing herself. She admits to making herself more of a fool than was in fact the case, to making herself look less efficient and incognito social investigator. She presents herself in 1902 as having presented herself in 1893 as less than capable, making mistakes that lessened her ability to interact fully with those whose lives she was investigated (and this holds true whether we are talking about those upstairs or those downstairs). This was done solely to improve her copy, she says, so we should perhaps amend our previous statement: she belittles herself as an incognito social investigator in order to aggrandize herself as a journalist. There are three levels at work here: she prefers to be a less capable servant, and thus a less capable incognito social investigator; as her incapacity as a servant is feigned, however, and feigned moreover to make for better, more entertaining copy, she is (in 1902) demonstrating how finely tuned is her instinctive capacity as a journalist to know what it is her readers want.

Banks's willingness to show her ineptitude not only as a housemaid but also as someone pretending to be a housemaid can be seen in her account of how she sets about becoming a servant. We have seen that she does this by placing an advertisement in a newspaper. This states that she is a 'refined and educated young woman, obliged to earn her living, and unable to find other employment'.[36] That this is a far from orthodox way to go about procuring such employment is clear from the array of baffled (and in some cases baffling) letters that she receives. Such calling attention to oneself, such standing out from the crowd, can surely never be a successful tactic for an incognito social investigator – that is, *if incognito social investigation is one's true aim*. As we have seen, Banks's true interest lies in presenting herself as entertaining and as a journalistic figure; incognito social investigation is for her a means to this end rather than an end in itself.

With regards to journalism, incognito social investigation is for Banks not an end in itself; the same status as means rather than end is held in turn by incognito social investigation in relation to a phenomenon often closely intertwined with it: philanthropy. Banks may inspire philanthropists, but is not one herself. As she (admittedly somewhat hedgingly) said in interview to Marion Leslie:

> 'Has the object of your adventures been chiefly philanthropic?'
> 'No, I do not pose as a philanthropist; but I do claim this, that my campaigns have done nobody any harm, and they may be the means of doing much good [ ... ]. I am hoping it will lead philanthropists and reformers to enquire into things'.[37]

Banks's 1902 autobiography also sees a far more detailed justification of her refusal to pose as a reformer. This is of huge importance, as nowhere else does an incognito social investigator speak so openly about his or her motives. Before examining this, however, it is worth returning briefly to Banks's explanation of how the idea for 'In Cap and Gown' first came to her. It was inspired by the outraged outburst of a young seamstress to whom Banks had suggested domestic service as a more lucrative and less onerous form of employment; the journalist had already been pondering how to help the sewing-woman for two months before offering in her ignorance to employ her as a maid.[38] This is the version given in *Campaigns of Curiosity*; that given in *The Autobiography of a 'Newspaper Girl'* matches this almost exactly vis-à-vis Banks's suggestion (although it is of generic 'domestic service' rather than employment in her own household).[39] There is, however, one crucial difference between the 1893 account of the relationship between Banks and the seamstress and the 1902 account. The earlier story of Banks's epiphany has her noting that 'I had been so interested in this girl, and for the past two months had vainly tried to think of a plan whereby I could help her.'[40] The version presented as autobiography – and where, therefore, the presumed identity of the narrative voice is much more known to the reader – is quite different.[41] She is taking her dog for a walk, and decides to let him lead the way. He takes her to Camberwell, where she strikes up a conversation with a young girl whose sister, she learns, takes in sewing. Banks is about to continue on her way when her dog, hearing his mistress say 'goodbye', automatically puts out his paw for the girl to shake. She is enchanted by this, and begs the journalist to bring her pet up to show his tricks to her sister. To make conversation, Banks asks whether there might be other employment that would bring in more than sewing, such as domestic service. The result we know.

Why might there be such a difference? The answer lies, I think, in the increasing level of fame that Banks enjoyed. In 1893, she presented herself, however marginally, as a figure not totally alien to her readers, the philanthropic slum visitor, before undertaking her pioneering exploits. By 1902, such a figure as she was had become familiar (chiefly, of course, through her own activity!); there was no longer any need to sugar the pill of her strangeness, and she could tell a far more charming story. It will be noted that in neither case is it of particular importance whether the version given is 'true': all of a piece throughout, Banks's choice is always that which is most likely to help her win the interest of her readership.

This is key: Banks's goal is entertainment and her self-presentation as a journalist. It is not 'truth' or reform, and we should now look at the long diatribe in her autobiography against those who would in any way criticize her priorities or presume them otherwise. This is occasioned by a question from a 'woman writer' at a 'gathering of women' to which Banks is invited, and the questions that follow make it reasonably clear that the American's interlocutor is herself of that class whence slum visitors come:

> 'Now, tell me exactly what was your aim and object – your serious one, I mean – in going out to service and writing about it? It is a question we are all asking.'
> 'I did it for "copy",' I answered. 'To earn my living, you know. I knew it was a subject that would interest everybody.'
> [...]
> '"Copy"! you mean to confess you had no philanthropic aim, that you did it for mercenary reasons, merely to earn your living?'
> 'Yes [...] I'm not a hypocrite and I won't pose as a reformer.'[42]

The reader, however, is likely to read more than the 'woman writer' into Banks's statement of purpose 'To earn my living'. She has already explained how when she met the seamstress who inspired 'In Cap and Gown' she had run out of money, and even the pennies brought in by taking in sewing were in fact enviable to her.[43] Banks is absolutely open that the flash of inspiration that led to 'In Cap and Gown' saved her from penury, and she continues to express with increasing vehemence this point to the woman who finds her open admission that she carried out incognito social investigation for copy so shocking, especially when she contrasts her writing with the American Girl's:

'Oh, I really never thought any journalist would sink to such a level, or make such a confession even though it were true! I must say that I have never written anything except with the object of benefitting somebody by it.'

'Perhaps you have an income aside from your writing, which I have not,' I answered; 'and then, I am sure you have never undertaken the hard kind of work which I have done. Would you scrub floors, and carry water up four flights of stairs, and make yourself ill in mind and body, doing work to which you were not accustomed, from motives of philanthropy?'[44]

Banks continues after this with a defence of her realist position, which may be summed up by Brecht's *Erst kommt das Fressen, dann kommt die Moral*...She concludes with a vindication of the practicality and realism of her position that nonetheless leaves room for more altruistic motives:

Who that is breakfastless and dinnerless can write an article on 'The Need of a Christmas Feast for the poor' merely and solely for the sake of those known as 'the poor'? to that 'feast' the hungry journalist is not invited; for who suspects that she may be hungry and far 'poorer' than the 'very poor' of the East End of London or the East side of New York? The journalist writes of the need of the feast and receives as payment two guineas or ten dollars. That is what the hungry journalist writes for – the fee, and if she is honest she will admit it. But along with the fee and the satisfaction of having earned some food for herself there comes the added compensation of having helped to fill other empty stomachs than her own.[45]

Banks's self-presentation, then, is of a self-consciously professional journalist; her incognito social investigation may have results that sit comfortably with philanthropy, but this is an unlooked-for bonus. The one member of the working poor that Banks really wishes to help with her journalism is the one individual who certainly gains from it: the author herself.

There is, though, another possible level to Banks's self-presentation, a hidden meaning lying at the heart of her genius for self-presentation and self-publicity. As we have seen, at many points Banks seemingly presents herself as a figure of entertainment rather than instruction. On the one hand, the textual hand as it were, she wears clothes ill suited to the task in hand and she places that strange advertisement in the newspaper; on the contextual hand (if we may call it that), she is motivated by mercenary interests, and entertainment was always likely to sell better than instruction. However, a seeming contradiction arises. Textually, Banks displays a lack of professionalism (compare her approximations with Malvery's later meticulousness in having a room where she can hide a whole wardrobe of disguises); contextually, she displays an excess of professionalism that courts accusations of hard-heartedness. This supposed contradiction can be solved: she is a professional *entertainer*, and her bizarreries are part of that professionalism. She is so professional a journalist that she is willing to allow her readers to think her less professional if that makes for a better, more entertaining story.

This is part of the story, but the importance that she gives in her autobiography to this question of her motivations hints at another level. After all, if Banks's motivations were so simply mercenary, why devote so much time to defending their being so in a book less than ten years after the event? After all, she had been paid and her professionalism had been successful. This was on the one hand; on the other, from a commercial or mercenary point of view, a reiteration of views for which she was known was surely less likely to make her money than a repudiation of those views. Banks's stance vis-à-vis her working for reasons of money rather than philanthropy is clearly of great importance to her.

There is one obvious seeming exception to this stance: her account of time spent working as a laundress may, she claims in her preface to *Campaigns of Curiosity*, she hopes, 'not be without the effect of calling attention to a class of working girls who stand in great need of a helping hand from the better classes'.[46] However, this is balanced in the same paragraph by implicit praise for herself ('the most difficult task I have yet attempted, and that I lived through it [ ... ] still causes me to wonder'):[47] she is certain of her skill and bravery, but only hopeful regarding any philanthropic role that her text might play.

In general, the preface to her collection is not without a certain very slight vague air of possible philanthropic usefulness to her works; to this there is one clear exception, and it is this that offers us a key to Banks's secret, which is that she, a writer very clearly conscious of her role as a public figure and active in that figure's creation, was in fact very subtly making a point regarding the whole process in which she was engaged. If we presume a reader interested in this early media star, then that reader would have known not only of Bank's campaigns of curiosity, but also her autobiographical 'honesty' over her motives when that became particularly public in 1902; that 'honesty' combined with what appears to be almost a throwaway phrase in the preface to *Campaigns of Curiosity*, offers us a new way to read the incognito social investigation journalism of this pioneering figure. Speaking of the fact that she is republishing two pieces from the *English Illustrated Magazine*, those on flower-girls and crossing-sweepers, she appends a dismissive sentence: 'They do not take up any very serious social or moral problems, and so need not be further referred to here.'[48] Above, we have looked at this phrase as an example of how Banks highlights her role as an entertainer rather than as a 'serious' journalist; I believe it also serves another purpose.

Banks's stints as supposed street-cleaner and flower-girl touch upon in fact as many (or as few) 'social or moral problems' as any of her other incognito social investigation pieces, as the simple fact that other incognito social investigators were able to make (or attempt to make) philanthropic and reformist points with similar pieces demonstrates. Why then might Banks be so dismissive of these two pieces? Partially to highlight her status as an entertainer, but partially for a deeper reason. She brings into evidence here the little inconsistencies about her role and the degree to which was 'mercenary'; and by doing so hints at a vital truth.

Banks is clear in her autobiography that at the time of becoming an incognito social investigator, she was herself poor. Her incognito social investigation work, like all such undertakings, is about shedding light on the lives of the poor to those more fortunate. Yet it would not have been enough for Banks in her poverty to have chronicled her own life when she was still to become famous: she had to pretend to be poor in a different way. The *Autobiography* is her true social investigation: she can speak of something that she truly knows about the poor, which is to say her own experiences, the experiences of Elizabeth L. Banks and not of some nonexistent individual such as 'Elizabeth Barrows', the 'housemaid'. She realizes that 'poverty' has nothing to do with money – not in the sense of the benefits of the 'simple life', but in a much more socially intelligent sense. As a journalist with no money she is not 'poor'; that is, her social and cultural capital is such that she is not considered 'different' enough or 'unknowable' enough. A housemaid earning more than her, on the other hand, *is* 'poor': for all that her scarce earnings are more on occasion than the journalist's, the probable reader of incognito social investigation texts is unlikely to encounter her in a drawing-room unless she is unusually tardy lighting the fire – and in that case dismissal rather than a transfer of knowledge is likely to be the result. Banks's mercenary honesty and little inconstancies show up this central point, that incognito social investigation has nothing to do with 'poverty' as understood economically, but rather with a class system that approaches a caste system in its rigidity and refusal to allow speech that comes from 'below'. Banks is speaking *for* the 'poor' to whom she economically belongs, but not until she becomes famous can she speak *as* one of the 'poor', when she is no longer economically one of them. Banks's point has a very slight undercurrent of mockery towards her readers: as if she were a magician explaining how a trick is done, all the while knowing that the audience still will not see it, yet still applaud her for doing it. Her works, then, convey a point that almost always goes unrecognized within the genre(s) of incognito social investigation: the privilege that allows one to be an incognito social investigator means that however careful one may be, one is always reporting something not truly lived; something that one can only ever know less well than one's true life and real experiences. Yet incognito social investigators' readers, for all their implied clamouring after 'the truth', were not interested in hearing about the writers' descriptions of what they truly knew, only of what they could never truly know, as those who did know it and did live it were considered incapable of expressing it.

This vital point almost *had* to remain unrecognizable if incognito social investigation were to continue; were it made too obvious, were Banks to spell it out, then this would have been a failing in her professionalism; she would have been a Sampson destroying herself with the edifice that she pulled down, destroying the market for the partial truths that she supplied. This explains her reticence; her journalistic genius explains her desire to communicate nonetheless this truth about her work, however partial, masked and subtle that communication may have been. In doing so, she gave life to a new text form, Banksian incognito social investigation, and thus new and continuing life to the genre of incognito social investigation texts more broadly, guaranteeing its survival as a form of writing down to the present, whilst the older, Greenwoodian, form slowly faded away.

## NOTES

1. Schriber, Mary Suzanne and Abbey Zink. 2003. Introduction. Banks, Elizabeth L. *Campaigns of Curiosity: Journalistic Adventures of an American Girl in Late Victorian London*. Madison: The University of Wisconsin Press, pp. vii$_a$–xliv$_a$, pp. viii$_a$–ix$_a$.

2. Ibid., pp. ix$_a$–xi$_a$.
3. Ibid., pp. xv$_a$–xxii$_a$.
4. Ibid., pp. xxiv$_a$–xxv$_a$.
5. Ibid., p. xxv$_a$.
6. Originally published as: Banks, Elizabeth L. 1894. 'How the Other Half Lives: The Crossing-Sweeper'. *Illustrated English Magazine* 11, pp. 845–50; Banks, Elizabeth L. 1894. '"How the Other Half Lives": The Flower Girl'. *Illustrated English Magazine* 11, pp. 925–31. There was a third Banks piece published in this series (Banks, Elizabeth L. 1895. 'How the Other Half Lives: The Dressmakers Apprentice'. *Illustrated English Magazine* 13, pp. 539–45); all of what is said here regarding the republished pieces applies, *mutatis mutandis*, to this.
7. Banks, Elizabeth L. 2003 [1894]. *Campaigns of Curiosity: Journalistic Adventures of an American Girl in Late Victorian London*. Madison: The University of Wisconsin Press, p. xiv.
8. Ibid., p. 131.
9. Ibid., p. 140
10. Ibid., p. 133.
11. Ibid., p. 129.
12. Ibid., p. 130.
13. Ibid., p. 137.
14. Ibid., p. 138.
15. See Schriber and Zink, Introduction. Banks, Elizabeth L. *Campaigns of Curiosity*, pp. xx$_a$–xxiv$_a$ for further analysis of the role that humour plays in Banks's work, although the focus is somewhat different from that adopted here.
16. Although not all: her encounter (p. 137) with the prostitute who is the only person to give her any money whilst street-sweeping and her lack of comment upon the other woman other than to note that prostitutes are those who give street-cleaners the most money I would suggest are instances of genuine emicity.
17. Banks, *Campaigns*, pp. 150–1.
18. Ibid., p. 151.
19. Ibid., pp. 151–2.
20. Schriber and Zink, Introduction. Banks, Elizabeth L. *Campaigns of Curiosity*, p. xx$_a$.
21. Ibid., pp. xxi$_a$–xxii$_a$.
22. Leslie, Marion. 1894. 'An American Girl in London: An Interview with Miss Elizabeth Banks'. *Young Woman* 3, pp. 58–62, p. 58.
23. Ibid.
24. Ibid.
25. Banks, *Campaigns*, p. 3.

26. What Banks does not point out is that any knowledge of servants' working conditions that she gleaned from her own employee was likely to be anything but representative, insofar as her housemaid, Dinah Moore, was an African-American with a relationship with her mistress that, at least as portrayed by Banks, was far more informal than the late Victorian standard would desire. Banks, Elizabeth L. 1902. *The Autobiography of a 'Newspaper Girl'*. London: Methuen & Co., pp. 52–60.
27. Banks, *Campaigns*, p. 9.
28. Ibid., p. 20.
29. Orwell, George. 1997 [1933]. *Down and Out in Paris and London* [*The Complete Works of George Orwell*, ed. Peter Davison, vol. 1]. London: Secker & Warburg, pp. 16–7.
30. Banks, *Campaigns*, p. 21.
31. Ibid., p. x.
32. Ibid., p. 45.
33. Banks, *Autobiography*, p. 86.
34. See Davison, Peter. 2000. 'Publication of *Down and Out in Paris and London*'. In George Orwell, *A Kind of Compulsion: 1903–1936* [*The Complete Works of George Orwell*, ed. Peter Davison, vol. 10]. London: Secker & Warburg, pp. 299–300.
35. Ibid., p. 300.
36. Banks, *Campaigns*, p. 9.
37. Leslie, 'An American Girl in London', p. 60.
38. Banks, *Campaigns*, pp. 1–3.
39. Banks, *Autobiography*, pp. 66–7.
40. Banks, *Campaigns*, p. 3.
41. Banks, *Autobiography*, pp. 65–6.
42. Ibid., p. 94.
43. Ibid., p. 66.
44. Ibid., p. 93.
45. Ibid., p. 95.
46. Banks, *Campaigns*, p. xiv.
47. Ibid.
48. Ibid.

# CHAPTER 7

# The Astonishing Thing Is That They Listen to Us: Modern Work from Celia Fremlin to Polly Toynbee

In the 1890s, Elizabeth L. Banks breathed new life into incognito social investigation, and this Banksian interest in the world of low-paid work was continued chiefly by women. This is the incognito social investigation tradition that has proved most durable, surviving into the present. We have seen how, in Banks's work, there are raised the epistemological weakness inherent in the phenomenon: what those who read incognito social investigation texts desire is not the voice of the truly poor and their insights into their condition, but rather the voice of those considered to be nearer socially to their audience. That the accounts of the poor that we examine here can almost never be read as unmediated is not failure, but rather their *raison d'être*.

Open denunciation of this fact and the whole concept of incognito social investigation by one of its practitioners would have to wait until Celia Fremlin, almost half a century after Banks's hints. Fremlin was born to a middle-class family in 1914, and read Greats at Oxford, going up in 1933.[1] There she joined the Communist Party, and was an 'open' member thereof, although when interviewed by Angus Calder in 1980 she claimed to have had 'no overwhelming convictions' and suggested that part of the appeal of joining was simply that '[e]verybody who was anybody was in the Communist Party', as 'that was where all the fun was'.[2] Rather than following a typical middle-class route from an Oxford Classics degree to the wider world, Fremlin after going down worked behind the counter at an Express Dairy restaurant, before moving on to work as a domestic

© The Author(s) 2017
L. Seaber, *Incognito Social Investigation in British Literature*,
Palgrave Studies in Life Writing, DOI 10.1007/978-3-319-50962-4_7

servant, usually of the scullery maid type, and a cleaner.[3] How this came about she described to Nick Stanley in 1981:

> Well of course when you do Greats you land up with a Classics degree which is of no use to man or beast unless you're planning to teach. The one thing I was determined not to do was to teach. So I thought 'right, the thing I'm qualified in isn't a qualification for anything I want to do, therefore I must treat myself as unqualified, like any fourteen year old'. So what can you do if you are unqualified? – You can do low grade catering jobs.[4]

A caveat should be appended here. Fremlin's daughter Geraldine informed Chris Simmons that her mother 'was notorious within the home for embroidering the truth', although she attributed this not to any innate dishonesty or wish to deceive but rather to a 'creative streak, her ability to fabricate new identities for people – even for herself'.[5] As any examination of her novels will show, Fremlin was fascinated by the process whereby one constructs the image one presents to society; and although there is nothing to suggest that her factual statements about her personal history are anything less than reliable, those that concern her motivation must be approached with a certain degree of caution. Nonetheless, nothing that Fremlin is recorded as having said or written about her reasons for taking on 'lower-class' work after Oxford especially contradicts the version given here.

Fremlin wrote up her work experiences in a book published in 1940 by Methuen under the title *The Seven Chars of Chelsea*. This was read and reviewed by one of the founders of Mass-Observation, Tom Harrisson (or he read a favourable review: Fremlin's account varies), who thought that its unknown author would be perfect for the organization and wrote to her to invite her to work for it, which she duly accepted. Fremlin carried out various investigations for Mass-Observation. Some saw her as an incognito social investigator, some saw her conducting interviews, and she also collected 'overheards', as well as becoming more involved in the planning of surveys.[6] In 1943, the book *War Factory*, credited to 'Mass-Observation', was published; although often since credited to a collaboration of Harrisson and Fremlin, this account of life in a factory making secret electronics equipment was (barring Harrisson's signed introduction) all Fremlin's work.

After the end of the Second World War she became a housewife in Hampstead, but in 1958 published the first of her sixteen novels, *The*

*Hours before Dawn*. This, like all of her fiction work a psychological thriller, received much acclaim, winning the Edgar Award in the United States for best mystery novel in 1960. She died in 2009; her final novel, *King of the World*, had been published in 1994. By her final years her work was increasingly unknown, although 2014 saw Faber republish all of her fiction in a uniform edition.

The exact genesis of *The Seven Chars of Chelsea* is somewhat more complex than the brief description given above. In her interview with Angus Calder, Fremlin claimed that her reason for *changing* jobs whilst working in service was that she had begun to think about the possibility of publishing something on her experiences,[7] although this of course has no bearing on her choice in *taking* such jobs in the first place. However, beyond economic and social reasons, as well as those of curiosity and eventual publication (whether, as she claims, developed during the period or prior to it matters little in this context), Fremlin also had lighter, more personal (we might even say more frivolous) reasons for entering into a working world far removed from that which one might have expected to await her. In her interviews of the 1980s Fremlin said that she supposed that the 'driving force in my life has been to have as a many experiences as possible in my span on earth',[8] and not only did domestic work help her in this aim, it also less exaltedly made 'a nice change from intellectual slog' to do housework, which she had always liked, and get paid for it.[9]

*The Seven Chars of Chelsea*'s rather odd title gives very little away about the nature of the book, but Fremlin's preface soon explains what it actually is. The first chapter is a report of middle- and upper-class views on women in domestic service, but after this theoretical opening, Fremlin moves on to accounts of lived experience, detailing: her attempts to get work in service; her experiences as a live-in scullery-maid in a household where repressed female sexuality creates a 'Gothic intensity' (Judy Giles's apt term);[10] her time as a chambermaid in a chaotic and hilarious boarding-house; hospital cleaning with the titular seven chars. The sixth chapter presents a brusque change from what has preceded it. The preceding chapter ends with the eight chars, that is, the seven plus Fremlin (it is worth noting that notwithstanding the title, Fremlin will later in the book talk of there having been *eight* chars, 'we eight chars', making it explicit that she does not think of the group as being divided into seven chars and a writer),[11] saying goodnight to each other, and the symbolic concluding phrase is 'The day's work was over':[12] this signals the end of the incognito social investigation section *stricto sensu*, and heralds the chapters following, which offer Fremlin's analysis of her experiences, as well as looking at the results of a questionnaire to which she received 211 replies from mistresses of servants.

Judy Giles has sited Fremlin's book within the 'political allegiance to social realism and documentary' of the 1930s, recognizing its connections with Orwell and Mass-Observation.[13] Although she compares in passing Fremlin's intentions to those of 'those social explorers of late-Victorian London who visited the East End [ ... ] to reveal to the upper and middle classes the lives, experiences and attitudes of the poorer classes in the hope of activating reform',[14] Giles does not recognize that both the Victorian and the 1930s writers were part of the same phenomenon, and this lack of knowledge causes her to misrepresent somewhat the form of *The Seven Chars of Chelsea*, notwithstanding her acute analysis of its contents:

> [U]nusual in that its structure and modes of expression blur the conventional disciplinary boundaries between sociology and literature. It purports to be a social survey into the conditions of domestic service[ ... ]. Fremlin begins with a description of social reality – the conditions of domestic service – but her survey also incorporates a variety of fictional modes[.][15]

Fremlin *does* blur the boundaries between sociology and literature, but this is far from unusual in incognito social investigation texts – indeed, it could almost be a definition of the genre. Quite what is meant by 'fictional modes' is unclear here: Fremlin recounts her experiences and intersperses these with analysis and comment, and her recounting partakes to a greater or lesser extent of *literariness* (most visibly in the beginning of the chapter that gives its name to the whole work), but this stylistic point does not necessarily imply anything about the factual or fictional nature of what is being related.

Elsewhere, however, Fremlin *would* blur the boundaries between sociology and literature, but this was to be in the long series of novels beginning in 1958. *The Seven Chars of Chelsea* may appear to be an uneasy compromise between sociology and literature, but this is a view only tenable if we do not read it in light of the tradition to which it belongs. It is not in this that its noteworthiness lies.

No other incognito social investigator known to me is so frank about his or her failure; indeed, so frank about how the whole enterprise of incognito social investigation must be doomed to fail. The preface sets out

with disarming forthrightness the insoluble epistemological problem
facing the incognito social investigator:

> When I first embarked on the researches which led to this book I did so in
> that spirit of armchair socialism which is so prevalent among my class and
> generation. I thought that by coming down from Oxford and taking a series
> of jobs as kitchen-hand, charwoman, cook-general and so on I would get to
> 'know' the domestic servant class; would understand and appreciate their
> lives and conditions of work; would find out where the mistresses were
> 'wrong' and where the servants were 'right'.
>     Needless to say, I did not succeed in doing anything of the kind.[16]

> The reader must beware of the whole book. By working and living for a time
> among a class other than one's own one may learn a lot; may make many
> friends. But one will not become a member of that class. [ ... ] However
> much one may will the contrary, one will remain an outsider; everything one
> says or writes about one's experiences will, in the last analysis, be from the
> point of view of an outsider.[17]

This clear-sightedness about her project's inherent incapacity to meet its
stated aims is, as a post-factum conclusion, reasonable, although (it should
be repeated) quite unique in the genre for the strength and decidedness of
its dismissal of the genre. However, it should be recalled that the preface,
although written after the rest of the book (it begins with a reference to
how it must be out of date given that the experiences related in it took
place before the outbreak of war), will of course usually be the first piece of
text encountered by the reader: Fremlin's conclusion regarding her technique's relative uselessness is presented to the reader from the onset, and
she has the courage to trust in the reader's interest in the subject and her
own writing ability to carry them through a text that has already
announced, before the contents page is even reached, its own failure.

Fremlin's wider political point regarding the epistemo-methodological
shortcoming of her own book is made clearer and stronger in the opening
paragraphs of the first chapter; one has almost the impression of a gauntlet
being thrown down to the reader:

> I can think of no more striking condemnation of present-day society than
> the fact that there is room in it for books like this. And there are coming to
> be a good many more of them. It is becoming more and more the fashion
> for people like myself to come down from a university, or out of Mayfair,

and go and work as a charwoman, waitress or whatnot, to see what it is 'like'. And when we have found out what it is 'like', we come back among our old friends and tell them about it.

And the astonishing, and sociologically horrifying, thing is that they listen to us; we are considered to have a real function as purveyors of information.

Now it is obvious that any even partially efficient social system would have no use for amateur job-crawlers such as us. In such a social system, if you wanted to know what it was like to be a charwoman, you would read books written by experienced charwomen, and discuss the matter with them, not with dilettante adventurers who happen to have done charring for a couple of months.[18]

No other author in the incognito social investigation tradition shows this level of brutal honesty regarding the value of their own work; nowhere else can we see so high a point of self-reflection on the nature of what incognito social investigators are engaged in. *The Seven Chars of Chelsea* should be recognized as the one work in the tradition under investigation here that turns a genuinely critical gaze on itself.

Fremlin's reflections on what she is engaged in are indubitably a remarkable intellectual achievement, but can the same be said about what she actually writes? Lucy Delap has claimed that Fremlin places the sexually frustrated live-in servants that she describes into the traditional stereotypes of female servants as 'sexually repressed elderly maid[s]', as well as seeing in the 'vigorous, earthy, though also [ ... ] comic' chars who give the book its title an example of how the 'humorous dimension of the eroticized servant became concentrated on these older workers' in Fremlin's book.[19] This represents Fremlin as perpetuating stereotypes not only about women, but also, more germanely with regards to the current discussion, about working-class women. Analysis of Fremlin's writing, however, paints a rather more nuanced picture than that of careless perpetuation of stereotypes given by Delap.

Delap's reference to Fremlin's portrayal of female domestic servants as being sexually repressed is clearly a reference to the third chapter of *The Seven Chars of Chelsea*, entitled, not without irony or ambiguity, 'A "Good" Place'. This narrates the experiences that Fremlin (calling herself 'Margaret') has working as a scullery-maid in the London town house of 'her ladyship', of whom the reader knows only that she is elderly, aristocratic and rich, and keeps eight domestic servants who have very little to do. Her employer (whom she never in fact meets) is not, however, the focus of Fremlin's observation and analysis. The person to whom Fremlin devotes most description is Lydia, the under-housemaid. She is at least thirty, but is portrayed as 'not a woman at all, but a thirty-year-old child',[20] whose stockings the housekeeper still examines for holes as if she were a schoolgirl.[21] The chapter ends with an episode to which Lydia is central, an episode presented as unfixed in time; we do not know when in Fremlin's period in this job it takes place, occurring when Fremlin wakes one night, not even knowing what time it is. This vagueness fits well with the slightly dreamlike nature of the scene narrated, and the narration here becomes more 'literary', less 'scientific', as might befit a symbolic episode taking place outside normal time.[22] Fremlin, who shares a room with her, is woken by the sound of Lydia's humming. She is unconsciously quietly crooning as she watches the last guests leave a party in a house across the square. She shivers, blaming the cold on a warm May night, and they both return to bed:

> A few minutes later I heard Lydia crying. I went across to her bed.
> 'It's my nerves, Margaret,' she sobbed. 'Just my nerves. Stroke my head the way May [Fremlin's predecessor as scullery-maid] did. It'll quiet 'em.'
> [ ... ]
> So she fell asleep on that moonlight night in May; with her three blankets, her eiderdown and her hot-water bottle. And in her lustreless hair, twenty-four tight curling pins gleamed with unutterable pathos in the Maytime moon.[23]

The tone is clearly suggestive of sexual frustration, as the detail of the tightly pinned yet dull hair suggests. Equally, the scene of head-stroking, and the fact that May too had done this, recalls Fremlin's earlier hints towards Lydia's sexuality being stuck in a phase of adolescent same-sex crushes ('"But I'm relieved May's gone," [Lydia] went on. "She was a nice kid, but she used to be soft about me [ ... ]". She enlarged on these topics for a little, and once more I felt the room thick with a stale boarding-school atmosphere').[24]

To see these hints of sexual frustration as perpetuating a stereotype regarding unmarried female domestic servants is in itself reasonable. However, Fremlin presents what she is writing as reportage rather than fiction, and we have no reason not to take her at her word. In other words, Fremlin's implicit conclusion that Lydia is sexually frustrated may be conditioned by the existence of the stereotype of the prematurely aged repressed housemaid, but in reporting this conclusion she is trying to report reality as she sees it rather than construct a stereotype. In a genre as obsessed with questions of epistemology as incognito social investigation, this distinction is a key one: if Lydia is a stereotype, then this is not because the genre is one peopled with stereotypes but because the genre reports what people observe, and authors too may believe that those whom they are observing act stereotypically. In other words, eventual stereotyping in a text like Fremlin's is *observational* rather than *representational*.

This presumes, though, that the central point in Fremlin's description of Lydia's arrested sexuality is her sexuality per se rather than the fact of it being arrested. Fremlin's intentions are not, in fact, to focus upon questions of sexual frustration as an end in itself: her analysis is not psychological, although, for completeness' sake and the sake of rhetorical power, psychological analysis is of course not overlooked. Rather, it is sociological. Fremlin is interested in the psychosexual states produced by a given way of organizing a section of society insofar as they shed light on that organization. That she is interested in what has produced this arrested development rather than in how it manifests itself can be seen from her treatment of the butler, Mr Thompson. Although when dressed in his butler's wing collar he appears an imposing and dignified figure, his room, which Fremlin has to 'do', reveals his true character. It is a chaotic mess of objects scattered everywhere, including a photograph showing him in a normal collar that reveals his weak chin and timidity when his authority is not bolstered by his work clothes. The phrases that Fremlin uses to describe the state of his room are key: 'a schoolboyish mess' and 'the pathetic schoolboy muddle'.[25] Here too we have arrested development, but this time with no hint of sexual repression to go alongside social repression. The cause of this perpetual adolescence in the staff is very obviously the fact that they work in her ladyship's house, as is made clear from the description of the kitchen-maid Irene, who is twenty-six and 'the only one who was not contented with this nightmare boarding-school, full of children slowly growing grey. [ ... ] I wondered how long it would be before [ ... ] she too became queer as the rest of the household were queer.'[26] Once again, we have the rhetoric of the perpetual school; domestic service as infantilizing prison. Indeed, 'prison' is another metaphor used for life in this household, the chapter ending on a reference to Lydia's already having served 'a third of her time in this model prison';[27] but the most important metaphor for the lives of the servants with whom

Fremlin finds herself at this point is another: 'But the lives we lived were not those of adult human beings; [...but] those of contented poodles eternally on leads...'[28]

If the servants are infantilized and made pets of, then there must be the other side of this arrangement; there must be someone holding the poodles' leads. The employer class is guilty, in Fremlin's eyes, of creating this situation, and she devotes the whole of her ninth chapter to this question. She entitles the chapter 'The Slump in the Marriage Market', but the title is misleading. It is not an excursion into sexual politics and economics for its own sake, shoehorned into a discussion of mistress–maid relationships, as one might suspect upon coming across it in the table of contents. Rather, it is exactly what Fremlin claims it to be at the end of the preceding chapter, which deals with 'miscellaneous grievances' between employers and servants of the type that can be solved with local intervention. 'In the following chapter', Fremlin writes, 'I will discuss a more deep-rooted problem; one that is the most glaring and widely-discussed of all: the problem of Freedom.'[29] The chapter title links the personal and the societal; the unnamed connector is of course domestic service, which places young women into other people's homes to live, creating a situation mixing questions of economics and questions of one's personal life in a way that Fremlin sees as quite unique. Other jobs will of course involve both these aspects of the employee's life, but the infantilization inherent in going to live under another family's roof in a position of subordinacy means that the female domestic servants' problems are far greater. The fact that servants have their time off at a different point in the day from everyone else, and have to be home according to their employer's whims (infantilization again) means that they cannot make friends, as communal social life is organized around 'the assumption that [people] will be free from work from 7 p.m. onwards',[30] and domestic workers have their *afternoons* off. However generous the employer may be, however light the terms of employment, the female house-servant must perforce be cut off from the normal avenues of meeting perspective sexual and marital partners. Fremlin's conclusion is grim: 'Each girl when she enters service must choose between her own life and her duty to her employer. A hard decision for a child of sixteen when she starts work.'[31] The reader's inference is clear: the great risk for girls who enter service is that they remain emotionally and socially *girls*: although it is not their employers' conscious aim to infantilize and desexualize their servants, it is the inevitable result of the system as it stands, and the system is set up by, and in favour of, the employing class. What may be perceived as Fremlin's stereo-typing is not unthinking labelling of young maids as 'old maids' before their time; it is part of a sociological analysis of class relationships.

*Mutatis mutandis,* the same conclusion may be reached regarding Fremlin's description of the titular seven chars. The great majority of the chapter that deals with Fremlin's time as a hospital charwoman is taken up with giving the reader the chars' slightly surrealistic conversation during their breaks, full of repetition, non sequiturs and jokes. There is a little authorial commentary, but the overwhelming drive of the chapter is the Dickensian gusto of the torrent of inconsequential speech. As one reads this chapter, the book's fifth, it is perfectly possible to reach the conclusion that what the book is presenting one with is a series of vignettes, some comic, some pathetic, of what the author has witnessed in her time in service. The comic, salt-of-the-earth, chars could be read, as Delap does, as part of a long tradition of humorous depictions of elderly and jolly working-class women. As we have seen, however, the chapter ends with the 'The day's work was over',[32] ending not only Fremlin's experiences as a hospital charwoman, but also, more importantly, the whole descriptive section of the book. The chapter that immediately follows serves as an interval, detailing replies that Fremlin received to a questionnaire that she sent out to various mistresses of female servants. After this, we leave behind description and move into analysis. As with the question of sexually frustrated housemaids, the depic-tion of jolly chars quickly gains in complexity when considered as only half of a whole: the description that will be followed up by analysis.

The uncommented reporting of the chars' conversation should be considered background given the reader in preparation for the seventh chapter, '"Good Manners"' (here too the inverted commas in the chapter title signal Fremlin's unwillingness to make straightforward value judgements). This examines the belief amongst employers that working-class female servants are rude, sulky, offhand, hostile, abrupt and crude.[33] Fremlin sees the problem as residing in what she considers the erroneous belief that mistress and maid belong to the same culture and are to be judged by the same standards, those of the middle-class employer, according to which the working-class employee has bad manners. Instead, in Fremlin's analysis, servants and householders belong to two different cultures, and the problem is one of a lack of translation between those cultures that leads to the implicit imposition of the socially and economically dominant culture, an imposition that in its near-inevitable failure leads to accusations of a lack of manners.

Fremlin views working-class sociolect and culture as absolutely valid alternatives; more than almost any other incognito social investigator she is able to view both the class that she is investigating and the class to which she belongs with objective emicity, realizing that employers' lack of recognition of this is what is leading to accusations of rudeness, sulkiness and offhandedness: 'The average mistress thinks that working-class language and manners are merely crude and ill-developed imitations of her own. She does not realize that they are fundamentally different in both function and origin; that they are quite as highly-developed as her own, but on entirely different lines.'[34] Fremlin does not judge one group as better, one as worse; unlike many other incognito social investigators, she avoids both romanticizing workers' culture and criticizing it: her interest is not just to understand it in its own right but to understand it vis-à-vis the dominant culture to which she belongs. When Fremlin does show preference for aspects of working-class culture here, it is either clearly a personal and reasonably idiosyncratic preference, as with her dislike of middle- and upper-class verbal contortions to avoid giving offence when refusing an invitation,[35] or, insofar as possible, a preference based on a scientific view of an issue, as with her parenthetical observation that perhaps working-class openness regarding people's physical disabilities might be preferred by a psychologist to middle- and upper-class reticence as it 'does not make the cripple feel that his infirmity is something unmentionable'.[36]

One of the best examples of Fremlin's objectivity and emicity comes in a scene from her time as a hospital charwoman:

> One afternoon at the hospital where I was working as a daily cleaner we eight chars were filing out into the street after work. As we did so a hunch-backed dwarf wobbled past on a child's bicycle. Now, if we had been eight cultured ladies we would have averted our eyes and talked rather hard about something else until he had quite passed. Being eight chars, we did nothing of the sort. With one accord we dashed out on to the pavement with yells of laughter, pointing and gesticulating.
>
> 'Oi-oi! Where's Snow White?' screamed Mrs. Burridge. I had hardly time to be horrified at this blatant lack of feeling before I heard a delighted answering yell from the dwarf:
>
> 'Come and take me pick, shall I? Oo'd like a ride?' and with mutual yells we parted, he wobbling off on the bicycle with delighted grins all over his face, and we pointing and laughing till he was out of sight.

As I say, if we had been ladies we would, out of consideration for his feelings, have treated him as if he was something indecent.

Now, there is no sense in asking which of these ways of treating infirmity is the kindest. They are both purely conventional. A cripple of either class would be horrified at the treatment he received if he went to live among the others. There is no question of 'better' or 'worse' about it.[37]

We have once again the technique, by now familiar, and here made more obvious by the proximity of the two elements, of narrative evidence preceding analysis. The objectivity and emicity in Fremlin's conclusion here should be clear; what is even more interesting is the observer's identification with the observed. Her talk is of 'we' '*eight* chars': there is no suggestion of a split between observer and observed here; Fremlin clearly includes herself when talking of those who, with one accord, laugh at the dwarf, and all references to her being a 'lady' are couched as counterfactuals. The one seeming exception to this, her noting that she hardly has time to be horrified by how the dwarf is being treated, should be read as ironic: Fremlin herself is pointing and laughing, and any 'horror' at any possible perceived vulgarity or unfeelingness of Mrs Burridge's is potential rather than actual; what she should feel rather than what she does. The degree to which Fremlin becomes what she is observing here is deeply unusual in the annals of incognito social investigation; what makes Fremlin unique, though, is not so much this as the fact that she does not take sides. Whilst a char, she is fully a char in actions and feelings, but without allowing her immersive emicity to spill over into partisanship; the same holds true with regard to her status vis-à-vis the class from which she comes. The normal model of the incognito social investigator may be said to be a bipartite one: observer and observed. This may take two forms: Class A observes Class B but remains Class A; Class A observes Class B and (temporarily or otherwise) 'becomes' Class B. Fremlin in *The Seven Chars of Chelsea*, however, creates a tripartite model: observer and *two* observed. Class A observes Class B and 'becomes' (temporarily, in this case) Class B *and in turn observes Class A*. Fremlin, more than any other incognito social investigator, not only achieves this deep level of identification, but also manages to achieve it without ever allowing her identification with, or belonging to, Class A or B to affect her observation or analysis. More than any other incognito social investigator, she is scientific rather than impressionistic; her epiphanies intellectual rather than emotional; never does she risk mistaking her personal reactions for recipes for social change. With all of this in mind, it should come as no surprise that Tom Harrisson, who brought a scientist's eye to the founding of Mass-Observation, and always tried to keep that organization as a scientific rather than an impressionistic enterprise, should have been so eager to recruit Fremlin.

Although Harrisson's eagerness is understandable, given Fremlin's recognition of the problems of social investigation, incognito or otherwise, it may perhaps come nonetheless as a surprise to learn that she was as eager as she was to join Mass-Observation, a body, after all, that in many respects had as part of its rationale the possibility and praiseworthiness of finding out what it is 'like' and telling one's friends about it... The importance of Fremlin's time with Mass-Observation, however, does not lie in the incognito social investigation that she carried out for that organization. What the war years gave her, beyond the opportunity to continue carrying out research into working-class lives, was the chance to have time for reflection on what Mass-Observation could be used for. Once again, we see just how unique Fremlin is amongst incognito social investigators. No other had the opportunity to develop insights formed during individual incognito social investigation in a context of group incognito social investigation.

Fremlin's most important piece of work for Mass-Observation other than her *War Factory* writing was 'The Crisis', a long draft for an eventual book that was planned to be on the lives of middle-class housewives;[38] as Hinton says, Fremlin's 'ambitions for the book went far beyond its ostensible subject'.[39] It shows more than any other of Fremlin's projects for Mass-Observation the potentialities that she saw in the information that (incognito) social investigation could gather, potentialities that, although unrealized, are still breathtaking in their intellectual ambition. Hinton sums it up thus:

> What would happen to the 'ties of affection and emotion 'once the material needs of the family had been taken over by business and the state? This was a question that was to preoccupy critics of late 20th-century individualism. Fremlin had got there early[.][40]

Hinton is right in his conclusion regarding Fremlin's precocity. 'The Crisis' is a remarkable work of social psychology or psychological sociology in its exploration of how technological advances and economic change had contributed to a generation of middle-class women feeling that they had lost their purpose as housewives (or house-managers amongst those with servants). This was a gap that could be filled by voluntary activity; it could also be filled by a job; by hairdressers and manicurists; by bridge parties. In all of these cases, however, the important thing is to be busy, *purely in order to show that one is necessary*. One need not even be good at what one does: if one's failure or incompetence is criticized, it shows that one's actions, indeed one's very existence, has a purpose.

This is extremely exciting analysis, far ahead of other Mass-Observation workers' in its daring. It deserves to be read against Keynes's far better-known 1930 attempts to prophesy regarding the world of work. When, in some hundred years' time from when he was writing, the 'economic problem' was solved, deeper problems would emerge. His analogy for them prefigures Fremlin's work:

> To use the language of to-day – must we not expect a general 'nervous breakdown'? We already have a little experience of what I mean – a nervous breakdown of the sort which is already common enough in England and the United States amongst the wives of the well-to-do classes, unfortunate women, many of them, who have been deprived by their wealth of their traditional tasks and occupations–who cannot find it sufficiently amusing, when deprived of the spur of economic necessity, to cook and clean and mend, yet are quite unable to find anything more amusing.[41]

Keynes's solution, or rather his prophecy, strikes the modern ear as a voice from an age in which utopias seemed far nearer:

> For many ages to come the old Adam will be so strong in us that everybody will need to do *some* work if he is to be contented. We shall do more things for ourselves than is usual with the rich today, only too glad to have small duties and tasks and routines. But beyond this, we shall endeavour to spread the bread thin on the butter – to make what work there is still to be done to be as widely shared as possible. Three-hour shifts or a fifteen-hour week may put off the problem for a great while. For three hours a day is quite enough to satisfy the old Adam in most of us![42]

In this age of what the anthropologist David Graeber has recently and influentially dubbed 'bullshit jobs',[43] if we compare Keynes's implicit vision here of job-sharing as the antechamber to the earthly paradise with Fremlin's analysis of modernity as leading to a proliferation of ultimately pointless activities carried out only to give one a sense of self-worth, activities constantly underlain by the terror of finding oneself surplus to requirements, then we may begin to see just how intellectually exciting and clear-sighted the unknown author's analysis is and was. Fremlin saw in the 1940s that (incognito) social investigation could be put to uses that might perhaps have led to insights that the twenty-first century is still hungering after; the tragedy is that nothing came of her brilliance in this direction.

James Hinton convincingly attributes the disappearance of Fremlin's project to a combination of Bob Willcock and John Ferraby's inability to see the importance and originality of Fremlin's work and Fremlin's own lack of 'intellectual self-confidence'.[44] We may also suspect that this unfortunate lack of confidence is partially attributable to the unfortunate timing of the publication *of The Seven Chars of Chelsea*. Angus Calder's notes of his 1980 interview with Fremlin state that her 'book was well reviewed, just as the war broke out – and sank it'.[45] Although it attracted Harrisson's attention to her, and thus brought to her to Mass-Observation, *The Seven Chars of Chelsea* did vanish: the lack of visibility of her debut work, one suspects, contributed to her not completing 'The Crisis'.

This would have been all the more true if she recognized, as there is no reason to presume she did not, just how remarkable her all too rapidly forgotten first book had been. It deserves a place next to *The Road to Wigan Pier* as a masterpiece of insight into the problems of cross-class contact in Britain in the 1930s (and beyond). There is no other work like it in the corpus of incognito social investigation texts; nor did any other incognito social investigator develop from his or her work a set of insights that would bear fruit in a series of novels that are amongst the most acute observations of society and individual in Britain in the latter half of the twentieth century.

In her 1987 preface to the republication of *War Factory*, Fremlin talks of what she saw as the importance of Mass-Observation's work:

> I felt we were providing unique material for future historians. I still do. How exciting it would be had a record of the Trojan war through the eyes of an ordinary housewife or trader within those walls, and not solely through the eyes of warrior-kings and heroes, as interpreted by tragic poets.[46]

This, with its echoes of Brecht's great poem from the same years as Fremlin's book, 'Fragen eines lesenden Arbeiters',[47] was in fact

Fremlin's aim, knowingly or unknowingly, from before she joined Mass-Observation until long after she had left it; from *The Seven Chars of Chelsea* to a series of novels spanning the second half of the twentieth century: it was an aim she succeeded in with a brilliance not reflected in her now forgotten state. Alas, her papers are now destroyed; lost amongst them the manuscript for a 1980s book of social investigation into nocturnal London street life,[48] a topic that has become very fashionable amongst academics:[49] here too we see that Celia Fremlin, that acutest of observers of the home and perhaps greatest of all incognito social investigators, was so far ahead of the game once again when she turned her attention to those unhomed at night that her pioneering status has unjustly consigned her to oblivion.

Fremlin is yet another rarity amongst incognito social investigators in that she drew upon her experiences to write novels. Orwell too did this, of course, with various episodes in *A Clergyman's Daughter* using material garnered whilst researching what would become *Down and Out in Paris and London*. Where Fremlin differs from her far more famous male counterpart is in the fact that what she used in her fiction was not so much material that she had observed (after all, how relevant would a 1930s housemaid's experiences be as material for novels set in the 1950s and later?) as an epistemological stance.

The most important of Fremlin's novels from the point of view of the present study is her eighth, *Appointment with Yesterday* (1972), the story of a middle-class woman running from a terrible incident in her past who finds herself class-crossing and employed as a cleaner in middle-class houses. The newly and falsely working-class Milly finds herself through necessity in the role in which her creator had found herself through choice some thirty years earlier.

The middle-class and middle-aged Milly finds herself penniless and friendless in the south coast town of Seacliffe. Once she has found work, she takes a room in a lodging-house; the chaotic atmosphere of Mrs Mumford's, with her two fellow lodgers, the shambolic students Jacko and Kevin, recalls the hilarity of the boarding-house ironically described as a 'bad' place in the title of the fourth chapter of *The Seven Chars of Chelsea*, just as the opening words of her new employer (who always calls her 'Mrs Er'), 'Yes, well, can you start tomorrow?', and Milly's surprise at the ease with which she is employed,[50] recall Fremlin's experience in that same '"bad" place'.[51] Such things are relatively trivial examples of recycling lived experience into fiction; they are worth noting in this case, however, as they underline the degree to which *Appointment with Yesterday* is almost as much fictionalization as it is fiction.

Equally, barbed asides on class nominally coming from Milly, but similar examples of which can be found throughout Fremlin's fiction, take on special relevance when one considers this novel's genesis. For example, Kevin borrows a suitcase to lend to Milly from someone Jacko describes as 'a classy friend'; Kevin insists that he is not a friend but only an acquaintance:

> Milly understood at once that to admit to upper-class friends would be damaging to his status in the student community. Lads like Kevin and Jacko, busy trying to live-down their glaringly non-working-class backgrounds, had to be careful about this sort of thing.[52]

In themselves, such semi-authorial sociological musings, scattered as they are throughout the whole of Fremlin's oeuvre, do not necessarily imply a link, causal or otherwise, with her earlier social investigation experiences: after all, we might posit that what interested Fremlin in the 1930s is also what still interested her in the 1970s, and that the passing of time had not affected the way in which her original mind approached the issues that interested it. Nonetheless, it can be argued that Fremlin's novel is *the* great fictionalization of incognito social investigation.

Where *Appointment with Yesterday*, more than any other of Fremlin's novels, can be seen as the secret sequel to *The Seven Chars of Chelsea* is in how its undeclared fictionalization underpins the whole epistemo-methodological structure that events force Milly to experience. On one level, this is obvious: Milly's situation mirrors that of her creator some three decades earlier, and this is a central part of the plot of the novel. More important and more interesting, however, are those parallels that are unnecessary to the plot; the non-structural asides that make *Appointment with Yesterday* not just partial fictionalized autobiography but also a fictionalization of the whole process of incognito social investigation. By 'non-structural asides' are meant moments within the novel that on the one hand do not advance the plot and on the other give such insights as they do into character or atmosphere without it being necessary that they have the exact content they do. Perhaps the best example of what is meant here comes when Milly muses on the habits of one of the women whose houses she cleans, Mrs Day, whom she has never met in person, and on the existence (or otherwise) of Mr Day or Mrs Day's lover(s), insofar as any of this may be deduced from the incongruous mixture of clothes, furnishing and sundries found in the flat. As the narrator says, 'the only Mrs Day [Milly] knew was the one she had gradually constructed, clue by clue, from the trail of evidence left around the flat';[53] equally, Milly feels it rather sad that Mrs Day does not have the same possibility of playing this game of deduction regarding the woman who cleans her flat: 'But there were no clues that way round: no data on which to work. Just a clean flat in place of a dirty one[.] Even the most fanciful employer couldn't build much of a picture of her Daily Help out of that.'[54] This clearly is a reflection of the situation in which an incognito social investigator of the Banksian type finds herself vis-à-vis her employers. It also – more interestingly – encapsulates the epistemological problem that makes incognito social investigation necessary. Whereas the class that is the object of Banksian incognito social investigation of this type, that comprising servants, has a remarkable degree of free rein to collect information on its masters and attempt to draw inferences from it regarding the employer class, the employer class can have no such intimate knowledge of its servants without recourse to incognito social investigation. As well as this epistemo-methodological point, we should note too the comic scientific dryness of a term such as 'data': it both ironically undercuts Milly's far from serious pseudo-scientific analysis of the mysterious Day(s) and is a non-ironic pointer to the issues raised above. This section also sheds light on Milly's changing character. On the one hand we see her relaxing into her role as a cleaner and finding entertainment in it where she can; on the other, as the subtext clearly implies, this epistemological disparity between master and servant works in her favour: she can hide in the role of a daily help and be unknown and unknowable in a way that would have been impossible had she remained in the employer class. Although this episode does have a structural role to play within the novel insofar as it as it gives the reader insight into Milly's changing character and how the role that she has assumed is one made necessary by social conditions, the *details* of this episode are not ineluctable with regards to the plot. It is necessary to show how Milly's character develops; it is not necessary *to the plot* that Fremlin does this through reflection on incognito social investigation rather than, for instance, showing Milly increasing the speed and ease with which she cleans on the one hand and having her experience the social and psychological phenomenon whereby such people as cleaners are 'invisible' through simply being ignored by the people around her on the other. Her choice to do so makes it clear that *Appointment with*

*Yesterday* is not just the psychological thriller that it was marketed as; it is also a novel about social investigation. It should be stressed that this is not to say that what we are faced with here is an example of the same theme being worked out on two different levels. The theoretical issues surrounding (incognito) social investigation are not inherently connected with Milly's psychological and social situation; nor should we read the personal, plot-based, level of the narrative (Milly) as mirroring or being mirrored by the abstract, methodology-based, level (incognito social investigation). The abstract level is connected to the personal insofar as it provides a structure; other than that, however much Fremlin's quiet skill in writing may disguise it, the two levels do not require each other. The personal narrative level offers the author a way to make a treatise on incognito social investigation attractive; it is the easily digested bait hiding a far less enticing hook. *Appointment with Yesterday* is both a psychological thriller and a treatise on incognito social investigation with examples of the sort of insights that that methodology alone, Fremlin clearly holds, can give.

Fremlin's great achievement in this novel and elsewhere (all that has been said above regarding the two levels of narrative holds for all of her novels to a greater or lesser extent; they are all simultaneous sociological treatises and psychological thrillers, without it ever being clear which, if either, is the primary function) is to do what Judy Giles somewhat misleadingly claims she does in *The Seven Chars of Chelsea*: 'blur the conventional disciplinary boundaries between sociology and literature'.[55] This is not the only case where this happens with incognito social investigation, for the 1930s (to which *The Seven Chars of Chelsea* and the genesis of Fremlin's fascination for the field properly belong) are particularly rich with regards to this.

One of the most interesting cases of this slippage between texts that present themselves as reportage and texts that present themselves as fiction comes in one of the most famous examples of one of the most (stereo) typical interwar genres in Britain: the Golden Age whodunnit.[56] This has long been regarded as having been brought to its apogee by the 'Queens of Crime', Agatha Christie, Dorothy L. Sayers and Margery Allingham, and it is to the last of these that incognito social investigation provided a source of inspiration.[57]

On 5 February 1971 the *Los Angeles Times* columnist Charles Champlin wrote an elegiac eulogy for Allingham's Albert Campion novels; the occasion was the publication of *Mr. Campion's Quarry* by Allingham's widower, Philip Youngman Carter. In it Champlin recounts how he had sent a cutting of his previous appreciation of Campion, 'Early 007 Still at Work', published in the same newspaper in 1965, to the detective's creator. This was something he had never done before, and he was gratified by the response:

> 'One plods along sending one's work out into the blue and getting a fair share of reward,' Miss Allingham wrote me, 'but without ever knowing if anyone sees the main "grand programme" until suddenly, after years and years, one gets a splendid appreciation which shows that every point has been taken and the whole exercise has come off after all.'
>
> What I'd said was that the best mysteries, and Miss Allingham's most especially, revealed the social history of England over a 40-year period as clearly as many more earnest works.[58]

Margery Allingham's 'grand programme' in the Campion novels was something more specific than an exploration of 'the social history of England': it was rather an examination of the English class system and, more precisely, movement within it. This was intimately connected with Allingham's first-hand acquaintance with an incognito social investigator, albeit an anomalous one: her brother Philip.

Albert Campion first appears in *The Crime at Black Dudley* (1929), where he is not the protagonist. He is introduced as 'the fresh-faced young man with the tow-coloured hair and the foolish, pale-blue eyes behind tortoiseshell-rimmed spectacles' with a 'slightly receding chin and mouth so unnecessarily full of teeth'.[59] He is a stereotypical 1920s 'silly ass', a more fatuous, parodic, version of Lord Peter Wimsey. As the novel goes on, however, he is revealed both to be an adventurer ('"To cut it short, in fact, I do almost anything within reason – for a reasonable sum, but nothing sordid or vulgar – quite definitely nothing vulgar"'),[60] and an aristocrat who uses Campion (the name chosen as the red campion is a flower that recalls the Scarlet Pimpernel) as his pseudonym. *The Crime at Black Dudley* is of interest chiefly because it marks Campion's first appearance, and had Campion not become Allingham's lead character, then the question of his position within society would have been of little interest.[61]

The second Campion novel, *Mystery Mile*, is that in which Campion moves to centre stage. It marks too the appearance of Magersfontein Lugg, Campion's ex-burglar factotum, whose role would become more important in terms of questions of social class as the series went on. In some respects, just as Campion mirrors Lord Peter Wimsey, Lugg is

Allingham's riposte to Sayers's extremely proper Bunter, his lordship's valet and former batman, as Campion's exchange with Sir Leo in *The Case of the Late Pig* slyly suggests:

> 'Extraordinary fellow, your man [ ... ] Save your life in the war?'
> 'Dear me, no!' I said with some astonishment, 'Why?'
> [ ... ] 'I don't know. Thought just crossed my mind.'[62]

In the later novels *Flowers for the Judge* and *The Fashion in Shrouds*, we see Lugg exhibiting pretentions to gentility, a situation that Allingham presents as comic.[63] This might lead us to posit that Allingham is in fact a snob,[64] mocking working-class attempts to move about within the social structure whilst making her hero an aristocrat who is able to move downwards. This is difficult to sustain, however, when figures who are unable to adapt (such as the Faradays in *Police at the Funeral*) are presented in a quite clearly negative manner that in no way implies an uncritical approval of the upper and upper-middle classes. Equally, Lugg is comic because of the gap between his occasional attempts to become a 'proper' gentleman's gentleman and his refusal to dissimulate his origins and character in any way – it is his *inability* to change that is comic, not the desire in itself. This can be seen by comparing Lugg with Branch, the butler in *Look for the Lady*, who has undergone a similar trajectory from criminal to respected servant, with the difference that he is good at it, and can switch between classes, and is at no point presented as anything other than admirable.

Perhaps the novel that makes clearest the fact that in the person of Albert Campion beneath the amateur detective there lurks a social investigator is Allingham's fourth to chronicle his adventures: *Police at the Funeral* (1931), a strange tale of madness and murder in a cloistered Cambridge family still ruled by an octogenarian matriarch, Caroline Faraday. The family are a remnant of the Victorian upper-middle classes, and Campion is asked to investigate by the Faradays' solicitor precisely because he is 'a gentleman', and thus able to observe and question with an understanding of what is meaningful within such a class-bound situation;[65] equally, Stanislaus Oates, the (lower-middle-class) police inspector, implicitly complains to Campion that his inability to move between classes hinders him in the investigation in a way that the amateur does not experience.[66] Campion becomes a figure whose very fixedness in class terms (Mrs Faraday knows his true name as she knows his grandmother) paradoxically allows him to become a go-between: he is the only character in the novel equally able to talk to Mr Faraday, the tramp Old Bee and all classes in between. He is fixed *in others' minds*, but not his own, and is therefore willing and able to become a sort of social investigator.

Campion, therefore, is clearly inter alia an example of detective as social investigator (and vice versa); in order to see why this is not merely a case of an author making use in her fiction of a theme generally present in the culture in which she was writing in journalism and elsewhere, which would after all be very far from remarkable, we need to turn our attention to the Campion novels from 1931 and 1936: *Look to the Lady* and *Flowers for the Judge*. The former is the story, vaguely tinged with the supernatural, of the attempted theft of a legendary chalice, and its interest to us here would at first appear to reside in the opening chapter, where 'Percival St John Wykes Garth, only son of Colonel Sir Percival Christian St John Garth, Bt, of the Tower, Sanctuary, Suffolk' is found reduced to penurious homelessness,[67] having fallen out with his father over a youthful marriage. Much more important, however, is Campion's relationship with the Gypsies who come to his rescue late in the book, and to whom he is known as Orlando. Attentive readers may recall already having seen the name somewhere in the book: it *is* in the book, but not in the novel, for *Look to the Lady* bears the laconic dedication 'To Orlando'.[68]

Who is the mysterious 'Orlando' of the paratext? We have here to look at the curious career of Margery Allingham's brother, Philip. A few years younger than her, he left a series of unsuccessful office jobs in 1928 to become first a travelling palmist and then a circus barker. His nickname amongst the Gypsies whom he frequented in fairgrounds across the country was 'Orlando'.[69] It is no great leap to see in the story of Philip Allingham a partial source for Albert Campion, especially in *Look to the Lady* with, as Julia Jones puts it, its '*mélange* of full-blooded gypsies, fairground characters and race touts'.[70]

Margery edited the manuscript of what would become her brother's memoirs, published under the title *Cheapjack* in 1934, and soon a best-seller. Two years later she published *Flowers for the Judge*, in which the murder is not the only mystery solved. Also solved is the mystery of Tom Barnabas, who vanishes into thin air twenty years before the novel begins. It transpires that he has left the family job in publishing that so bores him to become a circus acrobat, a trajectory followed in the novel by his brother who after the events recounted joins his brother's circus as a clown. We have here both a Romantic idea of escape to a freer, simpler life and – more crucially, given its omnipresence in Allingham – the idea that class is not fixed, that one *can* change it and escape the constrictions that a belief in its fixity create.

Although a fascinating work, *Cheapjack* is not an example of an incognito social investigation text *stricto sensu*. On the one hand, as Francis Wheen notes in his introduction to the 2010 reprint, whilst people such as Orwell and the rest of the crowd of 1930s 'slummers' logically 'strove to look shabby, Philip Allingham chose a top-hat and tails as his working clothes with no hesitation or embarrassment'.[71] His class-passing was far more complex, in this sense, than in the usual case: the fact of his being middle class was an advantage in his new chosen trade, and the evening wear that he wore if anything projected a more upper-class background than was in reality his. More importantly, on the other, Philip Allingham was not living the fairground life to report back on it: he chose it as a job more entertaining and better remunerated than those he had essayed thitherto. The importance of *Cheapjack* and of Philip Allingham's life lies in how his sister and writing collaborator used the methodological questions raised by her brother's experiences in her fiction.

The most important of Margery Allingham's works in this regard is her 1941 Campion novel *Traitor's Purse*. This is the story of how Campion, notwithstanding the amnesia he is suffering from for much of the novel, discovers and destroys a forgery operation aimed at flooding Britain with counterfeit notes to undermine the economy (a plot that beginning as a pre-war Nazi stratagem but taken over by the megalomaniac British villain in order to leave him as the only person able to save the government). Part of the machinations to get the notes into circulation involve the collation of addresses of the unemployed, work that is carried out by an organization named Surveys Limited, founded and run by a certain Mr Pyne. One of the other characters describes Pyne's organization as follows:

> 'They're an information bureau. If you want to build a factory or start up a business in an unknown locality they'll get out all the dope on the place for you. They're remarkably thorough. Apart from all the usual stuff, they tabulate the most intimate details, including some very shrewd work on public opinion and estimates of local wealth. In fact they'll sound every possible depth for you in strictest confidence. Pyne told me once that he had ten thousand agents all over England. That probably means that he's employed about half that number at some time or other during his career. I imagine any man to whom he's ever given five bob for personal views on

local conditions in included in the aggregate, but still, to do him justice, he does seem to get the commissions.'[72]

An army of observers who record quantitative and qualitative data on the British public; a private concern that has moved into government work for the war effort; a gang of organized snoopers collecting information on those amongst whom they live: Pyne's Surveys Limited is clearly a version of Mass-Observation.

There are two *loci classici* of references to Mass-Observation in fiction from the late 1930s and early 1940s, both in novels, such as *Traitor's Purse*, that sit uneasily on the line between 'serious' and 'genre' fiction. These are in Graham Greene's *The Confidential Agent* (1939) and Nicholas Blake's (which is to say C. Day-Lewis's) *Malice in Wonderland* (1940), but these better-known uses of Mass-Observation for the purposes of fiction differ greatly from what Allingham does. In *Malice in Wonderland*, Paul Perry, although initially reticent – rather self-aggrandizingly so – about his position as a Mass-Observer, does when circumstances dictate come clean about what he is and why he is in the holiday camp: 'People are apt to draw in their horns if they think they're being got at, though of course Mass Observation is pretty well known to the man in the street by now, and I myself make no secret of being an Observer if asked point-blank.'[73] Equally, Mr Muckerji in *The Confidential Agent* is happy to mention (at however unsuitable a moment) that he is involved in Mass-Observation: 'You know how it is, Mrs Mendrill, we mass observers are always on duty.'[74] Their belonging to Mass-Observation is very much part of the 1930s cultural context;[75] it is on one level background. This is not to say that it does not also have other roles to play: Muckerji's up-to-date scientism is inter alia a contrast to D.'s history as a scholar of Old French, the changes in methodologies and epistemologies mirroring how D.'s past gentleness and humanity has been superseded by the world in which he now finds himself; Paul Perry's position as a Mass-Observer is also very much about giving Day-Lewis a way to explore class difference. In both of these cases, however, Mass-Observation, which is openly named, is shown as part of the 1930s scene (although *Malice in Wonderland* was not published until 1940, it is set before the outbreak of war). It is not in itself made part of any wider debate.

In *Traitor's Purse* the situation is more complex. Pyne's organization is obviously not the historical one founded by Harrisson, Madge and Jennings – the description of it as a 'small army of well-paid crooks' alone would have made it impossible even to hint at the real organization's name.[76] Above all, its existence within a novel that is a part of a series of works exploring class-passing, especially given the extra-textual detail of the adventures of Philip Allingham, mean that *Traitor's Purse* should also be read as a novel about differing incognito social investigation types. On the one hand we have the modern anonymous organization typified by Mass-Observation outside the novel and Surveys Limited within it; on the other, we have the more traditional individual(istic) type exemplified by Albert Campion within the novel and Philip Allingham (or George Orwell, or James Greenwood, or Elizabeth L. Banks) outside it.[77] These competing methodologies in incognito social investigation also reflect debates over amateurism and professionalism: the gentleman amateur Campion against the modern corporate businessman Pyne. The question of moral honesty and dishonesty is in fact irrelevant at this level: what matters is the battle between the lone figure who has to be able to change his own social status and run the risks associated therewith – it is no coincidence that Campion suffers from amnesia and doubt in his own identity for most of the novel – and the managerial figure who collects information from others who perform the actual tasks and run the actual risks. On the one hand we have a figure who has to combine the skills of the investigator who collects information with those of the analyst who makes use of it; on the other, we have the specialist in collecting, analysing or organizing, but not all three. Allingham dramatizes this clash of methodologies, and Campion's victory – and the victory of all those who followed Greenwood's example or Banks's – over Pyne and the currents that would change incognito social investigation into a branch of anthropology as Mass-Observation were attempting is neatly symbolized by the fact that the explosion in which the forged banknotes are destroyed kills not the megalomaniac who would become dictator but rather the much lesser villain, Pyne.

We have already touched upon the prevalence of various forms of class-crossing in 1930s Britain, of which incognito social investigation was only one facet. This prevalence is mirrored in the degree to which so popular an author as Allingham was willing to fictionalize the questions raised by the phenomenon in a series of mass-market books. It is also visible in the examples that we have seen of the presence of Mass-Observation in fiction in popular genres then and in the early 1940s.

Mass-Observation has already been mentioned several times in this study. However, I would argue that although individual examples of incognito social investigation in the various traditions classified here may be found taking place under the organization's aegis,[78] Mass-Observation itself should not be classified as belonging to the phenomena examined here. Jed Esty has argued that Mass-Observation was 'one of the most visible signs of the fact that the anthropological eye of British intellectual life began during the 1930s to train its gaze back onto England after years of colonial fieldwork',[79] and it is to the history of nominally more purely scientific methodologies and the texts arising therefrom that we should look for Mass-Observation's lineage rather than the journalistic tradition (s) created by Greenwood and Banks. Tom Harrisson, whose 'Worktown' investigation as part of Mass-Observation involved the most examples of incognito social investigation in its widest sense, himself observed in the account of the project's genesis that he wrote for the Mass-Observation book *The Pub and the People* in 1942 that 'While studiously tabulating the primitive, we had practically no objective anthropology of ourselves, despite many "social surveys" on a statistical basis. I determined, there-fore, to devote as much as possible of the rest of my life to studying the so-called civilized peoples of the world.'[80] The incognito social investigation side of Mass-Observation grew out of a tradition of scientific methodology rather than journalistic, and it is unsurprising but key that in the same piece Harrisson talks of having to turn for guidance in matters regarding 'techniques of observation not to any of the incognito social investigators of lesser scientific pretence discussed here, but rather to 'field work that has been done in America, where sociology is so much in advance of anything yet seen in Europe'.[81]

American sociology, through figures such as Walter Wyckoff and in his two-volume account of his time as a tramp and casual worker, *The Workers* (1897–8),[82] offered similar results to the British journalistic tradition, but with a respectable academic pedigree.[83] As Mark Pittinger observes, what Wyckoff, from 1895 a lecturer in sociology at Princeton,[84] saw before him was a new and under-explored field for 'an ambitious young *scholar*'.[85] The American tradition, inspired as it was by German sociological work,[86] was, at least potentially, academic and – for want of a better adjective – *respectable* in a way that the old British tradition, the bastard journalistic child of James Greenwood and Elizabeth L. Banks, could never be.[87] Mass-Observation, for all of its importance, represents an attempt to import the American incognito social investigation tradition to Britain far more than a stage in the history considered here, whether Banksian or Greenwoodian.

Respectability would finally be achieved by British incognito social investigation, and it would be achieved within the Banksian tradition, but it would remain a predominantly journalistic rather than academic respectability. George Orwell brought Greenwoodian incognito social investigation to literary canonicity in the 1930s; Banksian incognito social investigation was brought to journalistic and political respectability much later, by Polly Toynbee in the early years of the new millennium. To see how this latest chapter in the Banksian tradition came about, however, we need to look away from Britain for a while and turn our gaze to the other side of the Atlantic.

May 2001 saw the publication in the United States of a book that was to be a reasonably constant presence on the non-fiction bestseller lists in the coming months, a book described in the few lines that the *New York Times* allots to those on its lists as 'A social critic reports on what it was like to become a member of the working poor'.[88] The book was *Nickel and Dimed: On (Not) Getting By in America*; its author the veteran journalist and campaigner Barbara Ehrenreich. The speed with which the book became canonical can be judged by the front cover of the 2011 American edition, which has proudly emblazoned across the top 'THE TENTH ANNIVERSARY EDITION OF THE CLASSIC BESTSELLER'. The back-cover blurb goes further: the book 'has become an essential part of the national discourse'. The importance of Ehrenreich's book is not limited to the American context; in Britain too its influence was felt. The *New York Times* summary is ambiguous, though: Ehrenreich in fact 'became' a member of the working poor voluntarily and temporarily. She represents the most recent efflorescence of Banksian incognito social investigation, and thus of incognito social investigation more broadly. *Nickel and Dimed* explores its author's experiences in a series of low-paid jobs: waitress, house-cleaner, shop assistant.

Although *Nickel and Dimed* is pre-eminently a work coming out of the American situation, its role within the late history of British incognito social investigation texts is such that some attention needs to be devoted to it here. What is of interest is not Ehrenreich's emicity or eticity, but rather how the text presents itself. On one level, it fits squarely within the American tradition of incognito social investigation texts as an academic and quasi-academic phenomenon. Although much of that part of the paratext aimed at marketing – cover, blurb, the three pages of encomiastic quotes from reviews – presents the book as very much an accessible, popular, journalistic, work, the text itself is filled with detailed footnotes referring to official statistics, newspaper articles, government acts and academic studies. This paratextual semi-academicity, however, contrasts with much of the text, the tone of much of which is personal and informal, and feels far closer to the British, journalistic, tradition inaugurated by Banks. The tensions created by this dual nature of Ehrenreich's text can be seen early on in the book, when she is describing her time waitressing in Florida. She recounts her growing friendship with her fellow workers:

> Still, no one is homeless, or cops to it anyway, thanks usually to a working husband or boyfriend. All in all, we form a reliable mutual support group: if one of us is feeling sick or overwhelmed, another one will 'bev' a table or even carry trays for her. If one of us is off sneaking a cigarette or a pee, the others will do their best to conceal her absence from the enforcers of corporate rationality.[89]

The registers of language reflect Ehrenreich's own mixed role as observer and participant: the informality of 'cops' and 'pee' and the unexplained waitress's jargon of 'bev' is set against the more formal 'mutual support group' and 'enforcers of corporate rationality'. The final words, which clearly represent the observer's commentary rather than her 'neutral' reporting, are a defiantly polysyllabic stepping out of character, so to speak, emphasizing the personal and the subjective. However, owing to a convention of citation, the quotation as given above is not quite accurate. In the original text, the final full stop is followed by a superscript 5, directing the reader to a footnote beginning 'Until April 1998, there was no federally mandated right to bathroom breaks. According to Marc Linder and Ingrid Nygaard, authors of *Void Where Prohibited: Rest Breaks and the Right to Urinate on Company Time* (Cornell University Press, 1997)', which then gives a long quote from the academic study in question.[90] At a textual moment in which Ehrenreich asserts her subjectivity and thus implicitly the non-academic nature of her book, the footnote pulls the text back into the American academic sociological tradition, with a citation that both in form (the standard formula of 'according to $x$ and $y$, authors of $z$'; the careful giving of publisher and year) and content (the simple fact that the book being quoted is published by a university press) is indistinguishable from similar references in untold theses and dissertations.

Indeed, this tension between whether *Nickel and Dimed* is American science or Banksian belles-lettres is present in Ehrenreich's own account of the book's genesis. The introduction begins with her recounting her lunch with the editor of *Harper's*, Lewis Lapham, during which the conversation casually drifted to a topic in which Ehrenreich was known to be interested: poverty, particularly that of women amongst the working poor. The moment is presented as a mixture of epiphany and misunderstanding:

> Then I said something that I have since had many opportunities to regret: 'Someone ought to do the old-fashioned kind of journalism – you know, go out there and try it for themselves.' I meant someone much younger than myself, some hungry neophyte journalist with time on her hands. But Lapham got this crazy-looking half smile on his face and ended life as I knew it, for long stretches at least, with the single word '*You*'.[91]

On the one hand, we have the explicit placing of what Ehrenreich is being asked to do in a *journalistic* tradition, albeit an 'old-fashioned' one about which no details are given. This lack of detail about her antecedents as incognito social investigator journalists need not be read in any way as a deliberate lack of acknowledgement; as we shall see with Polly Toynbee, by the late twentieth century and early twenty-first awareness of the history of incognito social investigation had very much vanished from its practitioners' frame of reference. Equally, the clearly semi-ironic self-deprecation of her often having had opportunity to regret her suggestion combines with the immediacy of the description in the last sentence and the stress on its italicized paragraph-ending pronoun to make it clear that what the reader is about to read is no dispassionate social science text but rather a belletrist one, knowingly using all the rhetorical arsenal that scientific literature eschews.

Three paragraphs later, however, the tone very much changes. Ehrenreich has mulled over Lapham's suggestion, finding reasons not to take him up on it. Her conclusion is as follows: 'In the end, the only way to overcome my hesitation was by thinking of myself as a scientist, which is, in fact, what I was educated to be.'[92] *As a scientist*: notwithstanding the massive textual and paratextual claims the book makes to belonging somewhere on the journalism/belles-lettres scale, Ehrenreich insists on placing herself, and thus also her text, within a scientific framework, stating a few lines later, 'In the spirit of science, I first decided on certain rules and parameters' (and the relative scientificity of the last word is also not casual).[93] *Nickel and Dimed*, therefore, is a text with a split personality: it is almost aggressively part of the American tradition explored by

Pittinger, a tradition where incognito social investigation texts are at the very least on the margins of academia, if not firmly anchored therein; it is simultaneously alien to that tradition and far nearer to the British, Banksian, tradition of incognito social investigation as woman's work that talks about women's work.[94]

Just as it took the American Elizabeth L. Banks to breathe new life into the relatively moribund genre created by James Greenwood, it took an American, Barbara Ehrenreich, to revivify the Banksian tradition at the turn of the millennium, just over a century after the original 'American Girl' had carried out her campaigns of curiosity. Unlike Banks, however, Ehrenreich's influence was purely from afar: the actual task of carrying out incognito social investigation into twenty-first-century British society was performed by a British journalist – most interestingly, one who some thirty years earlier had already carried out similar research.

Polly Toynbee published *Hard Work: Life in Low-Pay Britain* to much acclaim in 2003. Whereas some incognito social investigators such as Greenwood or Banks became famous because of their activities in the field, although most remained in the obscurity of minor newspapers or little-read books, Toynbee was already a noted public figure, an influential journalist, most importantly for *The Guardian*; a recognized media presence. In this, she has more in common with her American contemporary Ehrenreich than with her British precursors. Indeed, whereas Ehrenreich writes of her fear of being recognized during her time as a waitress in Key West, because of its nearness to her home,[95] as well as reflecting more generally on the possibility of her nature as an 'imposter' from a different economic/social group being observed,[96] Toynbee's analogous fears are much more precise. One of the jobs that she takes on is working in a nursery in the Foreign Office. The part of the job that most perturbs her is taking her charges for their morning walk in Whitehall: 'In my usual life I walk down here many times a week. [ ... ] I rarely walk along Whitehall without bumping into another journalist, an MP or someone I know. [ ... ] There I was in my purple Kinderquest uniform [ ... ]. What would I say to some fellow political journalist, some MP?'.[97] Although she walks past two political figures who know her well, they fail to recognize her. This pre-existing public awareness of Toynbee is paralleled in its importance only by another late Banksian incognito social investigator, the French journalist and former hostage in Iraq, Florence Aubenas, whose *Le quai de Ouistreham* appeared in 2010 to much praise. Within the British tradition examined here, however, Toynbee's position is unique.

*Hard Work* details how its author moves to a council estate near to her home in south London to work in minimum-wage jobs. The jobs that she finds are various: hospital porter, school dinner lady, nursery worker, cold-caller, cleaner, care-home worker... Toynbee opens the book with her receiving a letter from the charity Church Action on Poverty suggesting that she endeavour to spend Lent 2002 living on the then basic minimum wage of £4.10 an hour.[98] She realized that merely living on that wage would not be enough to give an accurate picture of the problems people faced, as 'work has its own costs':[99] she decided not just to move into the Clapham Park Estate, with the agreement of the residents' board and the local council's neighbourhood housing office for the estate, and there live on the minimum wage, but also to work.[100]

Perhaps the most interesting point regarding the genesis of *Hard Work* comes in what Toynbee describes as having been the final coincidence that convinced her to undertake the project: she was asked to provide the introduction to the British edition of *Nickel and Dimed*.[101] This is a fact of key importance. Although Toynbee in moments of self-doubt before the project began criticized it as 'play-acting' and 'Marie Antoinette as a milk maid in the Petit Trianon',[102] her only other reference to there being any sort of tradition of such investigation comes in her reference to Ehrenreich's book. She had no knowledge of the almost 150 years of journalistic and literary tradition stretching back to Greenwood, other than the example of Orwell, on whom, she has said, her generation was brought up.[103] This, as with Ehrenreich's case, shows the degree to which incognito social investigation can be divided into two periods. The initial period begins in 1866 after the publication of Greenwood's 'A Night in a Workhouse' and has come to an end before Orwell publishes *Down and Out in Paris and London* in 1933. This is the period in which there is an awareness, however lacking in detail, of the existence of a tradition; incognito social investigators in this period do not write thinking that what they are doing is something new, and nor do their readers. Orwell's work then becomes the reference point, insofar as there is one, but other-wise there is no sense of writing in a tradition, no sense that works are being created that can – and perhaps should – be read against a whole host of other, similar, works.

In Toynbee's case, her relationship with the incognito social investiga-tion literature of the past is complicated by the fact that she herself had already contributed to it. In the opening chapter of *Hard Work*, as part of her musing over whether to carry out the investigation or not, she writes:

> I picked up the book I wrote some thirty years ago when I was starting out in journalism, a personal experience of a world of manual work I knew nothing about. In *A Working Life* I had travelled the country taking jobs as they came [ ... ]. I worked on the production line at Unilever's Port Sunlight soap factory, lodging in Lord Lever's model workers' village in Birkenhead. In Birmingham I assembled electrical car parts at Lucas's [ ... ]. In a Lyons factory I operated the cream spreader, watching the angel cakes fly past on the conveyor belt. I was a ward orderly in a West London hospital and I joined the WRAC, the women's royal army corps, to be bawled at and brutalised on the parade ground. For a while I lived in Rotherham, lodging with a steel-worker's family, visited a steel works and the coalface down a coal mine.[104]

Toynbee will go on to compare, in the last chapter of *Hard Work*, the situation in the early years of the twenty-first century with that of the early 1970s (*A Working Life* was published in 1971), a comparison already adumbrated here where she first mentions it.

Toynbee's account here, over thirty years after the event, of her first book of social investigation is interesting, and slightly misleading. The list of jobs that she undertook is accurate, but the presentation is ambiguous. 'I had travelled the country taking jobs as they came': this makes no comment on her motivations for doing so – was she taking these jobs in order to write about them, or did she write about them because, through no other reason than necessity, she had had to do them? If we turn to *A Working Life*, we find little clarification at first. The book starts with a description of careers advice sessions that Toynbee sat in on; this somewhat unexplained beginning *in medias res* ends with the observer wondering what the result would be of her taking one of the boys whose interviews she has seen to 'the factories and offices I had seen and worked in'.[105] The following chapter launches directly into an account of Toynbee's time working in a cake factory; the only information that the reader has at this point as to what the author's real status – social investigator? unusually fortunate working-class woman who has been able to publish? – in fact comes from the dust jacket. If we presume a hypothetical reader who picks up the book with no prior knowledge of who its author is, then the first information (other than the author's photograph on the back of the dust jacket) comes in the two-paragraph blurb on the front flap: 'Polly Toynbee spent several months living the material of this book' – a description as ambiguous in its way as that given at the beginning of *Hard Work*: 'The book is by no means intended to be a comprehensive survey of work in this country'; again, 'survey' could be either a collation of information acquired through chance or a deliberate attempt to acquire knowledge. This ambiguity continues on the biography on the back flap: 'Polly Toynbee, the author of *Leftovers*, now works as a journalist for *The Observer*'. Although the fact of her having another book already in print (*Leftovers* being her 1966 novel) points, albeit not unambiguously, to her status as someone who has lived the life she describes as an investigative choice, the presence of the adverb 'now' makes this ambiguous: if she is *now* a journalist, what was she before? Was she in fact the seemingly transient worker the book seems to suggest?[106]

This question is not answered for the hypothetical unprepared reader until the second chapter, where, in passing, she writes that 'In the evenings I had meant to take notes':[107] this is the first suggestion that the author's 'several months living the material of this book' were undertaken as research. This is finally confirmed at the end of the chapter: 'When I left the factory, I went back to see an executive of the department I had worked in. I told him I had worked there incognito and that I was writing a book.'[108] In other words, the true nature of *A Working Life* is not revealed until almost fifty pages in; the exact same ambiguity possibly causing opacity is found in the 2003 description of the book and its genesis. Indeed, the full picture of Toynbee's status in her first book of incognito social investigation only comes in the brief 'Note' appended to the end of the book: 'For some of the jobs that I did I needed the co-operation of the management as they were not the sort of places that employed casual labour. [ ... ]. To the best of my knowledge, while I was working there only the top management and personnel officers in these two factories knew what I was doing there. Neither the workers nor the foremen were told.'[109]

This ambiguity over Toynbee's role, mirrored to some extent by the book's uncertainty over its status (alongside incognito social investigation it contains interviews and normal reporting), may be attributed to how the text came to be written. Toynbee had left Oxford, which she hated, with the idea of working in a factory during the day and writing novels and poetry during the evenings; she found work in a sugar factory, but found that this left her too tired to do any creative or imaginative work in her free time. After this period of her life she was working as a journalist when she discovered people's interest in the manual work that she had done;

deciding that this could be a serious journalistic proposition, she embarked on the research that led to *A Working Life*.[110]

At the time of this first book of social investigation, Toynbee 'was not really political',[111] and although the work has a clear political message in favour of the workers that she meets, a certain lack of sophistication can be seen, leading to what may be read as a level of essentialism. This is most clear in the penultimate chapter, which is not incognito social investigation and talks of the Rotherham steel industry, where she writes: 'The nobility of work is a bizarre concept. In all the jobs I saw and did, in almost all of the jobs for the working classes, I found little that wasn't stultifying and degrading to any normal human intelligence.'[112] 'Jobs *for* the working classes': the preposition is key here – one is not working class because one does a certain job; one does a certain type of job because one is working class. This is not to question the accuracy of Toynbee's implied view of the absence of social mobility in Britain in the early 1970s; rather, it is to note that such a stance must necessarily preclude a certain level of emicity. Such implied essentialism must imply a non-working-class gaze that is unable or unwilling to compromise beyond a certain point, as in the chapter describing Toynbee's time working in a factory making components for cars, where it is early on commented that 'As factories go, it was a good one, but as factories are terrible and deadening places to work in, so was this.'[113] In the end, no evidence is presented as to the universal, essentialist, truth of the general part of the statement on the nature of factories, whereas much is presented in favour of the specific part regarding this particular one; nevertheless, the statement stands. Interestingly, however, Toynbee's youthful etic middle-class essentialism is not focused where one might expect, on the workers, but rather on the jobs that they do: a lack of emicity here does not translate, as it so often does elsewhere, into a lack of empathy.

The nearest that *A Working Life* comes to that negative essentialism that skirts prejudice is in the description of one of Toynbee's fellow workers in the car-part factory, Carla:

> Although she knew I was a student at Oxford [Toynbee had said she was a student doing holiday work], she entirely failed to grasp the fact that my life was and *always* would be quite different to hers. Her knowledge of a middle class life was *only* visualised through a cloud of smoke, as being like her own life if she had more money. [ ... ] Her frame of reference was *necessarily* narrow. She could *only* imagine what she knew, and she was more or less unaware of the privileges she didn't have.[114]

I have italicized those adverbs that imply a social essentialism (again, their accuracy vis-à-vis social mobility is not of importance; what they imply about the author's epistemo-methodological *parti pris* is); the idea that Carla is unable to change, unable to understand another social group's life (although note the specificity of '*a* middle class life' and its buried implication of middle-class individuality as opposed to working-class uniformity) is potentially as deeply anti-empathic as the most prejudiced of Victorian incognito social investigation texts.

Toynbee, however, although still unconsciously favouring middle-class eticity over emicity, still retains empathy, and how she does so leads us to *Hard Work*, a book that does not suffer from the same essentialist generalizations as its predecessor. Immediately after the unconsciously rather negative description of Carla quoted above, Toynbee says that she had found it easy to make friends with her whilst she was inhabiting the role that she set herself, but 'when I got back to my own life, I couldn't write to Carla and tell her I had lied, and had been talking to her only so as to write to her'.[115] The sadness and guilt implicit in this departure are the key to what makes Toynbee's work so interesting, for they provide the most important common thread that connects the rather naïve *A Working Life* with the far more sophisticated and nuanced *Hard Work* (a text, incidentally, intensely focused on the very question of social mobility that its forerunner misses). Guilt in silent departure is found too in the later book, most notably when Toynbee leaves her job working as a dinner lady in a Lambeth school: 'I felt ashamed at going and even more sorry at not explaining to Maggie and Wilma why it was time for me to move on. I missed their companionship as soon as I walked out of the door.'[116] This, as in the case of Carla decades earlier, is true empathy: that is to say, above and beyond empathizing with her colleagues' work situation, Toynbee shows empathy for them as human beings. They lose a colleague, perhaps a friend: this is a cause for guilt and sadness that has in it only recognition of shared humanity; all epistemo-methodological questions of emicity and eticity become irrelevant as the author's status as an incognito social investigator fades away to be momentarily replaced by normal quotidian human interaction.

This decrease in the importance of the questions of methodology and epistemology that we have focused on hitherto is not casual. Just as the younger Toynbee's essentialism unusually focused chiefly on jobs rather than on those who did them, both Toynbees' books have as their real focus not the poor amongst whom they live but the work that they do.

The voyeurism that has otherwise always characterized – however explicitly or implicitly – incognito social investigation is here almost completely absent, just as it is in Ehrenreich's work. There is no longer a necessity felt to describe the poor to the non-poor; the aim now is above all to explain and analyse situations rather than personalities. This, paradoxically, allows the greater empathy that I have described in Toynbee: when the poor lose their strangeness,[117] it necessarily becomes possible to treat them without an outsider's gaze, to empathize not with what is particular to them but with the commonalities they share with the author who is their primary observer and the reader who is their secondary.

It is perhaps too early to classify this neo-Banksian variant as Ehrenreichian incognito social investigation, but just as we have seen how the history of incognito social investigation texts can be divided into two periods – 1866–c.1933 and c.1933–present – according to how aware people were of the tradition existing as opposed to knowing at most Orwell's work, the appearance of *Nickel and Dimed* in 2001 may have heralded the arrival of a third period.[118] This characterized not so much by an increased politicization per se, but rather a new focus not on the poor themselves, nor on the author's adventures amongst them, but rather on the political and societal structures that create the *situation* of the poor. Polly Toynbee has spoken of her uneasiness with what she calls Orwell's romanticization and sentimentalization of the poor:[119] another, more comprehensive, way of saying this would be to talk of the tendency of incognito social investigation texts towards what we may call personalization. In other words, the pre-Ehrenreich tradition has as its overwhelming focus the *personal*, whether of the observed, the observer or both. With Ehrenreich and Toynbee the personal is no longer the focus, but serves rather to supply examples for description and analysis at the structural level.

*Hard Work* is the most recent work within the Banksian tradition analysed by this volume. It serves as a fitting end point, for it marks the beginnings of a potential shift away from incognito social investigation texts as entertainment or revelation of an unknown world towards their becoming actors in policymaking. The subgenre that began in the 1890s with Elizabeth L. Banks presenting herself and others to the gaze of a jaded public for their entertainment has by the early twenty-first century become a means for the politically engaged to present politicians and others with the realities created by what otherwise might risk being viewed as purely abstract structural inequalities.

## NOTES

1. Information regarding Fremlin's life comes unless otherwise noted from: Simmons, Chris. 2014. 'Celia Fremlin: A Biographical Sketch'. In Fremlin, Celia. *The Hours before Dawn*. London: Faber and Faber, pp. vii–xiii.
2. Brighton, The Keep, SxMOA32/32/4.
3. Brighton, The Keep, SxMOA32/32/5.
4. Ibid.
5. Simmons, 'Celia Fremlin', pp. vii–viii.
6. Hinton, James. 2013. *The Mass Observers: A History, 1937–1949*. Oxford: Oxford University Press, pp. 171–2.
7. Brighton, The Keep, SxMOA32/32/4.
8. Brighton, The Keep, SxMOA32/32/5
9. Brighton, The Keep, SxMOA32/32/4.
10. Giles, Judy. 2004. *The Parlour and the Suburb: Domestic Identities, Class, Femininity and Modernity*. Oxford and New York: Berg, p. 81.
11. Fremlin, Celia. 1940. *The Seven Chars of Chelsea*. London: Methuen & Co., p. 116.
12. Ibid., p. 86.
13. Giles, *The Parlour and the Suburb*, pp. 84–5.
14. Ibid., p. 81
15. Ibid., pp. 27–8.
16. Fremlin, *Seven Chars*, p. v.
17. Ibid., p. vi.
18. Ibid., p. 1.
19. Delap, Lucy. 2011. *Knowing Their Place: Domestic Service in Twentieth-Century Britain*. Oxford: Oxford University Press, p. 192.
20. Fremlin, *Seven Chars*, p. 29.
21. Ibid., p. 31.
22. Note the echo of *The Waste Land* in Lydia's talk of her 'nerves'; note too that Judy Giles chooses the *literary* adjective 'Gothic' to qualify the atmosphere of the household described in this chapter.
23. Ibid., p. 49.
24. Ibid., p. 33.
25. Ibid., pp. 44–5.
26. Ibid., p. 40.
27. Ibid., p. 49.
28. Ibid., p. 38.
29. Ibid., p. 131.
30. Ibid., pp. 140–1.
31. Ibid., 142.
32. Ibid., p. 86.

33. Ibid., p. 101.
34. Ibid., p. 103.
35. Ibid., pp. 110–1.
36. Ibid., p. 117.
37. Ibid. pp. 116–7.
38. Brighton, The Keep, SxMOA1/1/9/11/6.
39. Hinton, *The Mass Observers*, p. 317.
40. Ibid., p. 319.
41. Keynes, John Maynard. 1972 [1930]. 'Economic Possibilities for Our Grandchildren'. *The Collected Writings of John Maynard Keynes*, vol. IX, *Essays in Persuasion*. London and Basingstoke: Macmillan and New York: Cambridge University Press, pp. 321–32, p. 327.
42. Ibid., p. 329.
43. Graeber, David. 2013. 'On the Phenomenon of Bullshit Jobs: A Work Rant', *Strike! Magazine*, Summer 2013, pp. 10–11.
44. Hinton, *The Mass Observer*, pp. 319–20.
45. Brighton, The Keep, SxMOA32/32/4.
46. Fremlin, Celia. 1987. Preface to 'Mass-Observation' [Celia Fremlin], *War Factory*, London: The Cresset Library, pp. vii–ix, p. viii.
47. See Brecht, Bertolt. 1967 [1939]. 'Fragen eines lesenden Arbeiters'. *Gesammelte Werke*, vol. 9, Frankfurt am Main: Suhrkamp Verlag, pp. 656–7.
48. Personal correspondence with Margaret Kettlewell, Fremlin's niece.
49. See Beaumont, Matthew. 2015. *Nightwalking: A Nocturnal History of London*. London and New York: Verso.
50. Fremlin, *Seven Chars*, p. 50.
51. Fremlin, Celia. 2014 [1972]. *Appointment with Yesterday*. London: Faber and Faber, p. 26.
52. Ibid., p. 67.
53. Ibid., p. 114.
54. Ibid., p. 117.
55. Giles, *The Parlour and the Suburb*, p. 27.
56. It is no coincidence that the examples examined here of fictionalization of incognito social investigation material both involve 'mystery' fiction, albeit of different types (the psychological domestic thriller in Fremlin's case and the classic whodunnit in Allingham's – although in both cases the label, adopted here purely for the sake of convenience, is at best reductive and at worst misleading). Earlier detective fiction also engages with the possibilities offered by social investigation, whether incognito or otherwise. See Keating, Peter. 1991 [1989]. *The Haunted Study: A Social History of the English Novel 1875–1914*. London: Fontana Press, p. 365; Docker, John. 1994. *Postmodernism and Popular Culture: A Cultural History*. Cambridge: Cambridge University Press, p. 226.

57. For biographical information on Margery Allingham, see Jones, Julia. 2009. *The Adventures of Margery Allingham*. Pleshey: Golden Duck; for information on her brother and the remarkable family in which they grew up, see Jones, Julia. 2012. *Fifty Years in the Fiction Factory: The Working Life of Herbert Allingham*. Pleshey: Golden Duck.
58. Champlin, Charles. 'Final Chapter of Albert Campion'. *Los Angeles Times* 5 February 1971, §IV, p. 1.
59. Allingham, Margery. 1982 [1929]. *The Crime at Black Dudley*. In her *The Margery Allingham Omnibus*. Harmondsworth: Penguin, pp. 7–195, p. 14.
60. Ibid., p. 72.
61. Various hints at Campion's true identity are scattered throughout the novels; for an analysis of what Campion's 'true' social position is, see Johnson, Roger. 2004. 'Albert Campion – the Truth'. In van Hoeven, Marianne (ed.). 2004. *Margery Allingham: 100 Years of a Great Mystery Writer*. N.p.: Lucas Books. 2004, pp. 48–58
62. Allingham, Margery. 2005 [1937]. *The Case of the Late Pig*. London: Vintage, p. 23.
63. The best example can be seen in Allingham, Margery. 2006 [1936]. *Flowers for the Judge*. London: Vintage, pp. 61–4.
64. An accusation implicit in Alison Light's throwaway remarks on Allingham. See Light, Alison. 1991. *Forever England: Femininity, Literature and Conservatism between the Wars*. London and New York: Routledge, pp. 80 and 95.
65. Allingham, Margery. 2007 [1931]. *Police at the Funeral*. London: Vintage, pp. 32–3.
66. Ibid., p. 68.
67. Allingham, Margery. 1982 [1931]. *Look to the Lady*. In her *The Margery Allingham Omnibus*, Harmondsworth: Penguin, pp. 385–589, p. 389.
68. Ibid., p. 386.
69. Jones, *Fiction Factory*, p. 178.
70. Ibid.
71. Wheen, Francis. 2010. Introduction to Allingham, Philip. *Cheapjack: Being the True History of a Young Man's Adventures as a Fortune-Teller, Grafter, Knocker-Worker, and Mounted Pitcher on the Market-Places and Fair-Grounds of a Modern but Still Romantic England*. Pleshey: Golden Duck, pp. ix–xv, p. xii. Note that the book's subtitle firmly distinguishes it from the usual serious and quasi- or pseudo-scientific tone of incognito social investigation texts.
72. Allingham, Margery. 2006 [1941]. *Traitor's Purse*. London: Vintage, p. 91.
73. Blake, Nicholas. 2012 [1940]. *Malice in Wonderland*. London: Vintage, p. 39.

74. Greene, Graham. 1963 [1939]. *The Confidential Agent.* Harmondsworth: Penguin, p. 121.

75. See Cunningham, Valentine. 1988. *British Writers of the Thirties.* Oxford: Oxford University Press, pp. 333–7.

76. Allingham, *Traitor's Purse*, p. 167.

77. Note that Jed Esty has talked about the 'centralizing effect of Mass Observation, particularly with the onset of World War II'. Esty, Jed. 2004. *A Shrinking Island: Modernism and National Culture in England.* Princeton and Oxford: Princeton University Press, p. 45.

78. Fremlin's work that led to *War Factory*, for instance.

79. Esty, *A Shrinking Island*, p. 44. Esty also quite rightly states that 'the thirties witnessed a spike in autoethnographic discourses that projected England qua nation as newly representable in the holistic terms of anthropology' and that this allowed 'English intellectuals found a distinctive way to respond to the imminent collapse of British hegemony' (p. 10); here, however, I feel that he does not recognize enough that forms of writing like *Down and Out in Paris and London* also belonged to a much older tradition that had very little to do with the 1930s situation in itself.

80. Harrisson, Tom. 2009 [1943]. Preface to 'Mass Observation'. *The Pub and the People: A Worktown Study.* London: Faber and Faber, pp. 7–14, p. 7. As with any of Harrisson's statements, we should bear in mind his biographer's caveat: 'he was certainly devious and would sometimes tailor the truth to lead the unwary to a false conclusion'. Heimann, Judith M. 1999. *The Most Offending Soul Alive: Tom Harrisson and His Remarkable Life.* Honolulu: University of Hawai'i Press, p. 3.

81. Harrisson, Preface to 'Mass Observation'. *The Pub and the People*, p. 13.

82. Wyckoff, Walter. 1897. *The Workers: An Experiment in Reality*, vol. 1 *The East.* New York: Charles Scribner's Sons; Wyckoff, Walter. 1898. *The Workers: An Experiment in Reality*, vol. 2 *The West.* New York: Charles Scribner's Sons. For a detailed analysis of Wyckoff's incognito social investigation, see Prude, Jonathan. 2006. 'Experiments in Reality: Wyckoff's Workers'. In Schrader Lang, Amy and Cecelia Tichi (eds.), *What Democracy Looks Like: A New Critical Realism for a Post-Seattle World.* New Brunswick and London: Rutgers University Press, pp. 144–57.

83. It is worth noting that the distinctly non-academic Harry A. Franck in the draft of his unpublished autobiography mentions reading Wyckoff as research for his Sociology 22 thesis that drew upon his hoboing experience: 'Of course I read with pleasure Jack London's hoboing stories and Josiah Flynt's "Tramping with Tramps", not to mention the personal experiences of the late Professor Wyckoff of Princeton, the first avowed sociologist to put on overalls and go to see for himself.' (Ann Arbor, Special Collections Library University of Michigan, Franck, Box 5, *Tales of a Vagabond/*

*Making of a Vagabond*). The presence of Wyckoff alongside Jack London and Josiah Flynt is a significant mixture of academic and literary figures that supports Franck's status as being as much in the British, literary, tradition, as the American, sociological, one.

84. For details of Wyckoff's life and career, see sv. 'Wyckoff, Walter Augustus', *Dictionary of American Biography*, 1936, London: Humphrey Milford and Oxford University Press and New York: Charles Scribner's Sons.

85. Pittinger, Mark. 2012. *Class Unknown: Undercover Investigations of American Work and Poverty from the Progressive Era to the Present*. New York and London: New York University Press, p. 17. My italics.

86. Ibid., pp. 11–12.

87. Pittinger (ibid., p. 11) notes a line of descent in American incognito social investigation running from Charles Booth, whose work 'marked a shift within the British tradition from Greenwood's brand of individual journalistic [ . . . ] impressionism'; what he does not note is how the Greenwoodian tradition continued after Booth, providing not just a distant precursor to the American tradition, but also a whole parallel body of texts.

88. 'Adult New York Times Bestseller Lists for 2001', available at http://www.hawes.com/2001/2001.htm, accessed on 10 May 2016.

89. Ehrenreich, Barbara. 2011 [2001]. *Nickel and Dimed: On (Not) Getting By in America*. New York: Picador, p. 37.

90. Ibid., n. 5.

91. Ibid., pp. 1–2.

92. Ibid., p. 3. Ehrenreich has a PhD in biology.

93. Ibid., p. 4.

94. There is also an argument to be made regarding Ehrenreich's self-presentation as a scientist here in terms of politics: she clearly wishes both to emphasize the fact that the results of her research will not be dictated a priori by what she is looking for owing to her leftist convictions. Nonetheless, although the *presence* of this tension between scientificity and non-scientificity can be explained synchronically in this way, I would argue that the *strength* of that tension is only fully explainable diachronically in terms of the history of American incognito social investigation texts.

95. Ibid., p. 11.

96. Ibid., pp. 7–9. Regarding her very insightful conclusions about how it is in fact impossible to pretend in cases like this (if one is doing a job, one is doing a job: motivations are ultimately meaningless), see Chapter 3 above.

97. Toynbee, Polly. 2003. *Hard Work: Life in Low-Pay Britain*. London: Bloomsbury, p. 120.

98. Ibid., pp. 1–2.

99. Ibid., p. 11.

100. Ibid. See Chapter 7 below for discussion of Toynbee's living on the Clapham Park Estate.

101. Ibid., p. 10.

102. Ibid., p. 12.

103. Interview with Polly Toynbee, whom I thank for her generosity in being willing to discuss her incognito social investigation with me, 16 July 2014. Hereafter 'PT Interview'.

104. Toynbee, *Hard Work*, p. 3.

105. Toynbee, Polly. 1971. *A Working Life*. London: Hodder and Stoughton, p. 32.

106. It should be noted that Toynbee's family relations – the novelist and critic Philip Toynbee her father; Arnold Toynbee her grandfather – as given at the end of the back flap of the dustjacket do suggest to our hypothetical reader that the author's background is a privileged one.

107. Toynbee, *A Working Life*, p. 39.

108. Ibid., p. 45.

109. Ibid., p. 157.

110. PT interview.

111. Ibid.

112. Toynbee, *A Working Life*, p. 141.

113. Ibid., p. 60.

114. Ibid., p. 80. Italics mine.

115. Ibid.

116. Toynbee, *Hard Work*, p. 114.

117. Or, more accurately: when an author no longer feels the need to treat the poor as strange; it would be contentious to read into this a universal shift in society's stance on, and construction of, 'the poor'.

118. *A Working Life* is both too naïve a work to stand as the first of this potential new form and without the influence enjoyed by Ehrenreich's work. Regarding which, note that in *Hard Work* Toynbee is explicit about Ehrenreich as an inspiration (p. 10) in a way that she is not about her own earlier book. This importance of Ehrenreich also holds true for the two French examples of Banksian incognito social investigation that appeared in the first decade of the twenty-first century. See Fayner, Elsa. 2007. *Et pourtant je me suis levée tôt...: Une immersion dans le quotidien des travailleurs précaires*. Paris: Panama, p. 13, and Aubenas, Florence. 2010. *Le quai de Ouistreham*. N.p.: Éditions de l'Olivier, p. 9, where the reference is less explicit (I take the final example in Aubenas's list of precursors as referring to Ehrenreich).

119. PT interview; cf. *Hard Work*, pp. 87–8.

# CHAPTER 8

# Settling Down: From Jack London's London Holiday to Stephen Reynolds's Sea-Change

We have followed the development of the incognito social investigation text tradition from its birth in the cold January of 1866 in a blaze of journalistic scandal through the reinvigoration and change brought it by Elizabeth L. Banks in the 1890s, creating an offshoot that in time over-shadowed the parent form; the one dying out to all extents and purposes after a last flash of glory in the 1930s and the other surviving to become a respected political voice. We have also seen how there can be traced a related tradition recounting the experience of those who tramped the roads of England and the wider world, a phenomenon related but never identical to the Greenwoodian tradition. What all this web of social investigation forms has in common is impermanence. No-one sleeps in casual wards or doss-houses for more than the few nights necessary to gather information; no-one takes on a job merely for the purposes of researching the mores surrounding it for longer than is strictly required; no-one who has as the *raison d'être* of their investigation travel and movement can afford to stop for too long. Texts recounting episodes of incognito social investigation are necessarily conditioned and shaped by the fact that what they recount is *episodes*: as the pious cliché might have it in reference to the poor whom they chronicle, these narrators have no abiding city here.

There is a final type of incognito social investigation text, however, where this impermanence is not found. This we might call 'settling' as opposed to 'tramping', the verb chosen to recall the settlement movement

© The Author(s) 2017

L. Seaber, *Incognito Social Investigation in British Literature*,
Palgrave Studies in Life Writing, DOI 10.1007/978-3-319-50962-4_8

of the late nineteenth and early twentieth centuries. This, which saw middle-class men going to live in 'settlements' amongst the urban poor, has been acutely analysed by Seth Koven, who takes it as part of an overarching phenomenon including incognito social investigation as defined here, labelled 'slumming'.[1] Although, as this book has always argued, incognito social investigation *stricto sensu* should be recognized as a distinctly separate practice to other forms of slumming, one characterized by the presence of disguise, Koven is right to place them together as *related* phenomena. An example of 'slumming' that Koven does not use is that of C.F.G. Masterman, a brief star of Liberal politics in the early twentieth century, who for two years from April 1900 lived in a workman's flat in Albany Dwellings, Camberwell, whence he published anonymous articles about life there in the *Speaker* and *Commonwealth*.[2] These were collected into a book, published in 1902 under the title *From the Abyss*. The book consists of a series of impressionistic, highly wrought, chapters, almost all referring to the slum-dwellers who are the book's subjects in the first-person plural: 'we', 'our', 'ourselves'... More than this, the book's paratext repeats this identification of observer and observed. The original title page reads:

FROM THE ABYSS
OF ITS INHABITANTS
BY ONE OF THEM[3]

'One of the inhabitants': there is no technical falsehood here, for Masterman did indeed live in what he calls 'the Abyss', but as a temporary visitor rather than as one without choice. The explicit 'we' of the text, however, is not the same as the implicit 'we' of the paratext: whereas the latter may be disingenuously misleading, it is technically accurate, the former is deliberately inaccurate, as 'we' whose life it describes is not the life of the observing and narrating voice. Almost any passage will serve to illustrate this: 'We choke up the public-houses and the few uncertain open spaces still left to us; we overflow into canal barges, and railway arches, and disused drains. Lines of us are pushed into the gutters where we ply unwanted articles, and children's toys, and publications obscene to the legal limit, beside the heedless stream that ever hurries past us.'[4] It may be true that 'we' live in what 'we' refer to as 'the Abyss', but it is certainly not true that 'we' are amongst those who end up as street traders or living precariously on barges or under railway arches. Whereas for the paratext 'we' = 'I', for the text 'we' = 'they'.

*From the Abyss* may present itself a form of incognito social investigation text, but it is nothing of the sort. Although we learn that the narrator and observer went there 'willingly', 'preparing to descend into the Abyss' quite deliberately,[5] at no point is there anything to suggest that he has endeavoured to pass himself as 'one of them' to 'them'. His status as an outsider is reinforced by the incessantly pejorative, almost hysterical, descriptions of the 'weird and uncanny people' who 'have poured in as dense black masses from the eastern railways' with their 'bizarre and barbaric revelry'.[6] This is not the language of one who wishes to stake a claim for his emicity. This is true a fortiori of the extended analogy that ends the first chapter, with its parade of deeply dysphemistic adjectives. It begins:

> Remember, again, the South American forest. Tall trees insolently rise to heaven; surrounding them is the mass of tangled, choking vegetation; gorgeous colours of unequalled beauty; ceaseless, silent strife. Below are all forms of life driven under, forced to adapt themselves to unnatural surroundings distorted into repulsive, twisted, grotesque forms of existence; each seemingly prepared for any monstrous change if only it can preserve its life and propagate its kind.[7]

This trope, exoticizing as it criticizes, whereby the slums are equated with tropical rankness, had much history behind it by the end of the Victorian era, as Mariana Valverde has brilliantly explored, by which point there was 'a sheer abundance of slum-jungle metaphors in social discovery texts, whether fictional or sociological'.[8] The importance of it in Masterman's text lies in the link it provides with a much better-known text, one that deals with true incognito social investigation as defined here. It serves as a reminder and a warning that although this book has focused very much on a narrow field, it is a field always influenced by works with related but not identical epistemologies and methodologies. This is above all true with the works that this chapter will examine, as 'settling' is the form of incognito social investigation where the texts it produces most merge into other forms, above all autobiography.

The text that *From the Abyss* so resembles is perhaps the only incognito social investigation text other than *Down and Out in Paris and London* (which it clearly influenced) that may fairly be described as canonical: Jack London's *The People of the Abyss*. London's writing of the subculture of hoboes in the United States is a type of social investigation outside of what is being studied here, belonging strongly to another tradition;[9] his work in London, though, is of prime importance in the history of the British tradition, not least because of its influence on Orwell. It also held great importance in the author's own career; as Ronald Paul says in his excellent analysis of the book, when it 'was serialized in an American periodical, *Wilshire's Magazine*, in 1903, it was an immediate publishing success, transforming London's status as a popular writer'.[10]

*The People of the Abyss* is a key text in the transmission of the tradition examined here, coming as it does at a moment when the Greenwoodian strand is on its way to being replaced by the Banksian, and providing a *literary* model rather than a journalistic one to Orwell.[11] However, I shall argue here that the most important feature of London's book is how much it demonstrates an alienness to the world it describes that in fact places it in a deeply ambiguous position vis-à-vis the tradition to which it nominally belongs.

At first sight, the subject matter and themes are typical of British social investigation texts. The trope of the 'abyss', which so clearly links London's text with Masterman's, is immediately obvious from the title before either book is even opened.[12] Equally, just as *From the Abyss* makes use of the language of the slum as jungle, so too does London's book, in a passage that is the key to the text's ambiguousness. The book's first chapter is entitled 'The Descent', which seems to bear out Peter Keating's observation that there is an important difference between the tropes of jungle and abyss, for the social investigator does not 'journey *to* an abyss', but 'descend[s] or fall[s] into it. It is all very well claiming that a Dark Continent lies at one's doorstep but that metaphorically is more welcome than a gaping hole.'[13] Notwithstanding this, and London's vocabulary of 'sinking myself down into the East End of London',[14] the whole governing conceit of the opening of the book is one of horizontal rather than vertical travel. London states his intention to see life in the East End to friends whom he has asked for assistance in this task, but, having failed to dissuade him from this folly, they deny any knowledge of how such a thing may be achieved. He announces that he will therefore go to Thomas Cook & Son, the first and greatest of travel agents, to organize his journey. He meets with no success:

> But O Cook, O Thomas Cook & Son, pathfinders and trail-clearers, living sign-posts to all the world and bestowers of first aid to bewildered travellers –

unhesitatingly and instantly, with ease and celerity, could you send me to Darkest Africa or Innermost Thibet, but to the East End of London, barely a stone's throw distant from Ludgate Circus, you know not the way![15]

On the one hand, this is clearly humorous hyperbole, albeit humour behind which there lies a serious point about charity beginning at home. It also recalls not just the slum–jungle trope in general, but also, more specifically, George R. Sims's use of it in *How the Poor Live* in 1883. Sims had written of 'a dark continent that is within easy walking distance of the General Post Office',[16] the geographical specificity of the reference used to imply the shameful contrast in levels of knowledge functioning, alongside the touch of humour, exactly as it does in Jack London. In this sense, despite Keating's observations, in *The People of the Abyss* the trope wherein 'Darkest Africa' and 'Darkest London' are part of the dialectic of the familiar and the unfamiliar has by no means been replaced by the newer image of the abyss.[17]

London's use of this trope, however, is more complex than solely being part of a rhetorical tradition. By talking of Cook's so jovially so early in the text, London is at first sight being ironic, and rather heavy-handedly so. *Of course* he knows that Cook's will not help him; *of course* there is no system set up for Americans who wish to live in the East End. After all, regardless of ideological questions of telescopic philanthropy, there is a simple practical issue: London does not wish to *visit* the East End, he wants to *live* there. A travel agency could never be the right place to seek aid, however many tours it might run. I have laboriously unpacked this joke about methodology because it is in fact an example of what Chesterton has called an irony 'so large that it is too large to be seen'.[18] In other words, behind the irony of London never having really expected Cook's to help him even if they did offer tours to the East End (if the story is even true rather than just a symbolic joke), there lies a deeper irony: Jack London *was* a tourist in the East End, and this book *is* an account of the equivalent of a Cook's tour.

By calling London a 'tourist' I do not mean to disparage him or his motives for living amongst the poor of his namesake city, nor suggest that *The People of the Abyss* merely recounts poverty tourism as opposed to being an investigative denunciation of social ills. I mean something much simpler: when London, regardless of his motives, visited the East End, he was visiting not only an alien social space, but an alien space *tout court*. Elizabeth L. Banks may have marketed herself as the American girl in

London, but she never demonstrates the innocent ignorance of her sur-
roundings that Jack London does; he is not ignorant of the poor – Paul
rightly observes that owing to his upbringing and background 'London
knew himself what real poverty was like and how it could destroy people's
lives' – but he *is* ignorant of Britain.[19]

We may begin exploring this through an examination of a moment
where London the incognito social investigator risks revealing himself as
one who is not what he seems. London famously broke cover at one point
in his investigation, revealing to his starving companions that he is a social
investigator with a sovereign sewn inside his singlet; this, however, is not
the only moment when the supposed pauper reveals that he is in fact
wealthy enough to possess (and spend!) a sovereign. The twentieth chapter of *The People of the Abyss* is dedicated to coffee-houses and doss-houses,
and London, talking of the former, reminisces about a 'Cockney Amazon
in a place near Trafalgar Square, to whom I tendered a sovereign when
paying my score'.[20] This unexpected wealth from one seemingly poor
unsurprisingly arouses the girl's suspicions, and she bites it to test whether
it is a forgery. London relates this because he is interested in reporting the
chaffing he receives from this 'Amazon', but the very fact that he does not
dwell on the true importance of the scene is illuminating. London, who
has gone to some trouble to disguise himself, makes an obvious error:
what beached American sailor in cast-off clothes pays for a cup of a tea in a
poor coffee-house with a gold sovereign? This lowering of his guard,
however, and the concomitant risk of revealing his 'true' status, is not
thought worthy of mention – indeed, London gives no reason to believe
that he has even noticed what he has done here. His interest is in local
colour and Cockney repartee, *not* his position vis-à-vis that local colour.
This is far from saying that London is only interested in reporting what
he sees, and endeavours to make himself as unobtrusive a presence as
possible in his text: *The People of the Abyss* is full of its author's judgements,
voice and participation. London is rather insistently present in his book, to
the point of providing a double of himself in the figure of the elderly and
doomed docker and trades unionist Dan Cullen.[21] London, then, is not
trying to anonymize himself or remove himself and his situation from the
text, so why this blindness to the oddity of his actions in the coffee-house?
The key, I think, is to be found in the parenthesized information that he
gives between mentioning that he tried to pay with a sovereign and his
account of the conversation with the girl serving him: '(By the way, one is
supposed to pay before he begins to eat, and if he be poorly dressed he is

compelled to pay before he eats.)'[22] To whom is this off-hand ('by the way') statement addressed? It can only be to his American audience, as such a detail of correct social behaviour would surely be known to the majority of any potential British audience. This is more, though, than just London being 'a naturalist reporting from the field', as Jonathan Auerbach has called him with regards to *The People of the Abyss*:[23] London's statement here is more than just information given for its own sake, for it reads as *advice*. In other words, if you, reader, wish to pass yourself as a pauper in London, this is how you must behave in a coffee-house. London's silence regarding his error in showing the sovereign belongs to the same epistemological realm: he is a stranger in a strange land, and does not know that he has committed a solecism, and, not noting it, cannot warn other travellers against it.

In this reading, *The People of the Abyss* attempts to be an incognito social investigation text, but its reliability is forever undermined by London's status as a tourist. Auerbach is quite right when he writes of London's time in his namesake city that the author 'remains exempt' from a 'local set of circumstances' 'by virtue of his American identity', and that 'Nationality, rather than social class, becomes the operative concept to define difference' in *The People of the Abyss*.[24] This, when combined with London's own admission (in a letter of 28 July 1902 to John Spargo) that his '"main idea" in traveling to England was "to get a vacation"',[25] reveals London the social investigator as London the tourist, and highlights (as does the career of Harry A. Franck) the degree to which these two roles, the nominally serious and the nominally frivolous, are in fact extremely closely related.

London's position as a tourist helps to explain minor 'errors' in the text: these are not errors caused by incomplete or imperfect incognito social investigation, but examples of a lack of knowledge unrelated to London's journey in social space rather than his journey in physical space. For example, one of the first changes he notes when dressed as a pauper is that he is no longer asked whether he wants a first- or second-class ticket in railway stations, but is automatically given third.[26] We may presume that a British author, like a British audience, would know that by the early twentieth century second class had been phased out almost totally, although it did still exist on suburban lines in London, so a reference to so increasingly uncommon a phenomenon would be extremely jarring in a text for domestic consumption by a domestic author: again, this is a tourist's 'error' rather than a social investigator's. [27] Something similar happens when he visits Spitalfields Garden at night, and sees 'a mass of miserable and distorted humanity, the sight of which would have impelled Doré to more diabolical flights of fancy than he ever succeeded in achieving':[28] what British author, writing in 1902 on the London poor would have been likely to have shown thus his or her ignorance of Doré's celebrated illustrations to Blanchard Jerrold's 1872 *London: A Pilgrimage*?[29]

It should be noted that the most important thing here is not whether London does or does not report things accurately here (hence the scare quotes on 'errors'). He may be right about what tickets were offered him; he may be right that Doré never portrayed anything to match the horrors that he saw. Nonetheless, the *presentation* of these matters in such a way as to suggest that they were obvious and simple in a way that a British author or audience would not have considered them justifies their labelling as 'errors'.

The most important of these 'tourist's errors' leads us to an wider point. Chapter 7 is entitled 'A Winner of the Victoria Cross', and relates London's conversation in a queue for a casual ward with an eighty-seven-year-old man who had won the Victoria Cross but had forfeited it after a court martial, the lesson drawn by the author being implicitly one of the unfair harshness of the British punitive system and how it relates to the cruelty of the casual-ward system.[30] If we examine the details of the story, however, a problem soon emerges. Eight recipients of the Victoria Cross forfeited it, but not one of these for a crime in any way related to that recounted to London (attempted murder of a lieutenant).[31] This is not to deny that London was told this story: there is no reason to disbelieve his version of events. Nonetheless, the story as told him immediately suggests a yarn (or, in a more favourable interpretation, an exaggeration) spun to gain at least sympathy and possibly assistance. Given that 1902 saw the end of the Boer War, with a concomitant British interest in matters military, it is almost inconceivable that an equivalent British incognito social investigator would have accepted so unquestioningly so improbable a military tale. This brings us back to the problem adumbrated in Chapter 1 regarding the question of how readers recognize 'truth' in accounts of incognito social investigation. To expect a commonality of experiences that allows the reader to accept the author's account of events without merely falling back onto an argument from authority is already difficult enough when one is describing something that is only socio-economically distant; when one adds to this spatial distance, as in *The People of the Abyss*, the work risks undermining its own authority whenever its public ceases to be that geographical one for whom it was intended. In other words, although *The People of the Abyss* clearly presents itself as an incognito social investigation text, its claim to be such rather than autobiographical travel literature is severely weakened once one reads it with the knowledge and expectations that one might presume from a contemporary British rather than American audience.

Auerbach has spoken of London's 'problematic positionality in relation to his subject' vis-à-vis the East End that he describes and where he temporarily lives:[32] I would add to this the problematic positionality of the text itself in relation to where it sites itself as a text. Nominally a text within the incognito social investigation tradition, and certainly read as such by Orwell (and most critics), it also uncomfortably belongs to autobiography and travel literature. This is above all what makes it a text of 'settling' rather than a Greenwoodian text, notwithstanding its interest in doss-houses and casual wards. All incognito social investigation texts are as much, if not more, about their authors' complex, uneasy and shifting relation to their readers in one direction and the object of their investigation in the other, but settling texts add to this a further level of instability: are they texts recounting their authors' experiences as a pretext to talk of the poor, or do they recount the poor as a pretext to allow their authors to talk of themselves?

If, having decided this about the nature of *The People of the Abyss*, we turn to the book to which it is most famously a hypotext, then an unexpected but unavoidable conclusion has to be reached. *Down and Out in Paris and London* very much does descend from London's work, but the part that is the truer heir to the American author's incognito social investigation is the Paris section, not the London. At first sight, this may seem absurd. The two authors' writing on London deals with an almost identical subject matter of doss-houses, casual wards and hopping; the parallels are too many to list. Orwell, however, in the sections of his debut work that deal with Britain, is not writing as a 'tourist'. The fictionality of the underlying structure of 'London' removes it from the sphere of autobiography and (paradoxically, perhaps) makes it much purer reportage. In Paris, things are very different. Here, like London in London, Orwell is in an alien world geographically as much as socio-economically. He recounts what he sees, but what he sees is conditioned by his tourist status. Indeed, whereas *The People of the Abyss*, notwithstanding its fame as such, is difficult to classify as a pure incognito social investigation text, inhabiting an uncomfortable and shifting zone of ambiguity, Orwell's writing on his experiences in Paris is easier to classify, as it refuses the ambiguities of its model. Put simply, *the Paris section of Orwell's first book is not an incognito social investigation text*. It is autobiography, and it is travel literature, but its protagonist is neither disguising himself nor researching. He may, as he does, learn much, which information he will pass on to his readers, but this is something that only happens after he has had his experiences. He does not set out to learn and inform as he does in London; he sets out simply to recount an episode of his life, his poverty and low-paid work in Paris. We see here the complexity of classifying texts in the 'settling' tradition with regards to their nature as incognito social investigation texts as opposed to the simplicity of classifying those in the Greenwoodian. The London section is purely Greenwoodian, albeit partially disguised and made to look like autobiography by its fictional scaffolding. It is an account of episodic moments of investigation that only exist as investigation. Paris, on the other hand, is non-episodic, and what is described has an existence and justification in the author's life outside investigation. In other words, Paris is what London pretends to be: autobiography.

We may take Orwell's London and Orwell's Paris to be two ends of a conceptual chiasmus, as it were, the British city representing 'pure' incognito social investigation (although disguised as autobiography) and the French city representing 'pure' autobiography (although disguised as incognito social investigation). The point of metaphorical crossing is the space inhabited by *The People of the Abyss*, classifiable as a blending of the two forms of text that allows no separation.[33]

At this point, one may legitimately begin to ask oneself whether there are *any* texts classifiable as 'settling' that are also uncomplicatedly classifiable as incognito social investigation. There is in fact only one text known to me that does allow a relatively uncomplicated classification as 'settling' incognito social investigation. This is Hugh Massingham's 1936 book *I Took Off My Tie*, a product of the 1930s intelligentsia's obsession with class passing in all its forms. Massingham, a journalist, son of the important Radical journalist H.W. Massingham, editor of the *Nation*, undertook, with a decision by now familiar to us, to spend a prolonged period of time living in the East End of London.[34]

As we begin *I Took Off My Tie*, we might understandably be struck by a sense of continuity with earlier 'settling' texts. It begins with a discussion of the general ignorance amongst the class to which his readers implicitly belong regarding the class amongst whom he is going to live, an ignorance from which he too suffers and hyperbolizes thus: 'I could not get out of my head the astonishing fact that the East End is as unknown to us as the

Trobriand Islands, that the unexplored regions of the world are just round the corner.'[35] This all-too-familiar trope is repeated a few pages later, with talk of how easier it would have been 'had I decided to explore remotest Africa'.[36] However, there is a subtle difference here from the earlier trope. Whereas the reference to Africa fits in easily to what Mariana Valverde has described, the first reference, that to the Trobriand Islands, needs a little more unpacking. It recalls the anthropological work of Bronislaw Malinowski: this instantly situates *I Took Off My Tie* within an anthropological and sociological milieu of a far greater scientificity than the less complex 'Africa' reference does – or, more accurately, it situates it not only within the ongoing dialectic explored by Valverde but also within a more specific 1930s context where (incognito) social investigation, as with Mass-Observation, is (also) part of a very different set of discourses from those prevailing with its earlier counterparts.[37]

In *I Took Off My Tie*, Massingham is very much interested in going to live in the East End, rather than working there or exploring the life of the homeless (although when assailed by doubts over what he is doing he experiments briefly and ultimately inconsequentially with a more Greenwoodian form of investigation).[38] This leads him into a unique situation. He is so set on finding a place to live that he accepts the only dwelling that he is able to find, one that comes with the condition that he act as rent collector for the other properties that his landlord owns in the street. This causes him to begin his time as an incognito social investigator as a figure very much loathed by the great majority of those whom he is investigating – episodes include his losing his temper and punching Shepherd, one of his landlord's debtors,[39] and his returning home to find that someone has 'smashed the rest of my crockery and [has] then done his business in the frying-pan and left it in the middle of the table'.[40] It is unsurprising that after this Massingham has doubts over his presence in the street that lead to him returning to his flat and briefly talking up Greenwoodian investigation as a safer and more pleasant alternative.

Massingham, it should be noted in passing, does not disguise his origins – for example, he tells the Timmses, a family whose rent he collects and who are amongst his few early allies in the street, 'a vague story of past misfortune' 'in order to account for my presence'.[41] This is an interesting variant as far as pretending to be poor is concerned, one where the investigator makes no attempt to disguise his or her social class, but more narrowly (and, one suspects, more convincingly) disguises his or her economic situation.

After he decides to return to his life in the street notwithstanding the threats and intimidatory behaviour that he has received there (a treatment that bespeaks the success of his disguise, in fact!), Massingham finally achieves the insertion into society there he has so long sought. We might to some extent read *I Took Off My Tie* as autobiography, given how its author is recounting his experiences not only of what he observes but how he observes them – his self-doubt and temptations to quit are as much part of his story as are the lives of the Shepherds, Timmses and others – but in that case it would still be false to say that the *focus* here is autobiographical. It would be more accurate to say that Massingham includes in his text a reflexive element, the observer observing himself, that is far more pronounced than in the great majority of other incognito social investigation texts. Lacking from this reflexivity, however, is any awareness of just how close Massingham comes in the end to full identification with the people amongst whom he is living. *I Took Off My Tie* is also very much the account of how its author slowly changes his stance, and not only does the street accept him, but he also accepts the street – or rather, he becomes one with the people from whom he was once separate. Massingham recognizes this burgeoning change in himself, reflecting on how after his return he has come to be friends with Mrs Morgan, the street's heavy-drinking and occasionally violent amateur prostitute, who was at first one of those opposed to his presence in the street:

> What more did I want? I had come down to the East End to study conditions, and I had gained a safe vantage point from which I could observe everything without any danger to myself. It seemed an ideal end to the adventure, and yet I was not satisfied. I had by this time almost forgotten why I had once been so anxious to know Mrs. Morgan. I thought of her no longer as a type but as a human being whose friendship was important to me. I had much the same attitude towards the street. For my original purpose it was only necessary for me to watch its life as a detached spectator, but my interest had so increased that I now wanted to become part of it and to identify myself completely with the people who persisted in remaining aloof.[42]

Massingham will achieve his goal, but he will achieve it so completely that he will not notice it.

This shift takes place in the book's culminating episode, Johnston's funeral. Johnston is what Massingham is pretending to be: a member of the middle classes who for some unspecified reason has come down in the world and ekes out a precarious existence with occasional work as a clerk. Towards the end of the book he is diagnosed with consumption, of which he dies whilst Massingham is dozing sitting up over him. Johnston has planned matters so that Massingham is to organize his funeral with the money from the burial insurance, and Massingham deputes Mrs Morgan to deal with the actual practicalities. Although Johnston has long been presented as a rather pathetic figure of fun with his snobbish pretension and obsession with 'the old school tie', by the time he falls ill Massingham has had a change of heart over how he views him and presents him. While he is sitting up with Johnston one day, Massingham has something of an epiphany, although it is presented rather as a moment of aporia:

> Society had put Johnston on the spot. [ ... ] He made you feel awkward. So nobody cared whether he lived or died. Nobody? Did I care? Was I fond of him? Certainly not. Well, what was I doing here? Pity? Sentimentality? Perhaps I was fond of him after all. Hadn't Johnston become part of me, like the street? [ ... ] What was the reality about Johnston? The old school tie was the reality. But was it? You think yourself might superior, but what would you do if you were thrown out on your ear? I'd find work. Supposing you couldn't? I'd shine shoes. Would you? I don't know what I'd do. Would you look at yourself in the mirror and say: 'That's a picture of a failure'? I don't know what I'd do. Wouldn't you think your case was unique? Hell, I said to myself, I don't want to think about this thing any more.[43]

This confusion of pronouns, leading to a refusal to commit, is the point at which Massingham truly changes, realizing, perhaps unconsciously, that there is ultimately no firm epistemological or ontological ground on which to stand safely as an observer. There but for the grace of God goes he, and his mind shies away at the indeterminacy of it all.

Although he does not state it, Massingham comes out of this dark night of the soul a changed man, and realizes his desire to identify himself completely with the erstwhile objects of his observation. Whilst Mrs Morgan undertakes arrangements for the funeral, Massingham muses on the effect the death has had, and the funeral will have, on the street. Noteworthily, the long reflective passage in which this takes place is couched entirely in terms of 'we';[44] even more noteworthily, Massingham in no way draws the reader's attention to this switch. This suggests that identification is complete: not only has 'I' become 'we', but there is also no recognition of the importance of this change, for it has happened naturally rather than as part of a strategy.

Something similar, although yet more subtle, happens in Massingham's account of the funeral itself. As Massingham sits in the cortège with Mrs Morgan, his thoughts drift into philosophizing about life and death, using imagery based upon the trams that they pass. They then shift from the general to the specific, and return to the questions explored as he sat up over the dying man, before Mrs Morgan interrupts the train of thought:

> This man died in my arms. Well, not quite in my arms. The truth is I was asleep. No one saw him go. No one cared for him when he was alive and no one cares a button now that he is dead.
> 'We're 'ere', said Mrs. Morgan. 'It don't 'arf make yer fink'.[45]

In other words, it is suggested that through Mrs Morgan's head are running thoughts analogous to Massingham's. This is a yet further level of identification: not only does Massingham now identify himself with Mrs Morgan, but he also implicitly identifies her with himself. The destruction of social barriers is complete: we may be privy only to the thoughts of the narrative voice, but we no longer have any reason to believe that they are in themselves more interesting or more valuable than the thoughts of those around him, and neither does he.

Massingham's subtlety in not drawing attention to the changes that his status undergoes may or may not be a deliberate technique to assure his reader of the genuineness of his conversion. Whether it is a rhetorical trick or not is less important, however, than its effectiveness and the degree to which it denotes a level of identification with those observed truly rare.

However, a question remains that has to be raised about *I Took Off My Tie*. In the passage quoted above, in which Massingham discovers his desire to become part of the community that he observes, he says of his having become friends with Mrs Morgan, 'It seemed an ideal end to the adventure.'[46] Of course, his 'adventure' does not end with Mrs Morgan being reconciled to his presence in the street, nor with Shepherd's reconciliation thereto. It ends with Johnston's funeral, a far more apt moment in narrative terms. Johnston's death gives dramatic structure to the end of the book, just as Massingham's moments of doubt and depression over what he is doing give structure to its middle. We might begin to wonder whether the dramatic structure of *I Took Off My Tie* is not perhaps a little *too* perfect: the narrative structure suggests a novel far more than it does reportage. This is not to say that Massingham's account is either fiction or fictionalized. We do not have enough information, whether in the text or outside it, to investigate to what degree the author did or did not live the experiences related. The question is rather to what point Massingham has arranged the chronology of events as he narrates them to give a novelistic structure. An example of this in a microcosm can be seen in the episode where he challenges one of Mrs Morgan's children, Annie, who has befriended him, to recite the Lord's Prayer. Her version of it is a mass of mishearings and misunderstandings ('Harold be thy name'),[47] but as she reaches the end her errors create unexpected meaning: 'For thine is the king—dom-and the poor—and the glawry'.[48] It is the 'poor' that belong to God rather than the 'power': the (bitter) joke or commentary within the linguistic play is clear. Again, there is no reason to doubt in itself that Annie mangled what she recalled; we may legitimately doubt, however, that in doing so she produced so apposite a malapropism. That Massingham chooses to transcribe the word that Annie uses in quite this way is a literary device: it is not exactly invention, but rather selection done in such a way as to improve his text literarily. The same holds true *mutatis mutandis* for the whole structure of the book. *I Took Off My Tie* has a novel's structure. Although this makes it neither a novel nor fiction, nor even necessarily fictionalized, this deliberate move away from journalism towards 'literature' once again shows just how indeterminate a form 'settling' is, where every definition of the subtype runs up against the problem of the indeterminate nature of the texts exemplifying it.

Massingham's text, although on the one hand atypical as an example of 'settling' literature given its relatively novelistic nature, is of course on the other hand typical precisely because of that anomaly: it has that ambiguity over its status so central to texts of this sort, even though in this case the ambiguity does not have to do with the question of to what extent it is autobiography as opposed to reportage. *Mutatis mutandis*, something similar happens with Polly Toynbee's *Hard Work*, hitherto discussed as an example of a Banksian (or perhaps Ehrenreichian) incognito social investigation text. Although Toynbee's focus is clearly the world of low-paid work, she (like Barbara Ehrenreich) also has to deal with the problem of housing, and in so doing makes part of her text an example of 'settling'. *Hard Work* itself is emphatically *not* a 'settling' text, but (such are the anomalies created by this subtype) it does contain one of the most important examples of an incognito social investigator's writing on 'settling'. Toynbee goes into significant detail about the economics of moving into and furnishing her temporary home, as well as the expenditure necessary to keep body and soul together.[49] Her focus is very much on practicalities rather than on people; only in the ninth chapter, 'Clapham Park Neighbours', does she go into any real detail of the human, as opposed to economic, side of living her new life. This might suggest a lack of interest in the human face of settling amongst the poor, but I would argue that, perhaps paradoxically, it does exactly the opposite. Just as in the Banksian majority of her text, by focusing on the work done rather than on the people doing it, Toynbee achieves a non-voyeuristic empathy extremely rare in the history of incognito social investigation, in the 'settling' sections, by focusing on the *general* reality of the practical implications of living where she does as opposed to the *specific* human reality of individual cases, achieving identification between observer and observed. The economic and practical realities of poverty are the same for anyone in that situation: character, motivation, past history – these, which may otherwise be mitigating and implicitly moral factors, fade into insignificance. If you have '4p in your pocket and £70 of rent and other arrears already',[50] then questions of individual personality matter little: the problem is primarily and fundamentally the practical one of how to survive. This approach necessarily creates a true commonality between observer and observed, and by getting down to the dry details of single pennies suggests to the reader too that if he or she does not belong to that commonality, it is not because of any inherent virtue or character traits, but only the simple fact of having more money. As Hemingway might have said to Fitzgerald, the poor differ from us in that they have less money. This is a tautology less obvious than it seems, for, as we have seen, writers on 'the poor' have tended very much to focus on the non-economic, non-practical, side of poverty, preferring – some nobly, some voyeuristically, some empathetically, but none uncomplicatedly or unambiguously – to look at the human element, whether that of the writer or those written about. Toynbee, in recognizing the insight in the tautology and thus realizing that in such a case with such a focus there is no difference between writing about oneself and writing about others (a truly humble point of view, again perhaps paradoxically), manages to write a 'settling' text that is truly about settling; that this achievement should be in a book dedicated to working rather than living only underscores the problems this form poses.

In *I Took Off My Tie*, Hewins, the philanthropic pawnbroker who finds Massingham somewhere to live in the East End, acts as the well of hard-earned knowledge from which the more naïve author draws. He insists that he should 'go in a proper scientific spirit' and harden his heart,[51] something that Massingham never truly succeeds in doing. Whereas other authors and investigators undertake their work either in a spirit of sympathy that more often than not serves to underline the gap between observer and observed or in a direct sympathy of condescension, Toynbee unknowingly follows Hewins's advice, and thus in *Hard Work* gives the reader a clearer-eyed and truer portrayal of what poverty means than almost any other of the writers explored here.

The most remarkable 'settling' text of all is also one of the most remarkable of all incognito social investigation texts (although it would perhaps be more accurate to talk of *semi*-incognito social investigation here, as the dissimulation of the author's status as a social investigator is only partial). The text is *A Poor Man's House* (1908), and the author Stephen Reynolds.

Reynolds is little known now.[52] He was a middle-class author from Devizes, Wiltshire, who in 1903 visited Sidmouth on the South Devon coast, looking for a place to stay to recover from what was more or less a nervous breakdown; here he met a local fisher family, the Woolleys. In 1906, he moved from Devizes to Sidmouth on a permanent basis, lodging in the Woolleys' slum cottage and combining writing and work as a fisherman. In 1908 he published *A Poor Man's House*, an account of life – his, the Woolleys' – in Sidmouth amongst 'the poor'. It was a great success, earning him praise from Conrad, Bennett, Galsworthy and many other Edwardian literary luminaries. He published a little more in the years following (as well as spending some time as assistant editor of the *English Review*), but by 1913 had given up writing to undertake work for the government on fisheries. He died in 1919 in the flu pandemic.

*A Poor Man's House*, where Sidmouth appears as Seacombe and the Woolleys as the Widgers, is a strange book: a mixture of social investigation, nature observation and character sketches. Reynolds is semi-incognito: he is recognized as a 'gentleman' – sometimes to his distaste, as when his previous landlady from the 'nice' part of Sidmouth wonders aloud after hearing of his moving in with the Woolleys 'I can't think how you can live in such a horrid place!',[53] obviously expecting her middle-class interlocutor to show some agreement – sometimes merely as an observation. However, although Reynolds's (decreasing) middle-classness was known, what he was writing up was not, although before publication he did consult with his hosts. More accurately, his former hosts, for in 1907 he stopped being a paying guest as he had been, and became a partner in a fishing boat. Here too above all we see the ambiguity of his status: he was no longer 'playing' at fishing, nor was he doing it for 'copy', so to speak, yet he remained a middle-class individual in a working-class role, whose status was sometimes identified and identifiable and sometimes not.

Although *A Poor Man's House* might thus appear to be classifiable as nearer to autobiography, like Orwell's Paris writing, and therefore not a true incognito social investigation text at all, it nonetheless deserves attention, as it demonstrates features that cannot be found in any other incognito social investigation text, however defined. Before we examine this, it is worth looking at how the space of the Devon coastal town, so unlike the more usual urban or (in the case of tramping texts) rural spaces in which the works that we have examined usually take place, enriches the text, and in so doing further complicates our analysis of the tradition(s) as a whole.

Reynolds's experiences, I should like to argue, are facilitated by their taking place in coastal settings. This is because coasts are both liminal and interstitial, terms requiring a degree of clarification with regards to how they are employed here. The interstitial space par excellence is that of 'the road' (in a semi-metaphorical sense): that space of travel where contacts are made between groups and individuals that would not be made, or not be made in that way, in normal non-interstitial space. It is the space of pilgrimages, say, or airports; it is also the coastal space in those years when long-distance travel was very much by boat: the coast, with the port as its focalizing point, in the years before air transport, was a space in which disparate groups and individuals came into contact whilst waiting to leave it. Liminal space, on the other hand, is used here to refer to space that is truly a *limen*; that is, it is bordered by, and defined by, what lies on either side of it, what comes before and after. The liminal space, the *limen*, is a stage in a transition where individual identities can blur, and it has no meaning without its before and after; the interstitial space, the interstice, exists in its own right, and identities there do not blur in the individual, but instead ambiguities are created by encounters between individuals and groups outside usual social space. In this context we should also distinguish between 'socioliminality' and 'idioliminality'. The former is liminality in the more usual anthropological sense: a liminal state that is part of a social reality wherein it has a recognized place; the latter is liminality experienced by an individual as part of a personal process. Interstitiality, on the other hand, can only ever be social, as it implies an arena for mixing, and such a thing is only possible within a social rather than an individual context.

Sidmouth was idioliminal for Reynolds: he came there a man on the edge of a nervous breakdown who worked fruitlessly for recognition as a writer; there he discovered another way of living less injurious to his psychological well-being on the one hand, and published *A Poor Man's House* to great acclaim on the other; and he left the town for a new life outside the literary world. However, it was also a socioliminal space: a town like Sidmouth attracted people like the pre-limen Reynolds, those looking to recover their psychological health, and it was therefore a liminal space between illness and health in the wider social context: Reynolds could find his idioliminal space in Sidmouth because, as part of the 'health-giving', 'relaxing', coast it was already a socioliminal space. This liminality made it interstitial, a place where an 'educated' man such as Reynolds could move in with a fisherman's family – indeed, he was far from the only one to do so: one of the Woolleys' rooms served to take up overspill from a nearby hotel; Reynolds's particularity was not his social mixing, but the extremes to which he pushed it. Equally, the interstitial nature of the coastal resort – an interstitiality helped but not dependent upon such resorts' socioliminal nature – meant that Reynolds's ambiguity was as much vis-à-vis those of the 'gentleman' class who observed him as it was vis-à-vis 'the poor'. This can be seen in an episode recounted early in the book:

> This morning, the visitor from the hotel, who has Mrs Widger's front room, so far presumed on the fact that we were both educated men among uneducated – both gen'lmen, Tony would say – as to remark flippantly though not ungenially, 'The Widgers are not bad sorts, are they? I say, what a mouth Mrs Widger's got!'
> Mrs Widger has a noticeably wide mouth; I know that perfectly well; but I can hardly say how indignant I felt at his light remark; how insulted; as if he had spoken slightingly of someone belonging to me.[54]

A useful comparison for shedding light on Sidmouth's mixture of interstitiality and liminality can be had if we compare it with one of the episodes in Harry A. Franck's journey around the world. This excursus away from settling back to the world of tramping is necessary insofar as the richness and strangeness of Reynolds's stability on the coast is in certain ways shared only by Franck's movement on the coast. Once again, we find ourselves only able to talk meaningfully about texts recounting settling amongst the poor through the invocation of other types of text; 'settling' is where the classificatory schema that this volume draws up begins to break up and lose its certainty.

The episode in Franck's journey that is of interest to us here is his time in Colombo, then a city in Ceylon as part of the British Empire and now the capital of Sri Lanka. Here Franck became part of a shifting population of 'beachcombers' and worked in a circus. Franck's Colombo was equally both interstitial and liminal; its liminality, however, much more firmly social rather than individual. *This* coast was not the liminal space of the psychological recharging of the genteel resort, but rather that of the port; another space made possible by the coast and equally a limen. The port, as a coastal liminal space, is particularly interesting because it marks the limen between normality and interstitiality, whilst itself also being an interstitial space in its own right. The world of sea travel in the days when it was the only realistic option for long-distance travel was an interstitial space: decks were separated, but a certain degree of contact otherwise unlikely was inevitable; Franck himself in his passage as both stowaway and deckhand from Suez to Colombo is an example of this (for instance, whilst using a begged frock coat to cover his ragged clothes when delivering a letter begging for employment he is mistaken by a steward for a 'gentleman' and passenger).[55] One arrives in a port, and, in the days of liners, there one tends to have to wait, in a liminal space between national, non-interstitial, space on the land side and international, interstitial, space on the water side. This is socioliminal space; it was socioliminal space for Franck as he waited there amongst the beachcombing community of Colombo. It is also in itself interstitial: as the various groups disembark or wait for embarkation in their liminal space, they create too an interstitial space where people mix who otherwise would be unlikely to do so.

The interstitial group par excellence in this interstitial coastal limen is that of the beachcombers. The existence of this collection of men – I know of no records of female beachcombers – as a socially recognized category around the ports and shores of the world, distinct from the better-known 'beachcomber' class of the islands of the Pacific, is clear from Franck's account of meeting them and sharing their lives in France, British India and China. Franck would appear to be the only source offering any details of this community's lives (one of the few other detailed descriptions of beachcomber life can be found in the Marseilles section of *The Moon and Sixpence*; Maugham plagiarized this from Franck, as he admitted in a letter to the American author).[56] The men with whom Franck spent his days in Colombo were a curious mixture: Henderson, the American deserter; Arnold, rich with the spoils of a corrupt career in Tammany Hall politics and waiting for the war between Russia and Japan to end so that might open a bar in Port Arthur; Marten from Tacoma, ex-pearl diver on the Coromandel coast; John Askins, MA (Dublin), twenty years in the East, drifting in and out of employment on the strength of a knowledge of – supposedly – most of the subcontinent's languages; 'Dick Haywood', alleged Sing Sing escapee and thief. These men had little in common economically or culturally; they had in common a desire or need to live outside the usual social spaces of the day. This disparate group could live on the coasts; it was here one became becalmed, so to speak, between voyages working or stowing away;[57] as much as possible, one gravitated to the warmer coasts, where, as Franck said, one 'escapes the terror of the coming night'.[58] Such heterogeneous groups may be found, one imagines, anywhere where those whom society has rejected or who have rejected society gather; such groups, however, when not in an interstitial space tend not to have contact with those outside their social grouping. On the interstitial coast, however, this is not the case.[59]

The particularities of the coast translate into the presence in Franck's and Reynolds's works of features and insights not found in any other incognito social investigation text. Franck provides documentary evidence for communities otherwise almost totally unrecorded, and certainly unrecorded in any way *from the inside*, as he does. The presence in the colonial enterprise of a whole class of people made possible by colonialism but not belonging to it – as the incident of the problems caused by setting up the circus shows – is nowhere better recorded, and the issues raised by such a group's presence in British India and elsewhere have still to be explored. This precious knowledge comes from the happy coincidence of a social explorer and a coast; we must, however, note, alas, that – as anyone now who takes up Franck's laborious pages will know –Harry A. Franck was, quite simply, not intelligent enough to recognize what he was seeing and do anything interesting with it. *Vagabond Journey* contains almost every type of social investigation possible – open, incognito, semi-incognito; tramping, working, begging – but it is only when the coast is added to the mixture that Franck produces something new, something that cannot be found anywhere else in the corpus: a space where race and class rub up against one another in a way no other social investigator records.

Reynolds, on the other hand, does not find anything to observe in the coastal space that others have not found elsewhere. The remarkable thing about his book lies neither in what he observes, nor in his recounting of it, but rather in the observer's relationship with what he has decided to study. What is unique in the annals of social investigation about *A Poor Man's House* is how he shows a level of identification with those observed that leads him to desert the life of writing for which he had moved to Sidmouth to become first a fisherman and then a fisheries expert working to help those whom he had first observed from the outside. No other social investigator before or after did what Reynolds did: some returned changed, some unchanged, but none went over the limen; no other never returned from their investigation.

Edward W. Said in *Culture and Imperialism* mentions the existence of artists and intellectuals 'who have, in effect, crossed to the other side' vis-à-vis Western imperialism.[60] This is a rare phenomenon, and its equivalent in class terms amongst the ranks of (incognito) social investigators, those whose intellectual honesty or courage (the one not necessarily implying the other, and the two being potentially very separate things) leads them to follow an epistemological logic to an ontological conclusion, is rarer still; for Stephen Reynolds is the sole figure who not only 'went native' but never truly came back. He alone decided that the privilege of the observer's position was not enough, with the ineluctable distance it always implies, however disguised and denied. Reynolds moved beyond questions of emicity and eticity, through empathy and sympathy, into identity. This should not be thought of as a Romantic return to the 'simple life': Reynolds's concluding remarks, on 'why I have forsaken the society of educated people, and have made my home among "rough uneducated" people',[61] make it very clear that his is an a posteriori decision based on what he has observed rather than an a priori decision based on ideology. In this sense, *A Poor Man's House* stands as the pinnacle of achievement of incognito social investigation: as opposed to endeavouring to change its readers' views of the poor, or its author's, it changed its author's very being, and the observer became one of the observed.

Incognito social investigation would of course continue after this publication of 1908, where it was brought to a point beyond which there is no going; it still continues now, and there is no reason to presume it will ever fully end, for the drive to discover 'how the other half lives' will always be there, and the tool created by Greenwood and diversified by Banks will always remain a vital part of how 'the poor' are investigated and constructed.[62] However, although the phenomenon itself may still be going strong, its function as something that produces texts is not. Its main role now seems to have split into televisual entertainment – very often in the form of politicians' 'undercover' investigations into how hard (or perhaps how easy, depending on the ideological *parti pris*) it is to be poor:[63] Matthew Parris in 1984 for *World in Action*, Clare Short teaching in a London comprehensive, Michael Portillo taking on the role of a single mother, the *Tower Block of Commons* series; or charity stunts to raise money and awareness for charities helping the homeless.[64]

Incognito social investigation as a phenomenon producing texts may have lost much of its importance now, but for a century and a half it was a hugely important form of knowledge creation, one underlying 150 years of assumptions about society and culture in Britain. If we are to talk honestly about that most continually subaltern of subaltern classes, the poor, then an understanding of this forgotten and overlooked force that for so long mediated their experiences to a non-poor audience, very often thus constructing 'the poor' about whom politicians and others talked and legislated, is vital, for doing so will give us hermeneutic tools better to deconstruct a discourse that has kept so many voices unheard for so long.

## NOTES

1. Koven, Seth. 2004. *Slumming: Sexual and Social Politics in Victorian London*. Princeton and Oxford: Princeton University Press, above all pp. 228–81.
2. Hopkins, Eric. 1999. *Charles Masterman (1873–1927), Politician and Journalist: The Splendid Failure*. Lewiston, Queenston and Lampeter: The Edwin Mellen Press, pp. 33 and 39.
3. As reproduced in Masterman, C.F.G. 1980 [1902]. *From the Abyss: Of Its Inhabitants by One of Them*. New York and London: Garland Publishing, unnumbered facsimile title page.
4. Ibid., pp. 9–10.
5. Ibid., p. 82.
6. Ibid., pp. 2–3.
7. Ibid., p. 16.
8. Valverde, Mariana. 1996. 'The Dialectic of the Familiar and Unfamiliar: "The Jungle" in Early Slum Travel Writing'. *Sociology* 30:3, pp. 493–509, p. 494.
9. For a comprehensive overview of London's hobo writings, see Etulain, Richard W. 1979. Introduction. *Jack London on the Road: The Tramp Diary and Other Hobo Writings*. Logan: Utah State University Press, pp. 1–27.

10. Paul, Ronald. 2010. 'Beyond the Abyss: Jack London and the Working Class'. *Nordic Journal of English Studies* 9:3, pp. 25–40, p. 39.

11. It is worth noting just how much *The People of the Abyss* signals its literariness through its paratext: each chapter is named as well as numbered, and is accompanied by an epigraph.

12. Regarding the 'abyss' trope see Keating, Peter. Keating, Peter (ed.). 1976. *Into Unknown England 1866–1913: Selections from the Social Explorers.* N.p.: Fontana, pp. 20–1, and Epstein Nord, Deborah. 1995. *Walking the Victorian Streets: Women, Representation, and the City.* Ithaca and London: Cornell University Press, p. 231.

13. Keating, *Into Unknown England 1866–1913*, pp. 20–1.

14. London, Jack. 1982 [1903]. *The People of the Abyss.* In his *Novels and Social Writings* (ed. Donald Pizer). New York: The Library of America, pp. 1–184, p. 7.

15. Ibid., pp. 7–8.

16. Sims, George R. 1883. *How the Poor Live.* London: Chatto & Windus, p. 5.

17. Valverde, 'The Dialectic of the Familiar and Unfamiliar', p. 494.

18. Chesterton, G.K. 1991 [1932]. *Chaucer.* In *The Collected Works of GK. Chesterton*, vol. XVIII. San Francisco: Ignatius Press, pp. 149–374, p. 160.

19. Paul, 'Beyond the Abyss', p. 27.

20. London, *The People of the Abyss*, p. 139.

21. See Auerbach, Jonathan. 1996. *Male Call: Becoming Jack London.* Durham and London: Duke University Press, pp. 141–2.

22. London, *The People of the Abyss*, p. 139

23. Auerbach, *Male Call*, p. 114.

24. Ibid., p. 118.

25. Ibid., p. 117.

26. London, *The People of the Abyss*, p. 13.

27. Simmons, Jack. 1997. 'class distinctions'. In Simmons, Jack and Gordon Biddle (eds.), *The Oxford Companion to British Railway History: From 1603 to the 1990s.* Oxford and New York: Oxford University Press, pp. 84–7, p. 85.

28. London, *The People of the Abyss*, p. 39.

29. London's seeming ignorance of Jerrold and Doré's book is particularly striking given the degree to which *The People of the Abyss* makes use of the jungle trope, suggesting a level of research on London's part into Victorian textual representations of the London slum.

30. Ibid., pp. 42–4.

31. See Wright, Christopher J. and Glenda M. Anderson (eds.). 2013. *The Victoria Cross and the George Cross: The Complete History*, vol. I. York: Methuen and London: The Victoria Cross and George Cross Association, pp. xviii, 19, 178, 272, 278, 326, 381, 430 and 500.

32. Auerbach, *Male Call*, p. 114.
33. As a more recent example of the classificatory problem regarding texts of this sort (as well as the complexities that adding race to the question of class can cause), it is interesting to consider Hall, Tarquin. 2005. *Salaam Brick Lane: A Year in the New East End*. London: John Murray.
34. Very little information about Massingham is available. For his family background, see Havighurst, Alfred F. 1974. *Radical Journalist: H.W. Massingham (1860–1924)*. London and New York: Cambridge University Press.
35. Massingham, Hugh. 1936. *I Took Off My Tie*. London and Toronto: William Heinemann Ltd, pp. 2–3.
36. Ibid., p. 13.
37. It is suggestive to note that Tom Harrisson renamed the cottage that he and Reynold Bray moved to in 1933 'The Trobriands' (Heimann, Judith M. 1999. *The Most Offending Soul Alive: Tom Harrisson and His Remarkable Life*. Honolulu: University of Hawai'i Press, p. 40).
38. Massingham, *I Took Off My Tie*, pp. 143–71.
39. Ibid., p. 121.
40. Ibid., p. 130.
41. Ibid., p. 92.
42. Ibid., p. 217.
43. Ibid., pp. 265–6.
44. Ibid., pp. 275–6.
45. Ibid., p. 280.
46. Ibid., p. 217.
47. Ibid., p. 239.
48. Ibid., p. 240.
49. Toynbee, Polly. 2003. *Hard Work: Life in Low-Pay Britain*. London: Bloomsbury, pp. 19–27 and 39–54.
50. Ibid., p. 54.
51. Massingham, *I Took Off My Tie*, p. 113.
52. He has received some critical attention because of his coining of the concept of 'autobiografiction' (see Saunders, Max. 2010. *Self Impression: Life-Writing, Autobiografiction, and the Forms of Modern Literature*. Oxford: Oxford University Press, pp. 164–179); he is also the subject of a remarkably exhaustive biography for so minor a figure, from which all information regarding him is taken: Scoble, Christopher. 2000. *Fisherman's Friend: A Life of Stephen Reynolds*. Tiverton: Halsgrove.
53. Reynolds, Stephen. 1980 [1908]. *A Poor Man's House*. London: London Magazine Editions, p. 13.
54. Reynolds, *Poor Man's House*, p. 21.
55. Franck, *Vagabond Journey*, pp. 240–241.

56. W. Somerset Maugham to Harry A. Franck, 10 October 1948. Ann Arbor, University of Michigan Library (Special Collections Library), Franck, Box 7, Notes on the Family.

57. It is suggestive to recall here that London passed himself off as an equivalent to beachcombers of this sort whilst investigating the East End – see his encounter with the ship's fireman who asks him whether he came over (as Franck did) on a cattle-boat (London, *The People of the Abyss*, p. 25), as well as his general comments about the American sailors he sees 'on the beach' (ibid., pp. 75–6).

58. Franck, *Vagabond Journey*, p. 261.

59. This question of coastal cross-class contact is complicated in Franck's case by the question of race – see the circus episode discussed in Chapter 3. This cross-class contact complicated by cross-race contact is only possible because of Colombo's, the coast's, interstitial nature.

60. Said, Edward W. 1994 [1993]. *Culture and Imperialism*. London: Vintage, p. xxii.

61. Reynolds, *Poor Man's House*, p. 315.

62. Most recently, Ben Judah has published *This is London*, which contains episodes of Greenwoodian incognito social investigation. This, however, was published too late to be able to include any analysis of it here.

63. The degree to which such investigations are truly 'undercover' is uncertain, given the technological demands of using hidden cameras on the one hand, and the possible recognizability of participants' faces on the other.

64. One example from many: 'The Mayor of London sleeps rough with the Evening Standard's owner to raise awareness of our Homeless Veterans campaign', headline in the *Evening Standard*, 12 January 2015.

# SELECT BIBLIOGRAPHY OF CRITICAL TEXTS

Alatas, Syed Hussein. 1977. *The Myth of the Lazy Native: A Study of the Image of the Malays, Filipinos and Javanese from the 16th to the 20th Century and Its Function in the Ideology of Colonial Capitalism*. London: Frank Cass.

Auerbach, Jonathan. 1996. *Male Call: Becoming Jack London*. Durham and London: Duke University Press.

Beaumont, Matthew. 2015. *Nightwalking: A Nocturnal History of London*. London and New York: Verso.

Crone, Rosalind. 2010. 'Reading the Victorian Underworld'. *Crime, Histoire & Sociétés/Crime, History & Societies* 14:1, pp. 95–101.

Cross, Nigel. 1980. *A Select Catalogue of Applicants to the Royal Literary Fund 1790–1870 with a Historical Introduction*. Unpublished PhD thesis, University College London.

Cunningham, Valentine. 1988. *British Writers of the Thirties*. Oxford: Oxford University Press.

Delap, Lucy. 2011. *Knowing Their Place: Domestic Service in Twentieth-Century Britain*. Oxford: Oxford University Press.

Docker, John. 1994. *Postmodernism and Popular Culture: A Cultural History*. Cambridge: Cambridge University Press.

Donovan, Stephen and Matthew Rubery (eds.). 2012. *Secret Commissions: An Anthology of Victorian Investigative Journalism*. Peterborough: Broadview Press.

Driever, Steven L. 2011. 'Geographic Narratives in the South American Travelogues of Harry A. Franck: 1917–1943'. *Journal of Latin American Geography* 10:1, pp. 53–69.

Epstein Nord, Deborah. 1995. *Walking the Victorian Streets: Women, Representation, and the City*. Ithaca and London: Cornell University Press.

© The Author(s) 2017                                                                    257
L. Seaber, *Incognito Social Investigation in British Literature*,
Palgrave Studies in Life Writing, DOI 10.1007/978-3-319-50962-4

Esty, Jed. 2004. *A Shrinking Island: Modernism and National Culture in England*. Princeton and Oxford: Princeton University Press.

Etulain, Richard W. 1979. Introduction. In London, Jack. *Jack London on the Road: The Tramp Diary and Other Hobo Writings*, ed. Richard Etulain. Logan: Utah State University Press, pp. 1–27.

Freeman, Mark. 2001. '"Journeys into Poverty Kingdom": Complete Participation and the British Vagrant, 1866–1914'. *History Workshop Journal* 52, pp. 99–121.

Freeman, Mark and Gillian Nelson (eds.). 2008. *Vicarious Vagrants: Incognito Social Explorers and the Homeless in England, 1860–1910*. Lambertville: The True Bill Press.

Giles, Judy. 2004. *The Parlour and the Suburb: Domestic Identities, Class, Femininity and Modernity*. Oxford and New York: Berg.

Gold, Raymond L. 1958. 'Roles in Sociological Field Observations'. *Social Forces* 36:3, pp. 217–23.

Hacking, Ian. 1998. *Mad Travelers: Reflections on the Reality of Transient Mental Illnesses*. Charlottesville and London: University Press of Virginia.

Hall, Lesley A. 1992. 'Forbidden by God, Despised by Men: Masturbation, Medical Warnings, Moral Panic, and Manhood in Great Britain, 1850–1950'. *Journal of the History of Sexuality* 2:3, pp. 365–87.

Harris, José. 1998. 'Between Civic Virtue and Social Darwinism: The Concept of the Residuum'. In Englander, David and Rosemary O'Day (eds.). *Retrieved Riches: Social Investigation in Britain 1840–1914*. Aldershot and Brookfield: Ashgate.

Harris, Marvin. 1990. 'Emics and Etics Revisited'. In Headland, Thomas N., Kenneth L. Pike and Marvin Harris (eds.). *Emics and Etics: The Insider/Outsider Debate*. Newbury Park, London and New Delhi: Sage, pp. 48–61.

Headland, Thomas N. 1990. 'Introduction: A Dialogue between Kenneth Pike and Marvin Harris on Emics and Etics'. In Headland, Thomas N., Kenneth L. Pike and Marvin Harris (eds.). *Emics and Etics: The Insider/Outsider Debate*. Newbury Park, London and New Delhi: Sage, pp. 13–27.

Heimann, Judith M. 1999. *The Most Offending Soul Alive: Tom Harrisson and His Remarkable Life*. Honolulu: University of Hawai'i Press.

Hinton, James. 2013. *The Mass Observers: A History, 1937–1949*. Oxford: Oxford University Press.

Hopkins, Eric. 1999. *Charles Masterman (1873–1927), Politician and Journalist: The Splendid Failure*. Lewiston, Queenston and Lampeter: The Edwin Mellen Press.

Hughes, Michael. 2014. *Beyond Holy Russia: The Life and Times of Stephen Graham*. Cambridge: Open Book.

Jaffe, Audrey. 1990. 'Detecting the Beggar: Arthur Conan Doyle, Henry Mayhew, and "The Man with the Twisted Lip"'. *Representations* 31, pp. 96–117.

Jebb, Miles. 1986. *Walkers*. London: Constable.

Jones, Julia. 2009. *The Adventures of Margery Allingham*. Pleshey: Golden Duck.

———. 2012. *Fifty Years in the Fiction Factory: The Working Life of Herbert Allingham*. Pleshey: Golden Duck.

Keating, Peter (ed.). 1976. *Into Unknown England 1866–1913: Selections from the Social Explorers*. N.p.: Fontana.

———. 1991 [1989]. *The Haunted Study: A Social History of the English Novel 1875–1914*. London: Fontana Press.

Koven, Seth. 2004. *Slumming: Sexual and Social Politics in Victorian London*. Princeton and Oxford: Princeton University Press.

Moretti, Franco. 2000. 'The Slaughterhouse of Literature'. *Modern Language Quarterly* 61:1, pp. 207–27.

Paul, Ronald. 2010. 'Beyond the Abyss: Jack London and the Working Class'. *Nordic Journal of English Studies* 9:3, pp. 25–40.

Pike, Kenneth L. 1954. *Language in Relation to a Unified Theory of the Structure of Human Behavior*. Glendale: Summer Institute of Linguistics.

Pittenger, Mark. 2012. *Class Unknown: Undercover Investigations of American Work and Poverty from the Progressive Era to the Present*. New York and London: New York University Press.

Prude, Jonathan. 2006. 'Experiments in Reality: Wyckoff's Workers'. In Schrader Lang, Amy and Cecelia Tichi (eds.). *What Democracy Looks Like: A New Critical Realism for a Post-Seattle World*. New Brunswick and London: Rutgers University Press, pp. 144–57.

Rodden, John. 1989. *The Politics of Literary Reputation: The Making and Claiming of 'St. George' Orwell*. New York and Oxford: Oxford University Press.

Said, Edward W. 1994 [1993]. *Culture and Imperialism*. London: Vintage.

Sánchez, María Carla and Linda Schlossberg (eds.). 2001. *Passing: Identity and Interpretation in Sexuality, Race, and Religion*. New York and London: New York University Press.

Saunders, Max. 2010. *Self Impression: Life-Writing, Autobiografiction, and the Forms of Modern Literature*. Oxford: Oxford University Press.

Schriber, Mary Suzanne and Abbey Zink. 2003. 'Introduction'. In Banks, Elizabeth L. *Campaigns of Curiosity: Journalistic Adventures of an American Girl in Late Victorian London*, ed. Mary Suzanne Schriber and Abbey Zink. Madison: The University of Wisconsin Press, pp. vii$_a$–xliv$_a$.

Scoble, Christopher. 2000. *Fisherman's Friend: A Life of Stephen Reynolds*. Tiverton: Halsgrove.

Seaber, Luke. 2014. 'Edward Burton, Fish Porter, Drunk and Incapable: New Evidence on Orwell's "Honesty" from the Records of His 1931 Conviction'. *Notes and Queries* 61:4, pp. 597–602.

———. FORTHCOMING. '"Many Acquaintances, and Those in the Most Different Classes of Society": Sherlock Holmes as Social Investigator'. In Tom Ue (ed.) *Mapping Arthur Conan Doyle's Modernities: 1887–1929*. Manchester: Manchester University Press.

Simmons, Chris. 2014. 'Celia Fremlin: A Biographical Sketch'. In Fremlin, Celia. *The Hours before Dawn*. London: Faber and Faber, pp. vii–xiii.

Southworth, Helen. 2009. 'Douglas Goldring's *The Tramp: An Open Air Magazine* (1910–1911) and Modernist Geographies'. *Literature & History* 18:1, pp. 35–53.

Stevenson, David. 2004. '"The Gudeman of Ballangeich": Rambles in the Afterlife of James V'. *Folklore* 115:2, pp. 187–200.

Tickner, Lisa. 2000. *Modern Life & Modern Subjects: British Art in the Early Twentieth Century*. New Haven and London: Yale University Press.

Valverde, Mariana. 1996. 'The Dialectic of the Familiar and Unfamiliar: "The Jungle" in Early Slum Travel Writing'. *Sociology* 30:3, pp. 493–509.

Vorachek, Laura. 2012. 'Playing Italian: Cross-Cultural Dress and Investigative Journalism at the Fin de Siècle'. *Victorian Periodicals Review* 45:4, pp. 406–35.

———. 2016. '"How Little I Cared for Fame": T. Sparrow and Women's Investigative Journalism at the Fin de Siècle'. *Victorian Periodicals Review* 49:2, pp. 333–61.

Vorspan, Rachel. 1977. 'Vagrancy and the New Poor Law in Late-Victorian and Edwardian England'. *English Historical Review* 92, pp. 59–81.

Walkowitz, Judith R. 1998/1999. 'The Indian Woman, the Flower Girl, and the Jew: Photojournalism in Edwardian London'. *Victorian Studies* 42:1, pp. 3–46.

Welshman, John. 2006. *Underclass: A History of the Excluded, 1880–2000*. London and New York: Hambledon Continuum.

Williams, Raymond. 1979. *Politics and Letters: Interviews with New Left Review*. London: NLB.

Winter, James. 1989. 'The "Agitator of the Metropolis": Charles Cochrane and Early-Victorian Street Reform'. *London Journal* 14:1, pp. 29–42.

# INDEX

L. Seaber, *Incognito Social Investigation in British Literature*,
Palgrave Studies in Life Writing, DOI 10.1007/978-3-319-50962-4

London (*cont.*)
  Lambeth, 18–26, 37–38, 52n5
London, Jack
  letter to John Spargo, 237
  *The People of the Abyss*, 233–240,
    254n11, 254n29, 256n57
London County Council, 74
*Los Angeles Times*, 207–208
Lot (Biblical story), 9, 29
lowbrow, the, 127–128
lower middle classes, 84–86, 135
Lucas, James, 'Mad Lucas'
    (hermit), 113, 116, 124n87
luggage, 110–111
lumpenproletariat
  as term, 2
Lushington, Charles, 3


**M**
Malvery, Olive Christian, 156–157,
    163, 170
  'The Heart of Things'
    series, 156–157
  'Music in the Byways', 132
  *The Soul Market*, 156–162,
    166n60, 167n77
Management, 149
Margate Rotary Club, 59
Massingham, Hugh, *I Took Off My
  Tie*, 240–247
Mass-Observation (social research
    organization), 190, 192,
    201–202, 212–214,
    228n77, 241
  *The Pub and the People*, 214
  *War Factory*, 190
Masterman, C.F.G., *From the Abyss*,
    232–234
Maugham, W. Somerset, 250–251
Mayhew, Henry, 141

*London Labour and the London
  Poor*, 3, 18–19
*The Wandering Minstrel*, 6
Merrilies, Meg, 170
methodology, 2, 21–27, 32, 49, 63,
    108, 113, 132–137, 147, 155,
    159, 163, 211–214, 223
microsocieties, 91
middlebrow, the, 127–128
middle classes
  and early incognito social
    investigation, 21, 36, 62
  and low-paid work, 127–129, 135,
    140–142, 144–145, 189, 191,
    197–201, 204, 222–223
  and the military, 12
  and settling, 232
  and tramping, 101–103,
    106–109, 120
military, 12, 60
Miller, Henry, 90
minimum-wage, 219
*Minister* (Anglican periodical), 137
modernism, 62
Moore, Dinah, housemaid of
    Elizabeth L. Banks, 188n26
Moore, Leonard, agent of George
    Orwell, 72
moral judgement, 37–39, 41,
    138–141, 150, 163, 165n31,
    172, 199–200
moral status, 64, 115
Moretti, Franco, 'The Slaughterhouse
    of Literature', 87
Moritz, Karl, 102
motivations, 6–7, 9–10, 35, 61, 101,
    136–138, 151, 184, 190
motor traffic, 109
Mount Street workhouse, St George's
    Hanover Square, ('Sinai
    Avenue'), 43–44

Printed by Printforce, the Netherlands